No. 1655
$21.95

THE
WOODTURNING
HANDBOOK
WITH PROJECTS

BY LEWIS H. HODGES

TAB BOOKS Inc.
BLUE RIDGE SUMMIT, PA. 17214

FIRST EDITION

FIRST PRINTING

Library of Congress Cataloging in Publication Data

Hodges, Lewis H.
The woodturning handbook—with projects.

Bibliography: p.
Includes index.
1. Turning. I. Title. II. Title: Wood turning hand-
book—with projects.
TT202.H63   1984   684′.083   83-24210
ISBN 0-8306-0655-6
ISBN 0-8306-1655-1 (pbk.)

Contents

Acknowledgments

I wish to express my appreciation to the following companies for their generosity in supplying information and illustrations for this book. Addresses are listed in Appendix A.

American Machine and Tool Co.
Baer American, Inc.
The Crane Creek Co.
Diehl Machines.
Dremel.
Du-er Tools.
Emco-Lux Corp.
Fox Super Shop, Inc.
Frog Tool Co. Ltd.
Gilliom Mfg. Co.
Goodspeed Machine Company.
Hattersley & Davidson, Ltd.
Holz Machine Co.
International Woodworking Equipment.
Lemco Tools, Inc.
Mattison Machine Works.
Northfield Foundry and Machine Co.
Oliver Machine Co.
Poitras, Danckaert Woodworking Machine Co.
Polamco
Powermatic Division, Houdaille Industries, Inc.
Precision Concepts
Raab-Kirk Co.
Ring Master, Inc.
Rockwell International
Shopsmith, Inc.
Sprunger Corp.
Toolmark Co.
TOTAL Shop
Turnmaster Corp.
Turn-O-Carve Tool C.
Woodcraft

Introduction

WOODTURNING IS AN INTERESTING AND FAS-cinating hobby that, in some cases, becomes an occupation. For a few master turners, particularly in England, it becomes a profession.

Turning is an activity that requires the use of many senses. Most turners would agree that sight is the major prerequisite. Nevertheless, a number of sightless people have become expert woodturners. The sense of feel is a very important component of turning expertise. A person might have the best eyesight in the world, but if he cannot feel the reaction of the chisel to the wood, his efforts probably will be mediocre.

Although the lathe is a machine, in some ways it resembles a hand tool in that the craftsman is in full control over his actions. The function of a lathe simulates the action of a potter's wheel. The lathe turns in a horizontal position and uses steel chisels to shape the wood; the potter's wheel operates in a vertical position and the clay is shaped by the hands of the potter with the help of wooden and wire tools.

The woodturner gains satisfaction in that, in most cases, he can experience the beginning and the completion of a project on the same machine, and in most instances in a shorter time than on other woodworking machines. If the turning craftsman wants to make multiple turnings on a mass basis, he can purchase one of the many lathe-duplicating attachments to speed up the process. Many salable items can be made using this method.

After the woodturner has learned the basic skills and techniques, he can, and many do, let their imagination run wild due to the flexibility of the lathe. The woodturners might design and turn an object that might win an award at an art fair. Some of the best projects find their way to art museums or into a collector's possession.

The sources of material for turning are varied and many. Scrap lumber can be used for many small turnings. Lumber from demolished buildings is a good source and usually can be obtained for a very low cost. Toppled trees and fireplace wood can often be used to advantage.

It is surprising to the layman or the beginning turner when he realizes the number and variety of things that can be turned on the lathe. This book illustrates a representative cross section of projects that can be turned, but it is far from a comprehensive listing.

The turner of today often is far more sophisticated than his earlier counterpart. He not only has improved his skills and techniques, but he has a greater sense of line and beauty, particularly in his experimental projects. He also is more apt to use imported or exotic woods, either separately or in combination with other woods.

It is entirely possible for the beginning woodturner to learn how to turn by reading good books and magazines on the subject, but he can advance much more rapidly by taking an adult evening class in turning or by attending one of the many turning conferences and demonstrations held throughout the country. These conferences/demonstrations usually last for two or three days of intensive training and instruction.

As the turning craftsman builds up his bank of experience, his acquaintance with the different woods and their reaction to the turning process will become a valuable asset. His selection of woods for different projects will become more discriminating and, as a result, his projects will become more satisfying.

The discerning tuner will find that with experience his projects will be crisper and that he will be using far less sandpaper. Sandpaper has ruined more turnings than it has helped.

The fascination of working with wood is that, unlike metal, no two pieces of wood, regardless of size and shape, are exactly alike. There is no synthetic material that has more desirable working characteristics. Perhaps no other material has the versatility of wood. It can be turned, shaped, bent, formed, smoothed, and finished. It presents interesting grain patterns, varied coloration, and surface structure. Wood is generally warm to the touch; metals are usually cold.

Woodworking, including woodturning, has always been the most prevalent and rewarding of the craft activities. As a building and furniture material, wood is, by far, the best understood. It is part of our natural heritage, and Yankee ingenuity has made the most of it. But even with today's high prices, wood is probably the best bargain around. Far too long we have taken wood for granted. Unlike oil, gas and coal, lumber is a renewable resource.

This book is designed for the typical home craftsman, but it is also an excellent reference for the industrial arts and vocational education teachers and Junior Achievement and 4-H Club leaders and members.

It would be presumptuous of me to assume that this is a totally comprehensive treatise on the subject of woodturning. Very few could write with total authority on all facets of woodturning, particularly if limited to one book. From my viewpoint, probably the only person to approach this level of authority would be Peter Child, the eminent English professional turner. His book is *The Craftsman Woodturner*, published by Bell and Hyman, Limited, Denmark House 17-39 Queen Elizabeth St., London SE1 2QB, England.

Other TAB Books by the Author

No. 1315 *The Master Craftsman's Illustrated Wood-*
          working Manual—with projects
No. 1675 *46 Step-by-Step Wooden Toy Projects*

Chapter 1

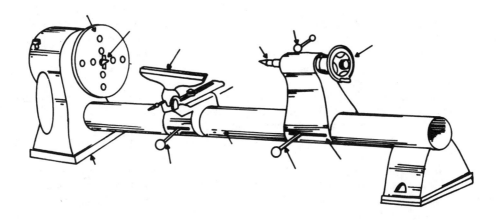

The Wood-Turning Lathe

THE HISTORY OF THE LATHE HAS EXPERIENCED many transitions from a clumsy, wood contraption with heavy string wrapped around the work—one end of the string fastened to a treadle and the other end to a springy, flexible pole above the lathe—to the modern, efficient lathe of today.

Because as this method caused the work to rotate in both directions, the operator had to apply the cutting tool to the work when the work was rotating toward him. Turning took place only half of the time. Naturally, the work had to be longer than necessary to allow room for wrapping the string around it. This lathe is sometimes known as the bodger's lathe.

Another similar version has the bow lathe. This lathe was used while the operator sat on the ground. The primitive Egyptian lathe had the bow string wrapped around the work. The bow was stroked by one hand, while the other hand and feet were used to steady the cutting tool.

More advanced nonpower lathes are the treadle lathe and the freewheel lathe. Jim Richey of Ponca, Oklahoma supplies drawings and instructions on how to build your own treadle lathe of wood. It differs from the primitive lathes described above in that it has a flywheel that allows the work to rotate in only one direction. (See

Fine Woodworking magazine, March/April, 1979 for details.)

Richard Starr of Thetford Center, Vermont, in the same issue of *Fine Woodworking* explains how a freewheel lathe can be built with a ratchet bicycle sprocket as the major component. He states that two lathes based on this drive system have been in use for several years in the Richmond Middle School at Hanover, New Hampshire.

With the advent of the steam engine, power-driven lathes came into being (along with the rather crude wood-bed lathes). This type of lathe accommodated a step-pulley, a saddle and tool rest, and a make-shift tailstock. When electricity replaced steam as a power source, many improvements were made to the lathe that lead to the highly efficient machine turning power tool of today. The development of roller and ball bearings was a major factor in this development. The older, poured babbitt bearings were a constant source of annoyance. They frequently burned out and new bearings had to be poured.

Power machines of all kinds should be kept clean and well lubricated. Belts should be checked for wear and pulleys for looseness. Craftsmen with air compressors should be careful to control the pressure when cleaning machines. William G. Ovens of Potsdam, New York, points out in *Fine Woodworking* magazine, Jan/Feb, 1979 that "section 1910.242 of the Occupational Safety and Health Administration required that 'compressed air should not be used for cleaning purposes except where reduced to less than 30 psi' . . ."

Some 40 or 50 years ago, all machinery was painted black, but currently colors are used to advantage. Green seems to be the accepted color for the body of most machines. Pittsburgh Paint and Glass has an excellent color system (sometimes called "color dynamics") not only for machines, but also for walls, ceilings and for marking safety zones on the floor. Operating parts on the machine are finished in strong contrast to the body of the machine; and machine controls, levers, and switch boxes are finished in high-visibility colors.

An industrial type of respirator should be available and worn. This is especially important when you are standing over the lathe for a prolonged period. If considerable sawing, jointing and planing, in addition to turning, are done in the workshop, it is almost a necessity to provide an industrial dust collecting system with metal and flexible tubing connected to the cyclone. Doyle Johnson of Crown Point, Indiana describes a damper-controlled dust collection system using plastic drainage pipe and clothes dryer vent hose in *Fine Woodworking* magazine, September, 1978.

A shop can be kept reasonably clean with a heavy-duty vacuum cleaner in the 10-gallon or 20-gallon size. If the home craftsman does only a minimum of turning and sawing—and no surfacing or jointing by power equipment—an ordinary household vacuum will be sufficient. Accumulated sawdust should be disposed of at the end of the day. A fire extinquisher should be located in a central position in the shop.

Most lumber for home workshops is stored in a horizontal position. If the shop has high ceilings, such as provided in a portion of a garage, the lumber can be stacked vertically. The rack for horizontal storage should be of sturdy construction. The main uprights should be 4×4 inches, or the equivalent, with 2-×-4-inch cross members or holes bored in the uprights and pieces of pipe at least 1½ inches in diameter inserted. This type of construction allows lumber to be removed from either side of the rack or from the ends. Make sure that plywood lumber lies flat; it should never be leaned against the wall.

All finishing materials should be stored in metal cabinets with metal doors to decrease fire hazards. No more than 1 gallon of each volatile liquid should be stored in the home workshop at a time.

Small aerosol spray cans of finishing materials can be safely used on small projects in the home workshop if adequate ventilation is provided by opening windows or doors. Commercial or industrial spray guns can be used only with a metal spray booth and a properly certified exhaust fan. It is best to check with the local fire marshall before installing such a system. Old paint and finishing cloths should be disposed of at the end of each day or placed in metal safety containers.

Provisions must be made for clamps. For the larger bar clamps, slots can be cut into hardwood 2×2 inches or larger in cross section and fastened to the wall with anchor fasteners. If a large number of bar clamps are used, it is advisable to mount an A-frame structure on a platform provided with large casters so that it can be moved about the shop. Bar clamps are stored on both sides of the slopes of the "A." Small clamps can be stored on the platform under the slopes of the "A."

Each piece of power machinery should be located so that there is plenty of room around it. The circular saw should be located near the entrance because it is usually the first power tool used when lumber is brought into the shop. The more well-equipped craftsman might have a power jointer, which should be located near the saw, and perhaps a thickness planer is added to make the triad complete. The other power tools (lathe, drill press, shaper, etc.) can be located wherever it is convenient.

Proper dress is very important. Goggles, safety glasses or face shields should be worn when operating woodworking machines. Long sleeves should be avoided. Finger rings should be removed before starting to work. Ties should be removed.

Always stop machines to make adjustments. Keep the area around each machine clear of cutter and debris. Do not approach too close to a person operating a machine. Expect the same from others while you are operating a piece of power equipment. Other safety precautions are required in connection with individual operations.

LATHE PARTS

The parts of the modern lathe are the *bed*, the *headstock*, the *faceplate*, the *live center*, the *tool rest saddle*, the *tool rest*, the *tailstock*, the *tail stock spindle lock*, the *tail stock spindle wheel*, and numerous locking and adjusting devices.

Figure 1-1 shows the parts of the very popular Myford lathe made in England. See also Fig. 1-2.

The Bed

Lathe beds come in numerous shapes. The most common

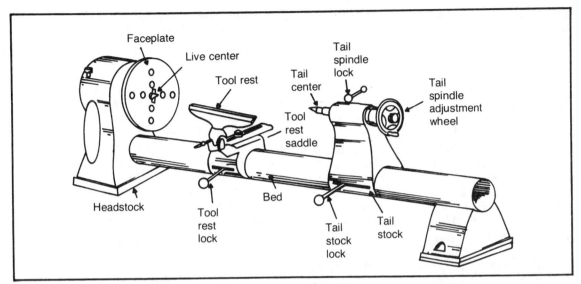

Fig. 1-1. Parts of the Myford lathe.

Fig. 1-2. The Myford lathe.

are the parallel flat bars, parallel round bars, and large, single tubular beds. Some lathes have a *gap-bed* designed to allow a larger-diameter faceplate turning to be turned on the inboard end of the headstock spindle. Nevertheless, the current trend is to make wood turning lathes with a continous bed and to make provision for large faceplate work on the outboard end of the lathe.

The Headstock

The headstock is the major component of a lathe. Most modern lathe headstocks are equipped with ball-bearings and are designed to resist side thrusts. The headstock spindle (sometimes called the *mandrel*) is hollow with the inboard end (the end to the right of the headstock) ground to accept a #1 or #2 Morse taper. The smaller lathes provide for a #1 Morse taper drive center or other accessories provided with a taper (e.g. Jacobs chuck).

The headstock spindle or mandrel extends both ways with screw threads on both ends. Right-hand threads are on the right end (inboard end). Left hand threads are on the left end (outboard end). See Fig. 1-3.

Naturally, the threads on the inboard and outboard faceplates must be threaded in a similar manner. If this were not true, any tool pressure exerted against the work on the faceplate would cause the faceplate and work piece to unscrew from the spindle and fly off the lathe—with probable damage to the faceplate and the work.

The headstock spindle portion between the two bearings is generally fitted with a three- or four-step pulley of different diameters. Power to the headstock pulleys is provided by V-belts or sectional belts attached to a similar step pulley fastened to a motor; however, the pulley attached to the motor is in a reverse position. In other words, the larger section of the headstock pulley is aligned with the smaller section of the motor pulley. Some provision is made for the tightening and loosening of the belt.

Faceplates

Any project that is turned from the headstock end only,

Fig. 1-3. Headstock and live center of the Myford lathe.

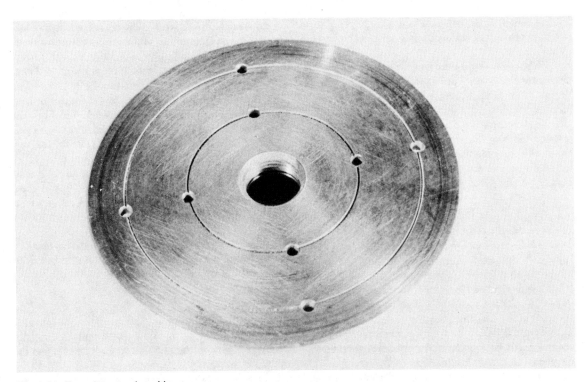

Fig. 1-3A. Faceplate, turning side.

Fig. 1-3B. Faceplate, reverse side.

without benefit of the tailstock, is usually referred to as faceplate turning. Chucks and other devices can be used to hold the work.

Faceplates are of different diameters and are pierced by countersunk holes to provide for short, squat, flathead screws that hold the workpiece or the base for the workpiece.

The standard faceplates for both the inboard and outboard ends of the spindle for the Myford lathe are identical except for the threads. Both faceplates are 6 inches in diameter and have eight countersunk holes. See Figs. 1-3A and 1-3B.

The Live Center

The live center (sometimes known as the drive or spur center) is inserted into the inboard end of the headstock spindle. Both the spindle and live center are ground to a Morse Taper. The #1 Morse tapers are used on the smaller lathes and #2 Morse tapers are used on the larger lathes. Any thrust against the live center will seat it securely in the headstock spindle.

Spindle turning or *turning between centers* is accomplished by holding the work between centers as distinguished from *faceplate turning.*

The most common types of live centers are the *two-spur* and *four-spur centers.* Each of these types have a cone-shaped point in the center where the spurs intersect. These points must be longer than the spurs. The four-spur center is more efficient on soft wood where the two-spur center might be apt to dig a hole in the end of the stock if too much pressure is exerted against the turning. See Chapter 3 for additional information concerning centers.

The Tool Rest Saddle

The tool rest saddle's main function is to provide a solid but adjustable base for the tool rest. The tool rest saddle extends across the bed of the lathe. It has a long slot and a bolt that locks it in place and can be moved and locked along the length of the lathe bed or locked in a position at different distances from the work.

The tool rest fits into a hole in one end of the saddle and can be raised or lowered or set at an angle to the work. The tool rest is locked into position by a butterfly nut or some other locking device.

The Tool Rest

Tool rests come in many sizes and shapes. Standard rests are T-shaped; the top of the "T" varies in length. The short tool rest is naturally used for short spindle turning or for small faceplate work. Why not use a long tool rest for short spindle turning? Because long rests will hit parts of the lathe before getting close enough to turn small diameters on short spindle turnings. Some lathes are provided with a special extra-long rest with two cylindrical stubs that fit into tool rest saddles. For temporary turning of extra long spindle work, a tool rest can be made of hardwood with dowels fitted to the upper part of the "T" in order to provide stubs to fit into the tool rest saddles.

The part of the rest on which the turning tool rests should be smooth and the cross section should represent a continuous curved surface. Even the tool rest for the Myford lathe could be improved by rounding over the top of the rest.

There are numerous rests that have the top member shaped like the letter S or L. These are used primarily to fit inside the interiors of faceplate work (bowls, etc.).

The Tailstock

The tailstock consists of the tailstock base, the tailstock spindle, the tailstock spindle lock, the tailstock spindle adjustment wheel, the tailstock locking device, and the tailstock center.

The tailstock base is usually a heavy casting and its main function is to support the tailstock center in a rigid and secure position. The tailstock spindle is similar to the headstock spindle. The left end is ground to a Morse taper. The right end has square threads on the outside of the spindle hat correspond to the threads on the tailstock spindle adjustment wheel.

The tailstock can be moved from one end of the lathe bed to the other and locked into the approximate position by the tailstock locking device. The tailstock center (sometimes called the dead center) is moved into its final position on the end of the work piece, tightened with the tailstock adjustment wheel, and secured with the spindle lock.

Although revolving centers are sometimes used for specific purposes, the most commonly used dead centers are the cone center and the cup center. The cup center is the most popular. See Fig. 1-5.

SIZES, CAPACITIES, AND LATHE SPEEDS

Lathe sizes are indicated by the overall length, the maximum distances between the live or spur center and the tailstock center or dead center, and the maximum diameter or swing, which is twice the distance from the bed to the line between centers. Some manufacturers also indicate the maximum diameters that may be turned

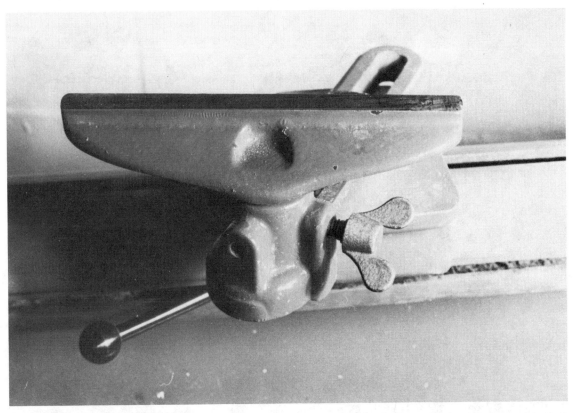

Fig. 1-4A. Tool rest for the Myford lathe.

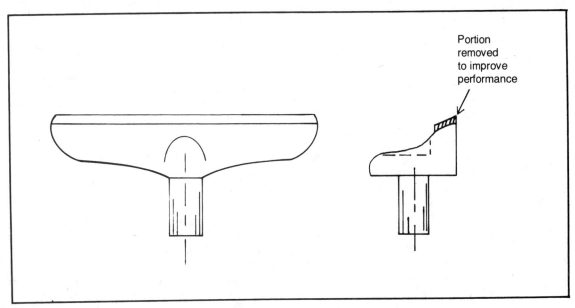

Portion
removed
to improve
performance

Fig. 1-4B. Myford tool rest altered to improve performance.

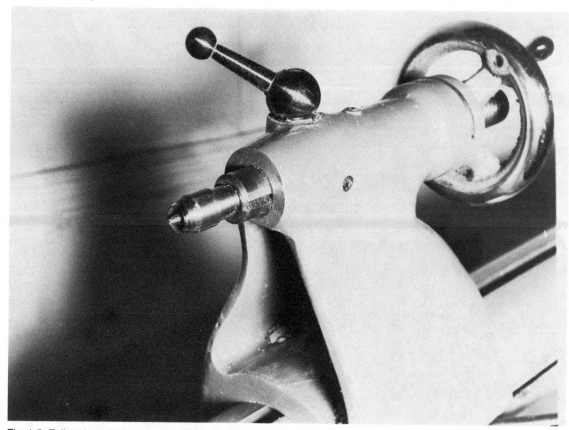

Fig. 1-5. Tailstock and tailstock center for the Myford lathe.

safely on the outboard end of the headstock. Some foreign manufacturers identify their lathes by the maximum radius that may be turned.

The identification of lathe sizes by maximum diameter or radius that may be turned is rather deceiving. No manufacturer specifies the size of the largest continuous turning (from one center to the other) that may be turned *over the tool rest saddle.*

Some lathes have a gap in the bed that allows faceplate turning of bowl-like objects to be turned to a larger diameter than permissible without the gap.

Wood turning lathes vary in size from the miniature Dremel with a swing of 1½ inches and 6 inches between centers, to the huge veneer cutting lathe used by plywood manufacturers that have a 4-foot wing and 8 or 9 feet between centers. The most popular size wood turning lathe for the home craftsman is one with a 12-inch swing and 36 inches between centers.

The standard four-step pulley and belt arrangement on many lathes has speeds varying from 900 rpm to 3300 rpm. Other lathes have variable speed control that is continuous over a wide range of speeds from around 350 rpm to over 3000 rpm. For large faceplate turnings and between center turnings of over 8 inches in diameter, the speed range should be in the 200 to 400 rpm range.

THE MYFORD LATHE

The Myford ML8 wood turning lathe, English built, is a traditional favorite of British turners and is rapidly becoming popular in the United States. The Myford lathe is cleverly designed and solidly built with fine castings and precision-machined parts. It is simple to operate and versatile. An extensive variety of accessories are available.

Specifications. The distances between centers in the three sizes of the Myford lathe and 30 inches, 36 inches and 42 inches. Bed sections can be supplied to give up to 72 inches between centers. The swing over the bed is 8 inches. Diameters of 16 inches or more can be turned using the outboard saddle and rest. The hollow spindle in the headstock is bored for a No. 1 Morse taper (as is the tailstock barrel). The four speeds, using a 1425-rpm motor, are 700 rpm, 1140 rpm, 1780 rpm, and 2850 rpm.

Standard Equipment. The Myford lathe has a tilting motor mount for belt pulley speed change and for tightening. The motor must be purchased extra. It has a four-step motor pulley, a ½-inch segmented V-belt that is easily repaired, lengthened or shortened. It has a four-prong spur headstock center, a cup dead center for tailstock, 6-inch and 10-inch tool rests, inboard, and outboard tool rest saddles, and 6-inch diameter inboard and outboard faceplates. See Fig. 1-6.

Special Features. The headstock is of one piece with totally enclosed drive pulleys. Provision is made for easy adjustment to angular contact ball bearings. Accurate threads are at the end of each spindle to facilitate the mounting of chucks and faceplates. The plunger indexing mechanism gives 24 fixed positions to the spindle. Quick-action clamping levers safely anchor the toolrest saddles and tailstock. Optional equipment and attachments are listed in Chapter 3.

SAFETY AND MAINTENANCE

☐ Wear a face shield or goggles when turning.

☐ Wear a nurse's mask if you are doing extensive sanding or turnings.

☐ Remove your tie and finger rings.

☐ Check to see if the tailstock spindle lock has secured the tailstock spindle.

☐ Never make adjustments when the lathe is running.

☐ Scan the work for any defects. Check glue joints.

☐ Run stock at a low speed until it is round.

☐ Use both hands and hold turning tools firmly.

Fig. 1-6. Power unit of Myford lathe.

Fig. 1-7. #159 Oliver lathe.

☐ Keep the tool rest as close to the work as possible.

☐ Remove the tool rest from the saddle when sanding or French polishing.

☐ Remove the live and dead centers from the lathe before driving them into spindle turning stock. Never try to force the centers into the stock by turning the tailstock spindle adjustment wheel excessively. Make sure that centers are in good condition. Sharpen or replace them if necessary.

☐ Keep lathe tools properly sharpened.

☐ Use SAE #10 when oiling. Do not attempt to oil motor as they usually have life-time sealed-bearings that do not require oil.

☐ Think about what you are going to do before you do it. What might or might not happen because of your actions.

☐ Keep your mind on your work. Do not allow anything to distract you. Respect the power of the lathe.

☐ If something doesn't look right or sound right, turn off the lathe at once.

☐ Faceplate work should be checked to see if the faceplate screws are in tight. Check carefully all glue joints in faceplate work. A section of the work might fly off with great force, and especially if a chisel or gouge catches in the wood.

☐ Turn the work over by hand before turning on the lathe switch.

☐ Be sure that spindle work turned from the square is absolutely round before using calipers. It is best to check roundness when the lathe is stopped.

☐ During turning, there should be no possibility of the operator coming in contact with pulleys, belts, or motors.

Fig. 1-8. #2200 Series Oliver lathe.

Fig. 1-9. Model 45 Powermatic lathe.

□ Dull tools are more dangerous than sharp ones.

□ Lathe tools should always be held firmly. Have one hand near the end of the chisel handle and the other hand holding the chisel tight to the tool rest.

□ When using cloths for French polishing on the lathe, watch for stray ends of threads that might get caught.

□ Always put down lathe cutting tools with the points away from you. It is best to put them back in the rack. Tools placed on the lathe bed or bed base are apt to vibrate and fall on the floor or against the operator.

□ Remove all finger jewelry. Wear shop coat with tight cuffs or roll up the sleeves.

□ Lights should be adequate and properly placed. Lights should be overhead, but should not shine in the eyes of the operator when turning.

□ Make sure that the floor space around the lathe is not slippery.

□ Check the stock before placing in the lathe. Lumber with cracks, splits, deep checks, or large knots should not be used.

LATHE MANUFACTURERS

Oliver Machinery Company of Grand Rapids, Michigan, manufactures a sturdy, 12-inch combination wood-turning-and-metal-spinning lathe. The Model 159 lathe would be more apt to be found in school shops and small woodworking shops rather than home workshops. There are many Oliver lathes still in service after 40 to 50 years of use.

Oliver lathes differ from most other lathes in that they do not have step pulleys for speed changes. The headstock is a double-ended, self-contained unit, consisting of a headblock with a ball bearing spindle driven by a suitable ball bearing motor, operating through a V-belt on adjustable cone sheaves giving speeds from 800 to 2750 rpm.

Another unusual feature is that the 1-hp motor is mounted directly to the headstock. The motor develops 1800 rpm and can be started only at the lowest spindle speed—assuring safety.

The Model 159 will swing a 12-inch diameter over the bed or 9¼ inches over the saddle and will turn 26 inches long between centers on 48-inch bed or 38 inches long on a 60-inch bed. The lathe is available on 6-foot, 7-foot, and 8-foot beds.

Outboard turning can be done on the double-ended spindle. The 8-inch faceplate on the outboard end is also a hand wheel.

Oliver also make a #2200 and #2300 series that are larger lathes starting at 6 feet in length and additional increments of 2 feet.

The #2200 series lathes are available with four, eight or variable spindle speeds, depending on the motor option ordered. The machines are available with a 1200-rpm, a two-speed 600/1200-rpm motor, or a variable-speed motor drive.

The #2300 series are available with two speed ranges. One range is 600/900/1200/1800 rpm and the other is 600/1200/1800/3600 rpm.

A hand feeding carriage is furnished as regular equipment on both series of lathes. It is built with a compound swivel rest. As an optional extra, all sizes of lathes can be furnished with a power feeding carriage. A handwheel is provided for fine adjustment if the power features are not required. See Figs. 1-7 and 1-8.

Powermatic Houdaille manufactures two 12-inch lathes. Model 45 is designated as a heavy-duty lathe and Model 90 as an extra heavy-duty lathe.

The Model 45 has an instant set-speed control. Optional straight bed and gap bed are available. The gap bed lathe allows a swing of 16 inches. The gap is 4½ inches wide. The distance between centers is 39 inches. The Model 45 can be used for metal spinning as well as for wood turning.

The headstock is available with a built-in variable speed drive from 330 to 2100 rpm, or with a four-speed drive of 600, 1100, 1800, and 3000 rpm.

The spindle has a 60-stop plunger type of index wheel, and is bored for a No. 2 Morse taper (as is the tailstock spindle). There is a 6-inch and 12-inch tool rest.

Fig. 1-10. Model 90 Powermatic lathe.

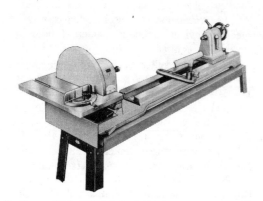

Fig. 1-11. Sprunger GBL-01 lathe.

A ¾-hp motor is recommended for the Model 45 lathe.

The Model 90 has a five-position limit stop so that instructors or shop foremen can enforce preset speeds. There is also a choice of straight bed or gap bed. The width of the gap is 5¼ inches. The gap bed allows a swing of 17 inches. See Figs. 1-9 and 1-10.

Sprunger Corporation manufactures a 10-inch gap-bed lathe that is 36 inches between centers and also a larger 12-inch lathe. Both lathes have sealed heavy-duty ball bearings that never need lubrication. Each lathe has an optional sanding disc and table for the outboard end of the spindle. Lathe speeds are 875/1150/2250 and 3500 rpm and are powered by a ½-hp motor.

The smaller lathe is designated Model GBL-01. It has a 13-inch swing over the gap. The larger lathe, Model GBL-21, will swing 15 inches over the gap. The headstock and tailstock spindles are bored for No. 2 Morse taper.

The faceplate for both lathes is only 3 inches in diameter. That is considerably smaller than for other lathes of similar size. Larger, 6-inch-diameter faceplates are available as extra accessories.

The two lathes weigh 125 and 132 pounds respectively. See Figs. 1-11 and 1-12.

Emco-Lux Corporation supplies an Austrian-built wood turning lathe with a 400mm swing (15.7 inches plus) and 1000 millimeters between centers (39.37 inches). The rigid, robust machine has four spindle speeds of 600, 1000, 1700, and 2700 rpm.

This precision-made lathe, identified as EMCO-DB5, is powered by a ¾-hp motor that is completely enclosed and dust and splash proof.

The DB-5 has many accessories such as a spindle brake attachment for spindle quick-stop; three- and four-jaw universal chucks; roller bearing, live, tailstock center; a 400mm tool rest, and many items.

American Machine and Tool (AMT) Company manufactures an inexpensive wood-turning lathe. Model No. 2731 is 36 inches between centers and has a 12-inch swing. It has a large, graduated tool rest and a screw action tailstock with a three-speed pulley. Optional ball bearings and bronze bearings are available. A lathe countershaft can be purchased at extra cost.

AMT also makes two larger lathes. The Deluxe ball bearing model has a 4-foot bed. The industrial long bed lathe Model No. 373 has a 55-inch bed. See Figs. 1-14 and 1-15.

Rockwell International manufacturers two 12-inch swing lathes: a heavy-duty lathe and a standard lathe. The heavy-duty lathe Model 11/14 with stand No. 46-150 has a 11-inch swing over the bed and a 36-inch capacity between centers. The gap bed allows a 14-inch swing. The gap is 3 inches wide. It has a 4-step pulley, a 3-inch faceplate and 4-inch-wide and 12-inch-wide tool rests. The spindles are bored for a No. 2 Morse taper. With a 1725-rpm motor, the speeds are 990, 1475, 2220, and 3250 rpm.

The standard lathe, Model 10 with stand No. 46-011, has a 10-inch swing over the bad and a capacity of 36

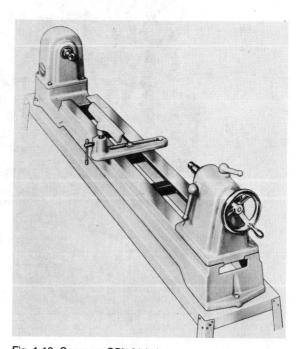

Fig. 1-12. Sprunger GBL-21 lathe.

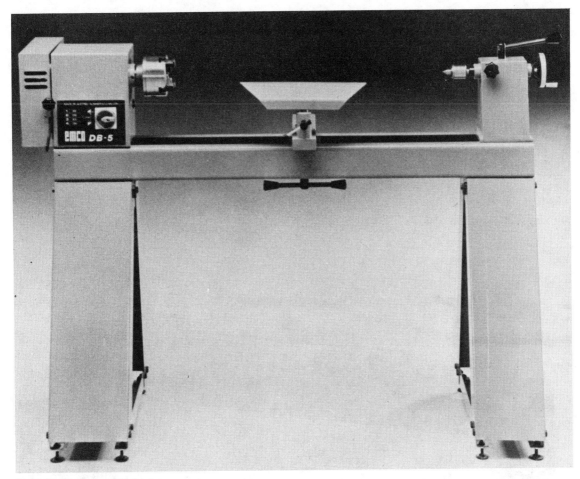

Fig. 1-13. Emco-Lux DB-5 lathe.

Fig. 1-14. AMT Model 2731 lathe.

Fig. 1-15. AMT Model 373 lathe.

Fig. 1-16. Rockwell Model 11/14 heavy-duty wood lathe.

Fig. 1-17. Phantom View of Fox Super Shop.

inches between centers. It also has a four-step pulley providing speeds of 800, 1350, 2200, and 3700 rpm. Model 10 will operate well with ⅓-hp motor while Model 11/14 works more efficiently with a ½-hp motor. The Model 10 is currently out of production. See Fig. 1-16.

COMBINATION POWER LATHES

Home craftsmen many times become very emotional when discussing the pros and cons of the combination power tool. The opponents contend that the constant shifting of the motor from tool to tool takes up too much time. They feel that individual tools, with their own separate motors, is the only way to go.

Many proponents argue that the combination tool is a godsend because their available space is much too restricted for individual tools. One manufacture claims that his combination machine takes up no more space than a bicycle.

The Fox Super Shop

Fox Super Shop, a subsidiary of Fox Industries, Inc., is a comparatively new product. Fox claims that the Super-Shop is the finest multipurpose power tool in the field. It works with metal as well as wood. With accessories, it can perform 15 operations with the following: 10-inch, heavy-duty, power-table saw, ⅝-inch wood or steel vertical drill press, all-purpose stationary router, 12-inch heavy-duty disc sander, high-speed shaper, 17-×-34-inch wood lathe, horizontal boring machine, a horizontal metal chucker, a 6-inch jointer, a molding machine, a

17

Fig. 1-18. Vertical Position, Fox Super Shop.

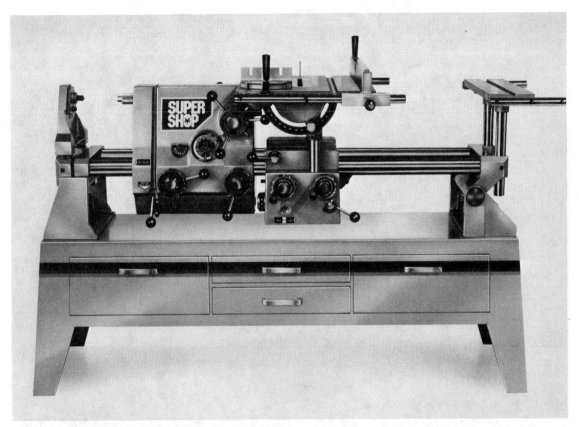

Fig. 1-19. Horizontal Position, Fox Super lathe.

6-inch planer, a 15-inch metal or wood bandsaw and a 16-×-34-inch metal lathe.

The Fox Super Shop is powered by a 1½-hp motor that provides speeds of from 30 rpm to 7200 rpm.

In its horizontal position, the Fox Super Shop is ideal for spindle turning. No mention is made of faceplate turning in their advertising literature. See Figs. 1-17 through 1-21.

The Shopsmith

The multipurpose Shopsmith has long been a favorite of the home craftsman. The contemporary Shopsmith Mark V has many improvements over the original Shopsmith invented shortly after World War II.

The Shopsmith multipurpose tool provides five major tools in one. It combines a 34-inch lathe, a 10-inch table saw, a horizontal boring machine, a 16-inch drill press and a 12 inch disc sander. It employs a single table, spindle, stand, and motor. And it requires less storage space than a bicycle (according to their literature).

The Shopsmith Mark V woodworking system provides nine power tools in a compact area. You can start with the Mark V multipurpose tool and grow with the system as you progress. Adding a bandsaw, jigsaw, jointer and belt sander is easy and economical because they can be mounted on and powered by Mark V. The four additional tools can be stored on a convenient wall shelf. Power stands are also available for independent operation.

The Shopsmith as a Lathe. The Shopsmith lathe will perform all the operations that a lathe of comparable size will accomplish. Spindle turning, faceplate turning, fluting and reeding, and spiral turnings are a few of the operations that can be done on this lathe.

The variable speed control on the Mark V offers a speed range of 700 to 5200 rpm at the turn of a dial. It is 34 inches between centers with a 16½-inch swing.

Total Shop

The Total Shop combination power tool is similar to the

Fig. 1-20. Tony Fox Displays Models of Super Shop.

Fig. 1-21. Wood Turning On Fox Super Shop.

Fox Super Shop and the Shopsmith. It is a 10-inch table saw, a 16½-inch drill press, a horizontal boring machine, a 12-inch disc sander, as well as a 34-inch lathe.

The Total Shop is powered by a 1¾-hp motor. It occupies only 12 square feet of floor space. It has a variable speed motor with a range from 900 to 5400 rpm.

In addition to turning spindles, faceplate turnings up to 16½ inches in diameter are possible.

Optional extras are an 18-inch jigsaw, a 11-inch bandsaw, a 6-inch belt sander, and a 6-inch jointer.

The HAPFO Woodturning Lathe

International Woodworking Equipment Corp. manufactures the Hapfo AHDK-125 and the smaller AHDK-110. The AHDK-125 is driven by a single-phase, 2-hp, 220-volt motor. Speeds are 630, 1000, 1600, 2330 and 3050 rpm by means of a five-step pulley.

The headstock is designed to extend the spindle bearing approximately 2 inches from the face of the housing to accommodate positioning the tool rest holder to allow turning on the work piece from the back side when doing faceplate work.

The height of the centers above the bed is approximately 8 inches and will swing 16 inches in diameter over the bed. The distance between centers is approximately 44 inches.

The tailstock and tool rest holder are equipped with a quick-acting clamping device. The tool rest holder is bored for a 1-inch steel column.

Chapter 2

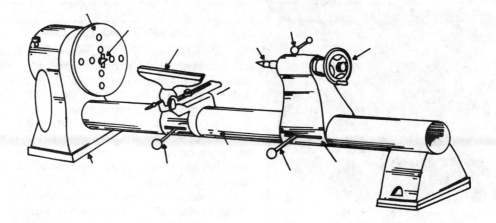

Chisels, Gouges, and Other Tools

CHISELS AND GOUGE SIZES ARE INDICATED BY the width of the blades. Sometimes the length of the blade is given, but more often it is the overall length including the handle. The overall lengths of the "long and strong" chisels and gouges is of considerable importance as the extra-long handles are necessary to properly control the tool.

The total range of chisel and gouge widths in inches are as follows: ⅛, ¼, ⅜, ¾, 1, 1¼, 1½, and 2. Only a few shapes are available in all the width listed. See Figs. 2-1, 2-2, and 2-3.

CHISEL AND GOUGE SHAPES

The standard shapes are the skew, single-bevel square-end chisel, double-bevel, square-end chisel, diamond or spear point, round nose, left corner, right corner, parting tool, gouge (fingernail), beading tool, and deep gouge (roughing out gouge, square end).

A set of turning tools for the beginner would probably include:

□ ¼-inch or ⅜-inch half round, spindle (fingernail) gouge.

□ ½-inch or ¾-inch shallow spindle or fingernail gouge.

□ ¾-inch or 1-inch half round, squared end roughing gouge.

□ 1½-inch or 2-inch skew.

□ ½-inch or ¾-inch skew.

□ Parting tool or parting/beading tool.

□ Two or three sizes of round nose or other shaped scrapers.

□ ⅜-inch or ½-inch "long and strong," deep-fluted, heavy-bowl turning gouge.

The standard skew is available in the widths given above, as is the square (single bevel) chisel. The square (double bevel) is not available in the ⅜-inch width, but it is available in all other widths.

The standard diamond or spear chisel is available in ⅛-inch, ⅜-inch, ½-inch, and ¾-inch widths.

The standard round nose chisel is available in ¼-inch, ⅜-inch, ½-inch, and ¾-inch sizes.

The standard left and right corner chisels are available in ⅜-inch, ½-inch, and ¾-inch sizes.

The parting tool comes in ⅛-inch, ¼-inch, and ⅜-inch sizes.

The fingernail, spindle turning gouge sizes extend across the entire range of sizes except for the ⅛-inch size.

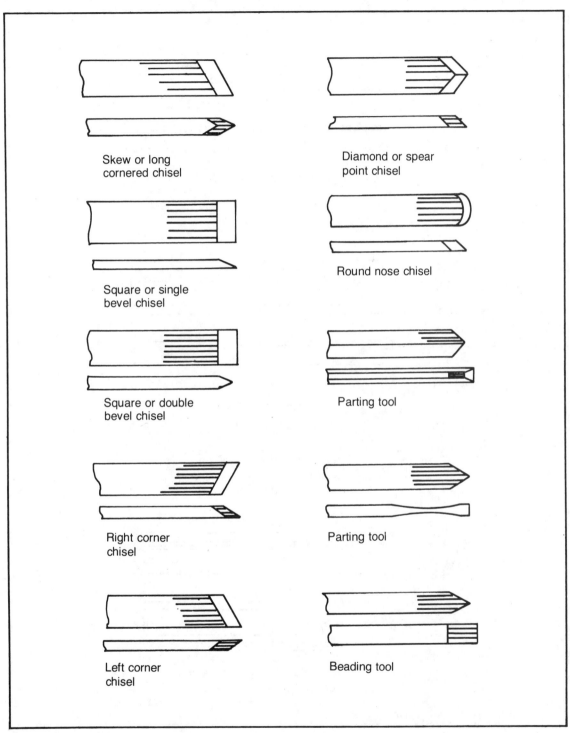

Skew or long
cornered chisel

Diamond or spear
point chisel

Square or single
bevel chisel

Round nose chisel

Square or double
bevel chisel

Parting tool

Right corner
chisel

Parting tool

Left corner
chisel

Beading tool

Fig. 2-1. Woodturning chisels.

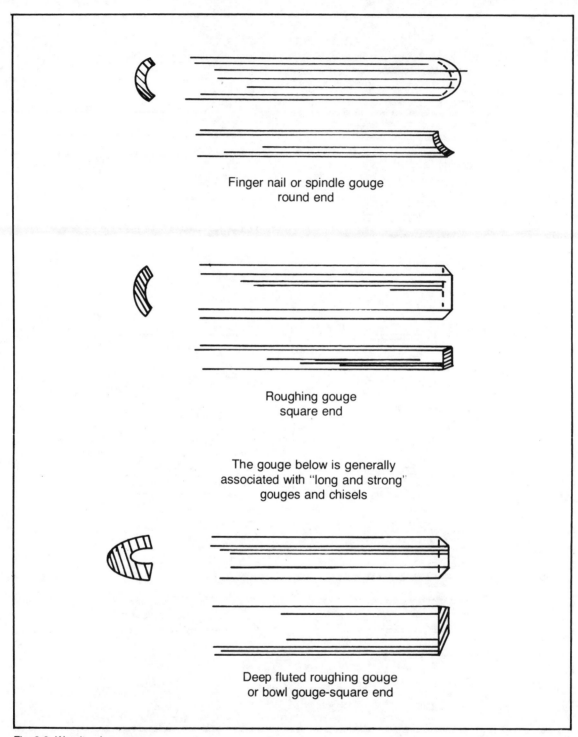

Finger nail or spindle gouge
round end

Roughing gouge
square end

The gouge below is generally
associated with "long and strong"
gouges and chisels

Deep fluted roughing gouge
or bowl gouge-square end

Fig. 2-2. Woodturning gouges.

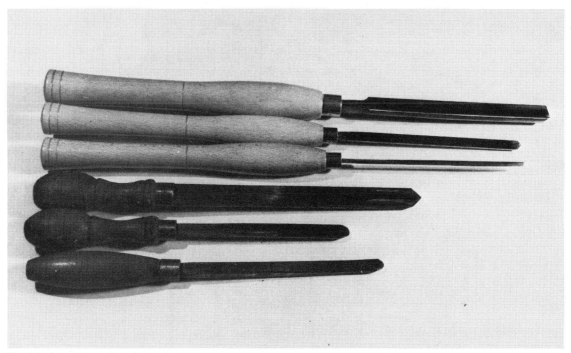

Fig. 2-3. Assortment of turning tools.

The beading tool is available in ¼-inch and ⅜-inch sizes only.

The deep gouge (square nose, roughing out) comes in ¾-inch, 1-inch and 1¼-inch widths.

Of the standard chisels and gouges, only the skew, the fingernail gouge, and the deep gouge are true cutting tools; all the rest (diamond, round nose, corner, parting and beading chisels) are in essence scraping or semi-scraping tools.

In the September, 1978 issue of *Fine Woodworking* magazine Peter Child wrote an article on spindle turning. The following three paragraphs are reprinted from *Fine Woodworking* magazine © 1978 The Taunton Press, Inc., 52 Church Hill Rd., Box 355, Newtown, CT 06470.

"For turning between centers, standard roughing-down gouges and coving gouges are best. These spindle gouges have only two shapes of blade. The roughing-down tool has a deep, U-shaped flute ground straight across with no pointed nose, and the coving gouge has a shallower flute with a pointed "lady's fingernail" nose.

"Roughing-down gouges have an even thickness of metal all around the cutting edge and a very short single bevel of 45°. Unlike bowl gouges, they have a keel. Three sizes are commonly available: ¾", 1", and 1¼".

The first and last sizes should both be the choice of the turner if possible; the 1-inch size is the economy combination tool.

"Coving (spindle) gouges have a longer bevel than roughing-down gouges. Four sizes will handle all the turner's requirements: ¼", ⅜", ½" and ¾". Any work requiring larger coves, hollows or long curves can be done better with roughing-down gouges, so gouges larger than ¾" aren't necessary. Both roughing-down and coving gouges should have long, heavy-duty handles to facilitate control—mine are at least 10" long."

LONG AND STRONG CHISELS AND GOUGES

All of these extra heavy tools are (or should be) fitted with long handles. These tools are well balanced and have a good "feel." The high-quality steel has excellent edge-holding characteristics. Ordinary chisels are hardened and tempered only for a short distance from the cutting edge, but these chisels are treated the entire length.

The long and strong skew is available in the entire range of sizes. The long and strong diamond or spear point chisel comes in ⅜-inch, ½-inch, and ¾-inch widths. The round nose has ¼-inch, ⅜-inch, ½-inch,

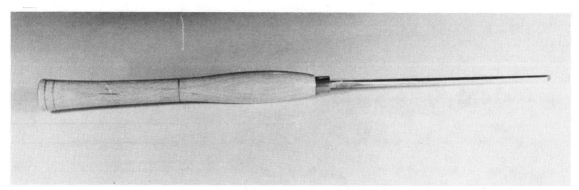

Fig. 2-4. One-quarter-inch long and strong gouge.

¾-inch, and 1-inch widths. The regular gouge (fingernail) is available across the entire size range, except the 2-inch size. The deep (square end) gouge's four sizes are ¼-inch, ⅜-inch, ½-inch, and ¾-inch sizes. These deep-fluted tools are used primarily for faceplate turning or roughing. See Figs. 2-4 through 2-7.

LONG AND STRONG SCRAPING TOOLS

These massive chisels are the brainstorm of Peter Child, the eminent English woodturning expert. They are 1½-inches wide and ⅜ of an inch thick, which eliminate any tendency for the blade to vibrate. After it is ground, the burr or feather edge is never removed. Sometimes it is turned over with a burnisher similar to sharpening a cabinet scraper. This helps in making a fine, silky shaving (thus getting rid of other tool marks).

The more common of the long and strong scraping tools are the right and left skew, the full round and the half

Fig. 2-5. Tip of ¼-inch long and strong gouge.

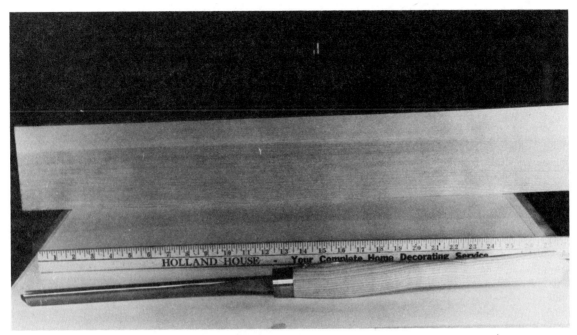

Fig. 2-6. Three-quarter-inch deep-fluted, long and strong gouge.

Fig. 2-7. Tip of ¾-inch deep-fluted, long and strong gouge.

round, the domed, and the straight. A lathe operator might want to grind them to his own preference. Many turners make their own scraping tools from old files. See Fig. 2-8.

Wood-Turning Scrapers. The scraper is generally used on faceplate work to obliterate gouge toolmarks. The bevel of the cutting edge is rather short. If it is too long it will not hold an edge because there is not enough steel to support it and the edge will heat up quickly. Differing from most other turning tools, the bevel does *not* rub against the work and the handle end is held higher than the cutting edge. When the scraper starts turning nothing but dust instead of small, silky shavings, it should be sharpened at once. See Fig. 2-9.

GRINDING, WHETTING, AND HONING

Grinding takes place when the cutting edge is excessively dulled or nicked; otherwise, only whetting and/or honing will be necessary. Many wood turners and carvers prefer the whetstone or grindstone to the dry, motorized grinder. Nevertheless, with proper care the dry wheel can be used effectively. The Whetstone grinders are apt to be expensive, nonportable, heavy, and large.

The dry, motorized grinder has to be used with caution because too much metal is sometimes removed and the tool edge is apt to be burned and lose its temper. The secret of good dry grinding is to exert little pressure against the wheel with the tool.

There is a small, 10-inch diameter, wet sandstone grinder that is motorized; professional turners and carvers are not too impressed with it. The grindstone turns *away* from the tool being sharpened, while the dry wheel grinder turns *toward* the tool. See Fig. 2-10.

If the chisel or gouge is excessively dull or nicked, the edge should be held against the wheel to straighten the edge. Of course, this will dull the tool further, but a true edge will be established to work from.

When grinding straight tools, hold the bevel side down against the grinding wheel, and place the index finger on the underside of it to slide against the rest on the grinder. Naturally, if the grinder is equipped with a tool holder, the freehand method is not appropriate.

Take a few passes across the edge of the grinding wheel to see if the correct angle has been established. If not, slide the index finger up or down until the correct angle is found. During the grinding process, check often for squareness and overheating. If the edge of the tool starts to turn dark in color, dunk it in water at once. Small tools are more apt to overheat than large ones.

If there is no shield on the grinder, the operator

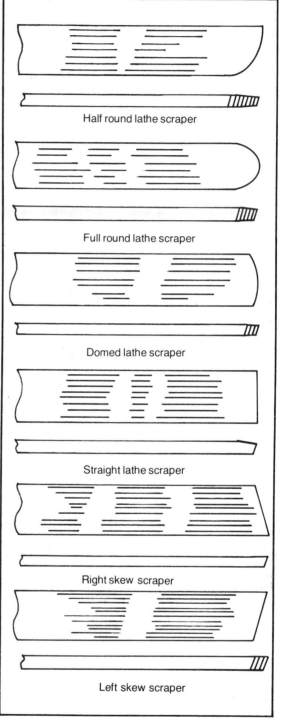

Half round lathe scraper

Full round lathe scraper

Domed lathe scraper

Straight lathe scraper

Right skew scraper

Left skew scraper

Fig. 2-8. Wood-turning scrapers.

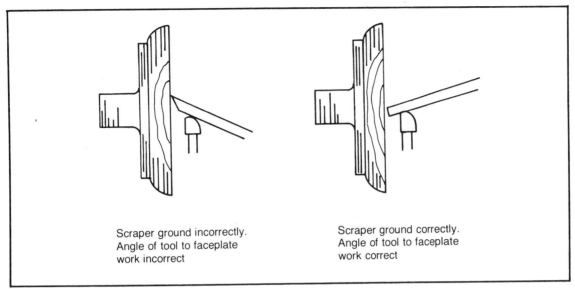

Scraper ground incorrectly.
Angle of tool to faceplate
work incorrect

Scraper ground correctly.
Angle of tool to faceplate
work correct

Fig. 2-9. Scraper angles.

must wear goggles or a face shield when dry grinding.

When grinding is complete, a wire edge will turn up on the side opposite the bevel. The wire edge will be removed in subsequent whetting and honing. On some turning tools (scraping tools and roughing gouges), the wire edge is not removed.

Grinding wheels or abrasive wheels are usually made of aluminum oxide and are available in fine,

medium, and coarse grits. The wheels range in diameter from 4 inches to 14 inches and in thickness from ½ inch to 2 inches. The wheel should not be allowed to glaze over because it will do a poor job of grinding. A wheel dresser should be used whenever the wheel is filled up with metal debris or is not perfectly straight across.

Spindle or fingernail gouges are ground to a round nose so they can turn concave sections on spindle turn-

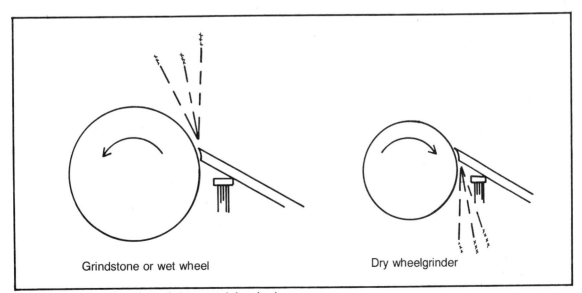

Grindstone or wet wheel

Dry wheelgrinder

Fig. 2-10. Direction of rotation: grindstone and dry wheel.

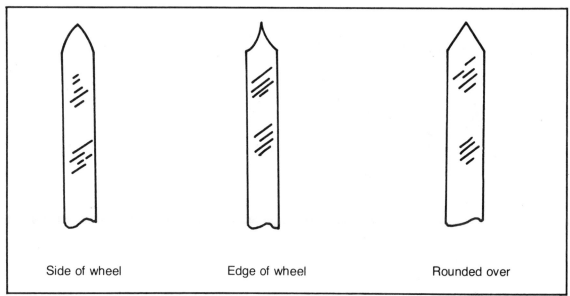

Side of wheel   Edge of wheel   Rounded over

Fig. 2-11. Grinding turning chisels.

ings. The grinding of spindle gouges—in fact all gouges—requires considerable practice and skill.

Some turners use the side of the wheel to grind turning chisels and skews, but I prefer to use the edge of the wheel because it is easier to observe what is taking place. Another advantage is that by grinding on the edge of the wheel a slightly concave edge is established. Grinding on the side of the wheel produces a flat bevel. It is easier to whet a concave surface as the two points of contact are easily observed and felt. A perfectly flat bevel is more apt to be rounded over. This results in poor performance because it is likely to dig into the wood. See Fig. 2-11.

Grinding Turning Chisels

The spindle gouge is held firmly against the rest while grinding. The gouge is slowly rolled from side to side with little pressure against the wheel. The grinding starts at the heel of the bevel and is slowly tipped toward the cutting edge as grinding proceeds. Some craftsmen prefer grinding right up to the very cutting edge (which they can ascertain by the sparks that come over the edge of the blade). At this point, the craftsman should look for signs of overheating. Because of this possibility, many craftsmen prefer to grind nearly to the edge and finish the sharpening with a whetting stone. See Fig. 2-12.

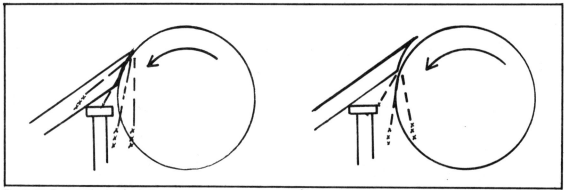

Fig. 2-12. Two methods of grinding.

Two Methods of Grinding

The roughing gouges and deep fluted gouges are a little less difficult to grind because the cutting edges are not ground to a a rounded nose (fingernail), but are ground straight across. The bevel of these tools is much steeper than on the spindle gouges—usually 45 degrees or less. The tool is rolled from side to side like the spindle gouge; but naturally it is rolled at a different angle.

Many turners argue over the exact angles that have to be ground on chisels and gouges. A lot depends on the height of the tool rest and the height of the operator. A short man with a high rest will probably grind his tools to a long bevel. A tall man with a low rest will grind his tools much blunter. The important thing is that the bevel must rub the work at all times to keep shavings curling away from the tool.

Bench Stones. Bench stones are used in a stationary position. Cutting tools are rubbed against the stone. Slip stones are rubbed against the tools. A bench stone often has a fine grit on one face and a coarse grit on the other. A typical bench stone would measure 8 × 2 × 1 inches.

Gouge Stones. Gouge stones, sometimes called *cone gouge slips,* are used for whetting the inside and outside curves of gouges. The taper of these stones takes care of a wide range of curvatures. Stones are about 6 inches long with a taper from 2 inches at one end to ½ inch wide at the other. They have both concave and convex surfaces. They are generally available in silicon carbide and aluminum oxide (India). These stones are used more often on carving chisels than on turning chisels.

Slip Stones. Slip stones are of different sizes and shapes. They are used to whet the cutting edges of chisels, gouges and many other edge tools. Sizes vary, but a typical slip stone is 4½ inches long and 1¾ inches wide. The thickest part is in the ¼-inch to ½-inch range, and the thinnest part is in the ⅛-inch to 1/16-inch range. The craftsman should possess at least two slip stones. Slip stones used on gouges should not be used on chisels because a hollow usually develops in a short time. Slip stones are available in India (aluminum oxide), soft Arkansas and hard Arkansas. See Fig. 2-13.

Whetting Stones. Two general classifications of whetting stones are *synthetic* stones and *natural* stones. Synthetic stones are made of aluminum oxide, also called India stones or aloxite, and of silicon carbide, a dark grey or black stone often carrying the name of Carborundum.

The natural stone comes from a small area in Arkansas. The soft, white Arkansas is relatively inexpensive when compared with the black, hard Arkansas stone. Both are more expensive than man-made stones.

Oiling Whet Stones. Synthetic stones are made

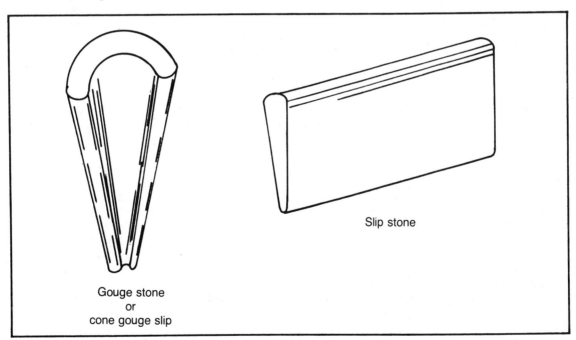

Gouge stone
or
cone gouge slip

Slip stone

Fig. 2-13. Whetting stones.

up of a multitude of very small crystals held together by an adhesive. As a result man-made stones are quite porous. As whetting takes place, small metal particles from the tool being sharpened—added to grain particles that are removed from the stone—has a tendency to clog the pores of the whetting stones. As a result the stone is much less efficient.

Oiling the stone's surface will keep these particles (metal and abrasive) in a slurry suspension that prevents the pores from becoming clogged. Of course, the oil will penetrate the stone. To counteract this high rate of penetration, silicon carbide and aluminum oxide stones are often filled with oil at the factory.

Whetting and Turning Tools. Turning tools should be held firmly against a stationary object; the tool rest or tailstock are convenient and nearby. They work fine. The stone is properly oiled and moved against the bevel with a continuous circular motion. Make sure that all parts of the cutting edges are covered.

Extreme caution should be taken not to roll over the cutting edge. For that matter, the entire bevel should not be rolled. Both defects will mean that the tool will have to be held much too high (which often leads to an automatic dig-in).

The major purpose of whetting is to remove the ragged edge (sometimes called the wire edge or feather edge) left after the grinding process. On some cutting tools the wire edge is left on.

"Sharpness" of the edge is not necessarily synonymous with the "finest" of edge. A long, sharp bevel can be ground on a chisel, but it will not be a fine point. It will dull easily and the edge is apt to break under pressure.

Honing. The difference between *honing* and *whetting* is sometimes controversial, but the author contends that honing is done only with a leather strop or a buffing wheel.

The leather strop produces a fine, sharp edge (remember the old straight razor!). Strops can be used with or without a specially prepared paste. All strops and stones should be kept free from dust, dirt, and grime when not in use.

The combination of a buffing wheel and buffing compound is, by far, the fastest of the honing methods. For the ultimate edge, use the compounds (fine abrasives mixed with wax) in the following order: *grey compound*, *tripoli compound* and *jewelery's rouge*.

Some manufacturers and suppliers contend that the dry and wet grinding wheels are old-fashioned and obsolete. They have developed a grinding and honing system in one package that they claim is much superior. The system revolves around a two-arbor motor. On one end is a buffing wheel. On the other end is a large contact wheel about 10 inches or 11 inches in diameter with a idler wheel just behind it. A long aluminum oxide abrasive belt rides on the contact and idler wheels. These belts have long life, do not glaze over easily, and can be changed rapidly if need be. The tools are held against the contact wheel (which is about the right curvature for hollow grinding). The sliding tool rest will handle extra-long tools.

MEASURING TOOLS

Outside Calipers. Outside calipers are available in 3-inch, 6-inch, 10-inch, and 12-inch sizes. The 3-inch and 6-inch size are the most commonly used for wood turning, and they are less cumbersome to use than the larger sizes. The sizes indicated above are the length of the calipers. Usually the maximum distance they can be opened to is a little more than their length.

Measurements are quite often transferred from a master turning or drawing to the work being turned. Calipers should not be forced, but should just touch the turning. A good turner can "feel" an error of less than 1/128 of an inch. Two calipers can be used as "go-no-go" gauges.

The most common type, and the most practical, is the spring-type calipers with a quick-acting nut. Friction-type calipers are seldom used except for extremely large turnings.

When the legs of the spring-type calipers are squeezed together, the nut breaks loose from contact with a tapered closing washer. The two half sections of the split nut open up so that the inside threads are no longer in contact with the external threads on the adjusting cross member and is free to move quickly up or down the adjusting cross member screw.

In use on the lathe, the outside calipers are usually held in the right hand after the dimension has been set. The parting tool is held in the left hand with the handle squeezed between the forearm and the body. By observation, the operator can ascertain when the diameter is near the required diameter. The calipers are applied frequently as the parting tool is slowly reducing the diameter. Calipers are *never* used with the stock turning unless the stock is perfectly round.

The nut of the calipers is generally clamped between the middle finger and the third finger so that the dimension will not change due to stock or lathe vibration. The nut should point away from the turning stock.

Dimensions are established on the outside calipers by placing one leg against the end of a steel scale or combination square and setting the dimension with the other leg. See Fig. 2-14.

Inside Calipers. Inside calipers are straight-legged with the points curving outward. They are available in the same sizes as outside calipers and are used to transfer or measure the diameter of internal holes or cavities. Inside calipers should *not* be used when the stock in the lathe is turning. See Figs. 2-15A and 2-15B.

Dividers. Dividers are used to scribe circles and arcs and to transfer or to take measurements. They can also be used to step off divisions of equal size. Great care should be exercised in scribing lines on round stock while it is turning. If the points should catch in the stock, they could cause injury to the user and are apt to ruin the dividers. It is best to angle the points down from the tool rest as there is less chance of injury.

I prefer a pencil compass for stepping off dimensions because there is only one sharp point to contend with. The dividers can be used for scribing circles on faceplate work as well as scribing dimensions on spindle turnings.

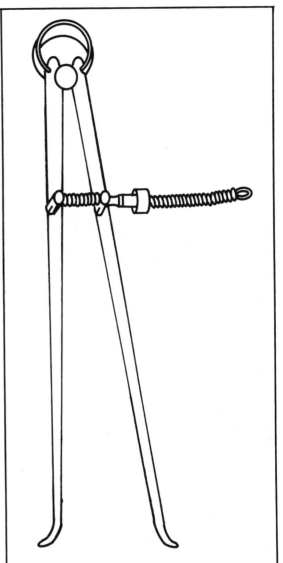

Fig. 2-15A. Inside calipers.

Care should be taken that the back point does not dig into the work. See Fig. 2-16.

There are two types of dividers: the spring dividers and the wing dividers. The wing dividers are my preference because they are a little more sturdy than the spring dividers. Furthermore, it has one fixed leg and one is removable so that it can be replaced with a pencil.

The diAccurate Chisel. The diAccurate, manufactured by Lemco Tools, Inc. are special chisels used for making duplicate cuts of the same size. It does away

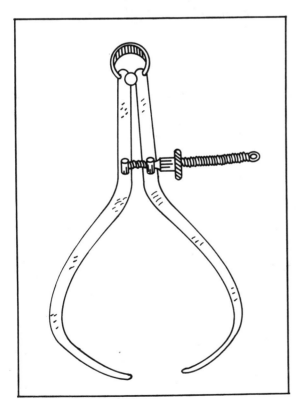

Fig. 2-14. Outside calipers.

small details. The narrow cutting edge will let the turner produce Vs or excellent square shoulders. It is also available with around nose-cutting edge for cutting covers. See Fig. 2-18.

Woodturner's Sizing Tool. This tool, also known as the woodturner's gauge, is used for making multiple

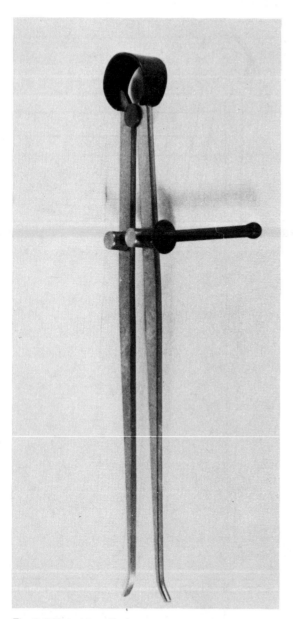

Fig. 2-15B. Inside calipers.

with the alternate use of the parting tool and the outside calipers. Tenons and dowels are made quickly with ease. Beads can be repeated over and over again.

There are 10 sizes (in inches) of diAccurate chisels: ⅜, 7/16, ½, 9/16, ⅝, ¾, ⅞, 1, 1⅛, and 1¼. See Fig. 2-17.

The #100 di Accurate Chisel is another Lemco product. It can be used as a parting tool or for finishing

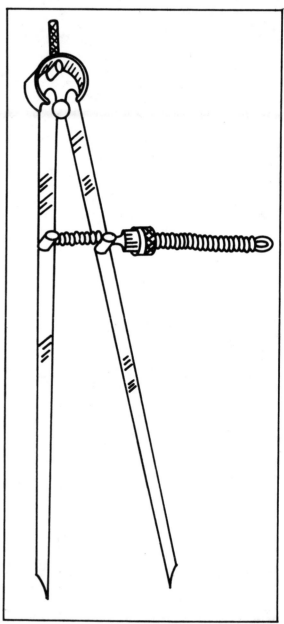

Fig. 2-16. Dividers.

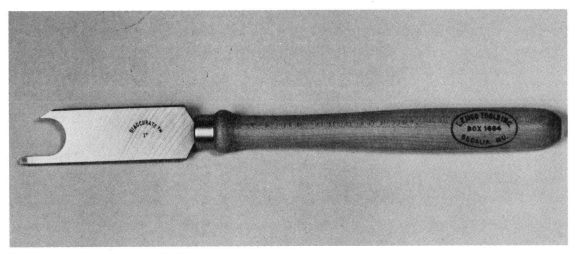

Fig. 2-17. One-inch diAccurate chisel.

cuts of the same diameter. This sizing gauge is generally used with a parting tool for making preliminary cuts and for making round tenons on turnings. Two wing nuts on the gauge are used to adjust the gauge to the proper diameter. See Fig. 2-19.

The Contour Gauge. The contour gauge is an excellent tool for comparing an original turning with work being turned in the lathe. It is made up of thin, sliding metal pieces that are pressed against the original and locked in place to be used until all turnings are reproduced. It eliminates the necessity of making templates or patterns for each turning.

The contour gauge can also be used for fitting floor coverings against door casings, moldings, bath fixtures, and pipes. See Figs. 2-20A and 2-20B.

The Centering Jig. The centering jig is used to locate centers on both square and round stock. Diagonals are drawn on square stock, and two lines at right angles to each other are drawn on the ends of round stock. The center is where the two lines cross. See Fig. 2-21.

DRILLING AND BORING TOOLS

The terms drilling and boring are used interchangeably. In general, however, boring is more often applied to woodworking. In other words, we bore holes in wood; we drill holes in metal. Boring is often necessary in many turned projects.

The easily available twist drill bits sold to many home craftsmen are designed for metal drilling. Experienced woodworkers depend on auger bits and drills spec-

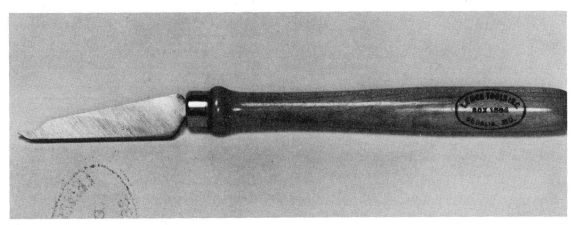

Fig. 2-18. #100 diAccurate chisel.

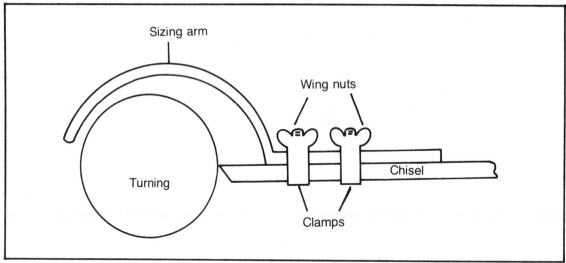

Fig. 2-19. Woodturner's sizing tool.

ifically designed for boring clean, smooth holes in wood. Properly used, these bits cut holes with more precision, more easily, and give a better-appearing final result.

Drill bits designed for metal have a tendency to "wander" in wood. Auger bits and other bits designed for wood are equipped with spurs and a screw point or spurs with an unthreaded point, often referred to as a brad point.

Auger Bits. Auger bits (square tang, spurs, and screw point) are ordinarily used with a hand brace. Machine bits (round shank, spurs, and unthreaded point or brad point) can be used in the lathe with a Jacobs chuck. They are also used in many other power-driven boring machines.

Auger bits can be converted into machine bits by cutting off the square tang and filing the threads from the screw point. This procedure, however, is not recommended except in an emergency.

Auger bits are available in sizes from ¼ to 1¼ inches in diameter. Sizes are indicated by a number indented on the tang of the bit. This number designates the size in sixteenths of an inch. A number six on the tang identifies a ⅜-inch (6/16-inch) bit.

The depth of the hole made by an auger bit can be roughly estimated by counting the number of turns the bit makes. Each revolution (turn) of the bit will pull the bit into the wood approximately 1/16 of an inch.

Auger bits are of two types: the *single twist* and the *double twist*. Deep holes are bored easier with the single twist bit, but the double twist bit cuts a cleaner hole. Figure 2-22 shows a single twist bit.

Not all square tang bits are auger bits. Other boring tools such as the Forstner bit, the expansion bit, and others are often equipped with a square tang.

The *tang* is the part of the bit that fits into the brace. A small tapered screw (feed screw) on the tip of the bit pulls the bit into the wood so that the *spurs* (knife-like projections) can cut the outline of the circle. The cutting edges or *lips* cut away the rest of the hole that follows up the *twist* of the bit.

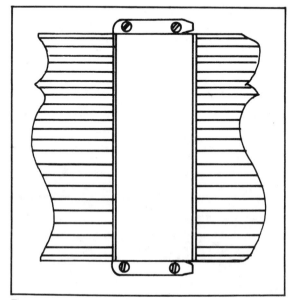

Fig. 2-20A. Contour gauge.

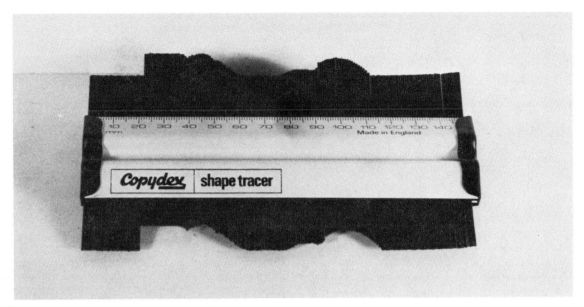

Fig. 2-20B. Contour gauge.

Fig. 2-21. Centering jig.

Drill Bits. Drill bits, although designed for drilling metal, can be sharpened so that they perform adequately in boring wood, by sharpening the bit to a sharper point, and by grinding a concave section on each lip.

Drill bits are available in *fractional* and *letter* sizes. Fractional sizes run from 1/32 to ½ inch in 1/64-inch increments. Letter size bits are available in ¼-inch to ½-inch sizes where fractional sizes are not applicable. Fractional sizes are generally adequate for boring in wood. See Figs. 2-23 and 2-24.

Lamp Standard Shell Auger Bits. Lamp standard shell bits are used on the lathe in conjunction with a hollow boring guide. These bits will bore perfectly straight holes in end grain up to their length. The hollow portion is kept on the uppermost side to collect the wood shavings. The shavings should be removed often while the bit is in use.

These bits are used frequently in making holes in turned lamps and in making musical instruments. The most commonly used bit is 30 inches long. Diameters are 5/16 of an inch and ⅜ of an inch.

Spade Bits. Spade bits, sometimes known as zip or whiz bits, are used exclusively for boring in wood. The flat, spade-shaped bits are available in sizes from ¼ inch in diameter to 1 inch, in increments of 1/16 of an inch. The shanks of all spade bits are ¼ inch in diameter so that they can be used in portable electric drills. Spade bits bore faster and neater than many other boring tools, but

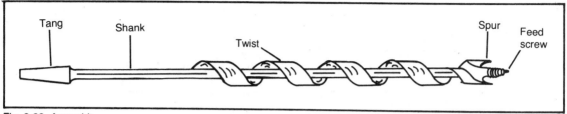

Fig. 2-22. Augur bit.

care has to be taken to prevent puncturing the reverse side of the stock. See Fig. 2-25.

Multi-Spur Bits. Multispur bits are available in sizes from ½ inch to 1 inch, in increments of 1/16″, and in sizes 1 inch to 1¼ inches in increments of ⅛ of an inch.

The multispur bit has a round shank of ¼-inch diameter so it can be used in a portable electric drill. It is a very fast, clean-boring tool. In addition, it will bore at an angle, overlapping or on close center, without splitting the wood. See Figs. 2-26 and 2-27.

Forstner Bits. Forstner bits are ideal for boring flat bottom holes. They are available in sizes from ⅜ to 1 inch, in increments of 1/16 of an inch. Stamp sizes are the same as those stamped on the tang of auger bits. There are also Forstner bits available in sizes from 1¼ to 2 inches, in increments of ¼ of an inch.

Forstner bits (Fig. 2-28) are used for counterboring and the multi-sput bit will bore a hole close or on the edge of stock without tearing. The multisput bit will bore nearly through wood without the spurs or feed screw

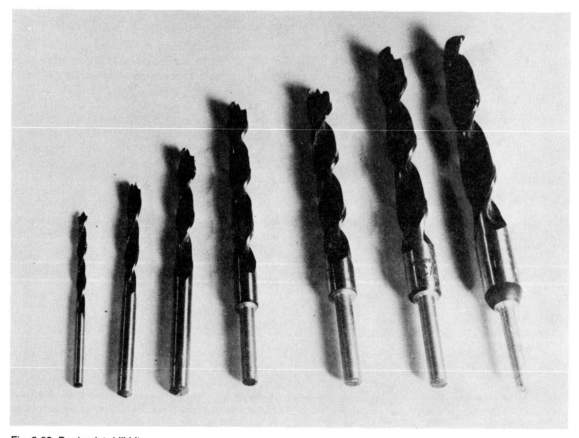

Fig. 2-23. Brad point drill bits.

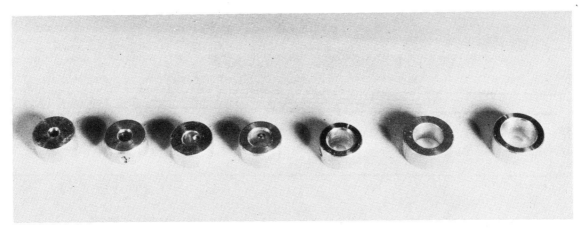

Fig. 2-24. Drill bit depth collars.

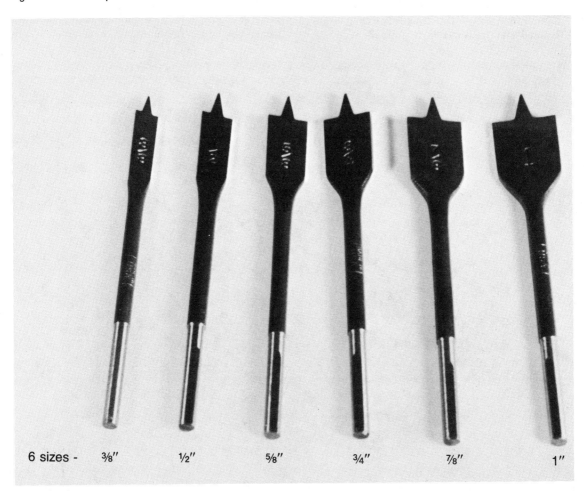

6 sizes - 3/8"   1/2"   5/8"   3/4"   7/8"   1"

Fig. 2-25. Spade bits.

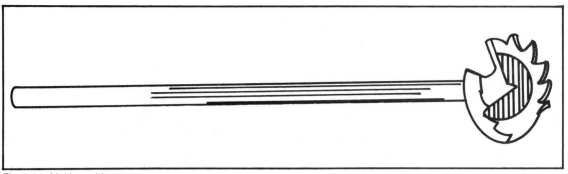

Fig. 2-26. Multispur bit.

coming through, puncturing the reverse side of the stock.

Power Bore Bits. Power bore bits are available in sizes from ⅜ to 1 inch, in increments of ⅛ of an inch. Each bit is 5½ inches long. The shank is ¼ inch in diameter. The brad point feeds evenly. See Fig. 2-29.

VERTICAL LATHE TOOLS

The Raab-Kirk Company present an entirely new concept in wood turning. The basics stressed are safety, controlled cutting per revolution, and simplicity of opera-

Fig. 2-27. Multispur bit.

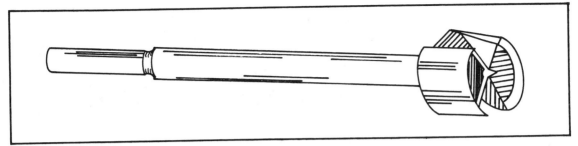

Fig. 2-28. Forstner bit.

tion. The bits are engineered with a design that controls wood removal per revolution along with simplicity of sharpening. It is an easy task that takes less than one minute of sharpening time for every hour of turning. All of these are accomplished without sacrifice to the flexibility of the Raab-Kick Vertical Wood Lathe Tools. Even the selection of woods is easier and less expensive with the ease and simplicity of cutting through voids and knots.

The three types of vertical wood lathe tools are: the *Spindle Turning Tool*, the *Bowl Turning Tool*, and the *Parting* and *Design Tool*. See Figs. 2-30 and 2-31.

BOWL-TURNING DEPTH GAUGE

In the Nov/Dec 1979 issue of the *Fine Woodworking* magazine, Percy W. Blandford describes a practical bowl-turning depth gauge. The following four paragraphs

Fig. 2-29. Seven-eighth-inch power-bore bit.

VERTICAL WOOD LATHE TOOL

SPINDLE TURNING TOOL

The VERTICAL WOOD LATHE TOOL is an entirely new concept in wood turning.

The *safety* of this tool enables novices - men, women and children - to learn in a short period of time (20 minutes or less) how to *safely* shape wood. To do the same shaping and design work with conventional tools for wood turning, extensive training would be required.

The tool is held in a vertical position. No tool rest is needed, only a flat table surface across the ways of any lathe. The operation of the tool is such that the hands are automatically placed *safely* away from the danger of the spinning wood.

The uniquely-designed cutting bit gives you precise, controlled cutting, with unbelievable stability for cutting through knots and voids with fingertip control. The VERTICAL WOOD LATHE TOOL turns square wood down to round with ease.

The SPINDLE TURNING TOOL takes the place of many chisels.

The cutting bit has a round and a pointed bit that extend 3/32 of an inch. Use the round bit for rounded and sloping cuts and the pointed bit for small designs and flat square ledges. To cut a deep design, turn the tool on its own axis in a semicircle. To make a sloping cut, lean the tool from side to side, while keeping the base of the tool in one place.

To sharpen the cutting bit, place the top of the cutting bit's flat surface on a sharpening stone and rub it back and forth until the cutting tips have a sharp edge.

MONEY BACK GUARANTEE

MEMBER EDUCATIONAL EXHIBITORS ASSOCIATION ☐ SHIP

RAAB-KIRK Co.

P.O. Box 208 • Corvallis, OR 97339

Phone (503) 752-6698

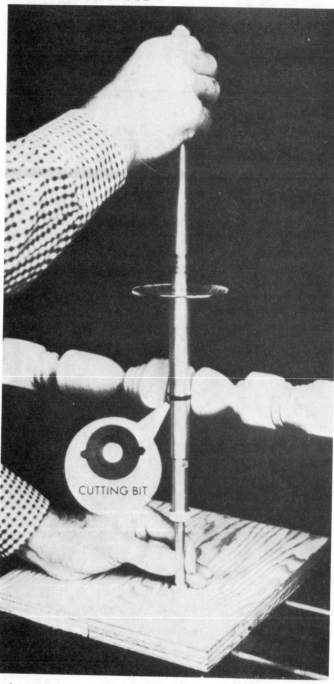

CUTTING BIT

Fig. 2-30. Vertical wood lathe spindle turning tool.

ALL TOOLS DESIGNED FOR PRECISE, CONTROLLED CUTTING, PER REVOLUTION.

BOWL TURNING TOOL

This tool is used to cut the interior of a bowl 2¼ inches deep and undercut its edges.

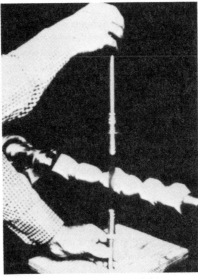

PARTING AND DESIGN TOOL

This tool is used to part off multiple work and cut extremely tight designs in spindle turning.

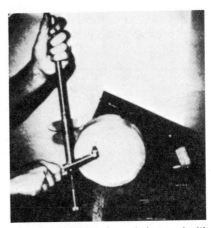

BOWL EXTENSION shown being used with the Bowl Turning Tool.

BOWL EXTENSION

This tool is used to cut the interior of a bowl 4 inches deep and has the same cutting bit that is used in the Spindle Tool.

The extension can be used with either the Spindle Turning Tool or the Bowl turning Tool.

TOOLS
Designed for Safety

BY RAAB-KIRK COMPANY

Fig. 2-31. Bowl-turning, parting and design tools.

"When turning a hollow, as for a bowl, it is difficult to estimate how deep a cut has been taken. Although the best curves may be made by eye, it is necessary to know the depth to check on the remaining thickness of wood and avoid turning through. A ruler can be held against a straightedge across the rim of the bowl, but that is an improvisation. The tool described here is a more efficient way to check depth.

"Make the stock wide enough to span the largest diameter bowl your lathe can turn. The base must be flat. The other parts can be shaped as you wish, but edges should be rounded for a comfortable grip. It is easier to get the peg hole perpendicular to the base before other shaping is done. The wedge hole can be cut at the same time.

"The peg may be a length of dowel rod. Its working end should be slightly tapered and finished with a little doming where it will touch the bowl.

"The slot for the wedge has to be made with its edge cutting through the peg hole by a small amount. An overlap of 1/32" should be enough. Make the wedge and measure the thickness of the stock centrally on it. From the distance across the wedge at these points, mark the width of the hole at each side. The ends of the wedge can be rounded and decorated, but a plain wedge works just as well." See Fig. 2-32.

HOW TO MAKE TOOL HANDLES

Many times lathe tools and other chisels can be purchased without handles. As a result, considerable savings can be achieved by turning your own tool handles. The procedure below applies to all-round tool handles—not just to lathe tools—such as carving and sculpturing tools, bench chisels, paring chisels, garden tools handles, file handles, etc.

Most straight-grained hardwood make fine tool handles. Beech, hickory, boxwood, ash, hornbeam, and maple seem to be the favorites. See Chapter 5. Procedure:

☐ Select proper ferrule stock. The best ferrules are made of brass or copper; stainless steel is sometimes used. Brass and copper tubing or pipe make excellent ferrules. They are much less expensive than ferrules purchased separately. The purpose of the ferrule is to prevent the splitting out of the handle when the tang of the tool is driven into the handle.

Ferrules should be at least as long as the diameter of the ferrule. The diameter of the ferrule should be large enough to provide considerable supporting wood between the ferrule and tang.

☐ Cut ferrules to length. Tubing and pipe can be cut with a fine-toothed hacksaw. Stay away from coarse blades. The distance from one tooth to the other should never be greater than the thickness of the tubing or pipe.

☐ True up the ferrules. File the ends of ferrules

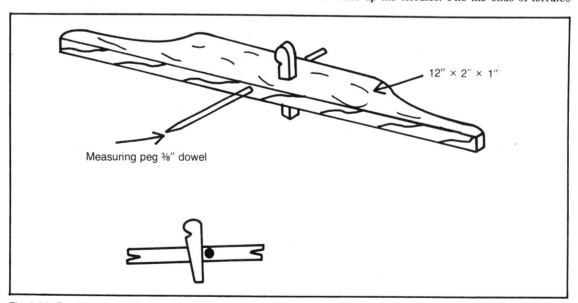

12" × 2" × 1"

Measuring peg ⅜" dowel

Fig. 2-32. Bowl-turning depth gauge.

straight and true. Remove the burrs on the inside with a needle file or small, round file.

☐ Cut rough stock for handles on the circular saw. The width, thickness, and length will depend on the function of the tool. For example, tool handles for the "long and strong" woodturning gouges and chisels will be considerably longer than handles for other lathe tools.

☐ Prepare and mount stock in the lathe. See Chapter 6 on spindle turning.

☐ Turn the entire length round with a gouge.

☐ Establish length of ferrule. Mark the length of ferrule plus ⅛ of an inch on the tailstock end of the stock.

☐ Set calipers. Set the outside calipers about 1/32 of an inch larger than the internal diameter of the ferrule.

☐ Turn diameter. Turn to the diameter set on the calipers with a parting tool on the right side of the mark made two steps earlier.

☐ Turn ferrule part to size. Turn the rest of the ferrule to size (first with a small gouge and then with a skew or scraping tool). A beginning turner should use the scraping tool for the entire cut. Taper the ferrule slightly on the part closest to the tailstock center.

☐ Turn off the lathe. Turn off the lathe and grip the turning with the left hand so that the turning will not slip off the spur (live) center in the headstock.

☐ Try for size. Back off the tailstock center and try the ferrule for size. If the ferrule part of the handle is still too large, put the handle back in the lathe and reduce the size. Be careful not to remove too much stock.

☐ Check the ferrule for length. When the correct size of the ferrule is arrived at, measure the ferrule against the ferrule tenon on the handle to make sure that the tenon is long enough. The ferrule should fit tightly on the tenon.

☐ Square up the shoulder. Square up the shoulder of the ferrule tenon with the point of a skew.

☐ Registration mark. Place a registration mark on the handle and spur center in order that the turning can be returned to the same position to complete turning of the handle.

☐ Fix the ferrule to the handle. Remove the handle from the lathe and drive the ferrule end of the handle into the ferrule.

☐ Reposition handle. Reposition the handle with the attached ferrule back in the lathe between centers.

☐ Round over the ferrule. Start the lathe and round over the end of the ferrule next to the tailstock center with a file.

☐ Polishing the ferrule. Polish the ferrule with a strip of emery cloth. Keep the emery cloth moving using the entire length to the cloth.

☐ Apply liquid polish. Polish the ferrule with a little liquid metal polish on a pad. The pad should be free of loose threads; otherwise the pad might be caught in the lathe.

☐ Establish the length of the handle. Mark off the length of the handle. It should be from ½ to ¾ of an inch from the headstock end of the stock.

☐ Make an incision. Make an incision at this mark with a parting tool about half way through the turning.

☐ Turn the shape of the handle. Turn the handle to a comfortable and pleasing shape with a small gouge. Finish off the ferrule ends of handle with a skew.

☐ Decorate the handle. Decorate the handle with V cuts or beads. The V can be enhanced by burning in the V with the corner of a chisel held tightly against the turning handle.

☐ Sand. Sand the handle lightly with fine sandpaper.

☐ Burnish. Some turners burnish the turning with a handful of shavings held against the underside of the turning with the tool rest removed.

☐ Mount the drill bit in the chuck. Insert a drill bit—slightly smaller than the tang of the tool to be inserted into the handle—into a Jacobs chuck.

☐ Reverse Tailstock. Back off the tailstock and remove the handle and tailstock center.

☐ Mount the Jacobs chuck in the tailstock. Insert the Jacobs chuck with drill bit into the tailstock. Turn back the tailstock spindle to allow for a movement of the Jacobs and bit equal to the length of the tang.

☐ Replace the handle in the lathe. Reinsert the handle in the lathe using the registration marks previously established.

☐ Move up the drill bit. Move up the tailstock until the drill bit enters the center indentation left by the tailstock center. Lock the tailstock.

☐ Bore the tang hole. Advance the drill bit into the ferrule end of the handle to the desired tang depth.

☐ Remove the Jacobs chuck and handle. Stop the lathe, back off the tailstock, remove the Jacobs chuck and handle, and reinsert the tailstock center into the tailstock.

☐ Handle goes back in lathe. Place the handle back in the lathe between centers using the registration marks.

☐ Headstock end turned. Turn the headstock end of the handle with a skew leaving about 3/16 to ¼ inch of stock.

☐ French polish. Sand and polish the headstock end of handle. Some turners apply a French polish to lathe projects while they are turning in the lathe. A small amount of thinned shellac is applied to the center of a strip of folded cloth. Apply a drop of linseed oil or machine oil to the shellac. Apply cloth to the handle while it is turning using considerable pressure. This finishing process builds up a high gloss finish. Apply three or four coats with a short interval between coats.

☐ Finish turning. Cut through the remaining 3/16 or ¼-inch stock at the headstock end with the skew held in one hand. Catch the falling handle with the other hand.

Chapter 3

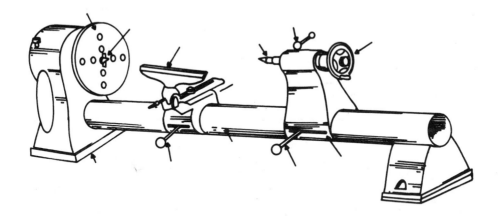

Lathe Accessories

IN ADDITION TO STANDARD, SINGLE-COLUMN TOOL rests there are extra-long, *double-column* supports that require two tool rest saddles on the lathe. The *right-angle* tool rest is useful when you are doing both spindle and faceplate work on the same piece. This tool rest alleviates the necessity of moving the tool rest when switching from one type of turning to the other. See Fig. 3-10.

The *S-shaped tool rest* is designed specifically for internal faceplate turning.

JACOBS CHUCKS

Jacobs chucks are used primarily on drill presses and lathes to hold drilling and boring tools and occasionally other tools or devices. Jacobs chucks are also used with portable electric drills.

The Jacobs chuck has a teeth ring that operate (open and close) the three jaws. A chuck key engages the teeth ring that operates the jaws. The Jacobs chuck used with the lathe is fitted with a tapered shank (usually a #1 or #2 Morse Taper) that fits the taper in the headstock and tailstock.

Jacobs chucks are used quite often to bore into faceplate work or chuck work to start an internal cut such as

goblets and egg cups or to bore holes simply to hold an object (e.g., candlesticks). When boring holes with the Jacobs chuck in either the headstock or tailstock, there is little need for caution because the pressure against the chuck keeps the Morse tapered shank well seated in the spindles. When the Jacobs chuck is used to hold other accessories used for grinding polishing, buffing, sanding, etc., the tailstock center should be brought up close to the outside end of the accessory to prevent the accessory from flying out of the lathe that could cause an injury or damage to tools. See Figs. 3-2 and 3-3.

Special attention must be given to the chuck key. If the chuck key is left in the Jacobs chuck, it can be thrown out with great force when the lathe or drill is started and might cause an injury. Sizes of Jacobs chucks are designated by the sizes of drill bits that they will hold. The sizes (in inches) are 0-3/8, 0-1/2", 1/8 to 5/8, and 3/16 to ¾.

UNIVERSAL OR COMBINATION CHUCKS

Woodcraft Supply Co. supplies a new, refined version of the six-in-one combination chuck claimed to be the ultimate in holding devices for faceplate turning. This chuck is manufactured by Hattersley & Davidson, Ltd. of Shef-

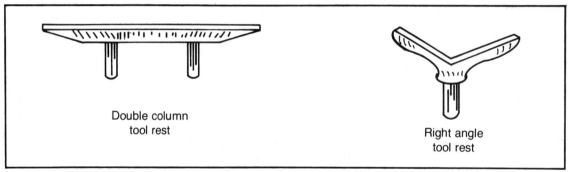

Fig. 3-1. Double-column and right-angle tool rest.

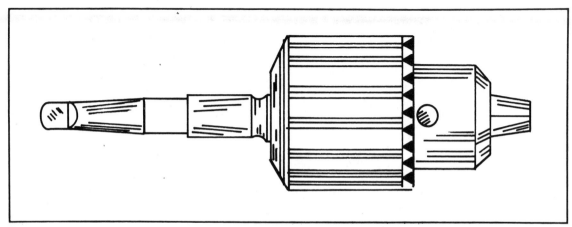

Fig. 3-2. Jacobs chuck.

Fig. 3-3. Jacobs chuck.

field, England. The expanding collet system is safe and easy to use. The wood is mounted in the traditional way on a faceplate and shallow dovetailed recesses is turned in the bottom. The dovetailed recess can then be mounted over the collets that are expanded into the recess by tightening the outer ring with the two spanner wrenches. The system provides automatic self-centering and the work can be removed and replaced without any loss of strength. Glue blocks are not necessary and unsightly screw holes are eliminated. In addition, there are no projecting parts to catch tools or clothing while turning.

There are four parts to the combination chuck: *Body, Center Boss, Split Ring,* and *Outer Ring.* These four parts are used in different ways to make up four different chucks: the expanding-collet chuck, split-ring chuck, screw chuck, and ring chuck.

The Expanding-Collet Chuck. The expanding collet chuck uses three parts: the body, the center boss, and the outer ring. To prepare stock for use in the expanding-collet chuck:

☐ Mount the stock on a faceplate and mark out the 3½-inch diameter with dividers.

☐ Turn the recess maintaining a flat base, and finally reduce the dovetail with a skew.

☐ Assemble the chuck on the lathe with the collets close together.

☐ Mount the recess over the collets and tighten the outer ring with the large spanner. See Fig. 3-4.

The Split-Ring Chuck. The split-ring chuck uses three parts: the body, the split ring, and the outer ring. To prepare stock for use in the split-ring chuck:

☐ Mount the wood between centers and produce a square end face and a ⅜-inch groove.

☐ Assemble the chuck on the lathe and grip wood as shown. *Note*: This chuck is suitable for wood between 1¾ and 2½ inches in diameter. For stock larger than 2½ inches, prepare the wood between centers and turn an additional 1 5/16 inches of 2 1/4 inch diameter as shown to allow for the ⅜-inch groove before assembling the split ring. See Fig. 3-5.

The Screw Chuck. The screw chuck uses four parts: the body, the center boss, the split ring, and the outer ring. To preparing stock for the screw chuck:

☐ Plane or cut true the side to be mounted against the chuck.

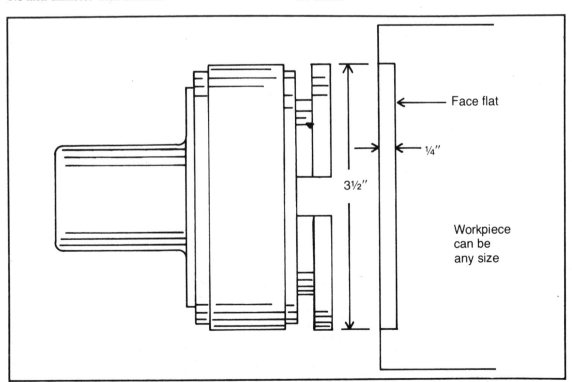

Fig. 3-4. Expanding collet chuck.

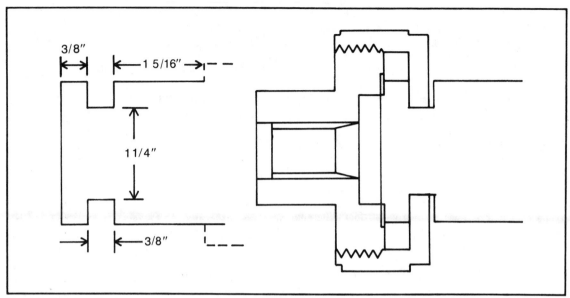

Fig. 3-5. Split ring chuck.

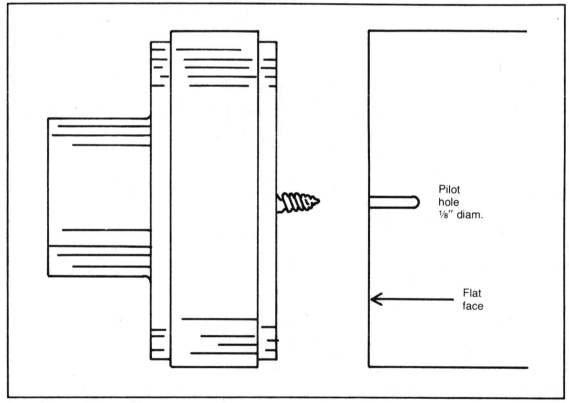

Pilot hole 1/8" diam.

Flat face

Fig. 3-6. Screw chuck.

□ Drill a small pilot hole in the center of the work piece and mount on the screw chuck.

□ Place a folded piece of abrasive paper on end grain work to prevent slippage.

□ Place a wood disc between the work and the chuck face to provide easier access to the rear of the work. *Note*: The No. 14 wood screw can be quickly replaced or adjusted to protrude the required length by using the Allen key. See Fig. 3-6.

The Ring Chuck. The ring chuck uses two parts of the 6-in-1 combination chuck: the body and the outer ring. To preparing stock for use with the ring chuck:

□ Mount the stock between centers.

□ Turn the flanges as shown in the drawing. The diameter must be between 2¾ and 3 inches. The rest of the stock must be 2½ inches in diameter or less to allow the clamping outer ring to pass over it.

□ True up the end of the stock with the parting tool to ensure a firm seating.

□ Remove the work from between the two centers and mount within the chuck using the C-spanner. See Fig. 3-7.

The Collet Chuck. The chuck described below is not a combination chuck but it seemed appropriate to place it here. This collet chuck from Woodcraft represents the state of the art in split-ring chucks for woodturning. The metal body has sufficient rigidity to withstand the stress of turning tools while the designed aluminum collets allow some of the flexibility normally associated with wooden chucks. Aluminum has been used wherever possible to reduce weight and to reduce wear on the headstock spindle bearing.

The interchangeable collets are tapered externally and tighten onto the stock as the outer ring is tightened onto the main body of the chuck. The method of holding the workpiece is similar to the principle of the Jacobs chuck. It simplifies rechucking turned work for finishing, holding spindle tenons, and working from dowels for full-size or miniature turning projects. Capacity of the chuck is ¼ to 1⅛ inches. Each chuck includes the follow-

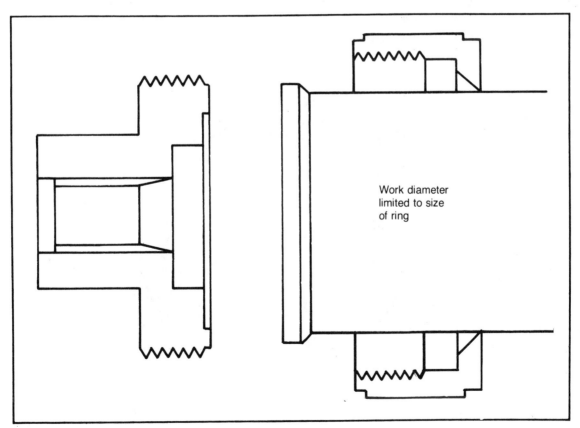

Work diameter
limited to size
of ring

Fig. 3-7. Ring chuck.

Fig. 3-7A. 6-in-1 combination chuck, outer ring.

Fig. 3-7B. 6-in-1 combination chuck, body.

Fig. 3-7C. 6-in-1 combination chuck, center boss.

ing: chuck body, chuck outer ring, tightening bar, C-spanner, and three sets of collets (½, ¾, and 1 inch).

There are three sizes of internal threads to fit the inboard headstock spindle of the lathe. All are right-hand threads. The 1-inch diameter, 8 threads per inch, will fit the Rockwell 11-inch and 12-inch lathes and the Powermatic Model 45 lathe. The 1½-inch diameter, 8 threads per inch, will fit the Viceroy and Powermatic Model 90 lathes. The ¾-inch diameter, 16 threads per inch, will fit the Craftsman and Coronet Minor or Consort lathes. More recently, Woodcraft is providing a chuck that will fit the Myford lathe with a 1-inch diameter, 12 threads per inch chuck.

The Myford Three-in-One Combination Chuck. Myford manufactures a special three-in-one combination chuck that fits only the Myford ML8 woodturning lathe. See Fig. 3-8.

The *backplate* can be used as a faceplate. The *screwplate* can be used as a woodscrew chuck. The *collet* is used as a collet chuck. The *clampring* can be used as a screwgrip chuck. See Fig. 3-9.

The internal threads are 1 inch in diameter with 12 threads per inch. The Myford combination chuck fits on the right-hand headstock spindle nose. As a *faceplate* it is 3-inches in diameter. As a *woodscrew chuck* the abutment face for work with a plain end is 2 inches in diameter or 3¼ inches in diameter, if recessed. The maximum

Fig. 3-7D. 6-in-1 combination chuck, collets.

Fig. 3-7E. 6-in-1 combination chuck, split rings.

Fig. 3-7F. 6-in-1 combination chuck, disassembled with spanner wrenches.

54

Fig. 3-7G. 6-in-1 combination chuck, screw chuck (body, center boss, split ring, outer ring).

finished diameter of work held in the *screwgrip chuck* is just over 2 inches. The stock used is at least 2¼ inches, but preferably 2½ inches square. The Myford three-in-one chuck is an excellent device for holding spindle stock on one end only. See Figs. 3-9 through 3-10.

The Simple Screw Chuck. Although the universal or combination chuck can be used as a screw chuck as one of its functions, it is best to use a series of small screw chucks varying in size from 1¼ inches to 3 inches in diameter.

There are a number of simple screw chucks available, but the turner who is engaged in turning a large number of small faceplate turnings, where the tailstock would be a hindrance, might better have a number of different-size screw chucks turned on a metal turning lathe. Of course, the craftsman so equipped can turn his own screw chucks. Aluminum is an ideal metal for this purpose.

For the smaller screw chucks, 1¼ to 1¾ inches in

Fig. 3-8. Myford 3-in-1 combination chuck, disassembled.

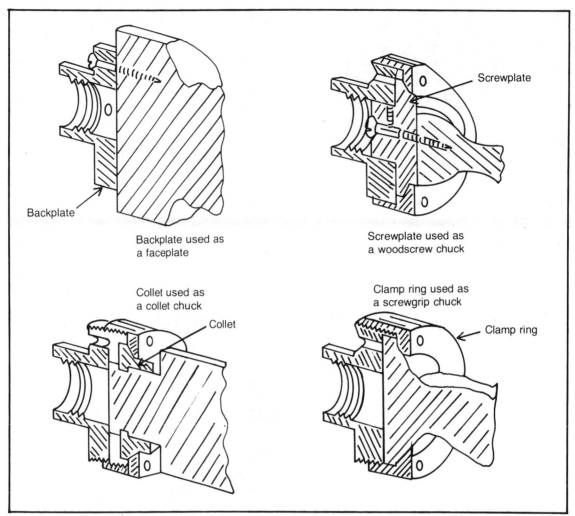

Backplate used as a faceplate

Backplate

Screwplate used as a woodscrew chuck

Screwplate

Collet used as a collet chuck

Collet

Clamp ring used as a screwgrip chuck

Clamp ring

Fig. 3-9. Multiple uses of the Myford combination chuck.

diameter, the best bet is a screw chuck fitted with a Morse taper to fit inside the headstock spindle. For the larger screw chucks, 1¾ to 3 inches in diameter, an internal threaded protrusion fits over the outside of the headstock spindle nose. Both screw chucks fit on the inboard end of the headstock spindle. See Fig. 3-11.

When turning the chuck on the metal lathe, follow the procedure below:

☐ Turn the body to the desired diameter.

☐ Turn the cap to the same diameter. The cap should be at least ¼ of an inch thick.

☐ Clamp the cap to the body.

☐ Drill at least three holes in the cap. The diameter

of the holes should be slightly larger than the self-tapping screws that will be used. Use a depth stop or collar on the drill bit so that the drill bit will not penetrate the body.

☐ Drill holes into the body slightly less in diameter than the diameter of the self-tapping screws using the cap as a template.

☐ Remove the clamp. Drive in the screws holding the cap tight to the body.

☐ Return the chuck to the lathe. Even up any differences between the body and the cap and roll over the outside edge of the cap.

☐ Place a small drill bit in the Jacobs chuck and insert the Jacobs chuck and drill bit into the tailstock.

☐ With the lathe running, advance the drill bit into the cap (thus drilling a pilot hole). A depth stop will prevent drilling into the body.

☐ Remove the cap from the body. Using the pilot hole as a guide, drill a hole in the cap the size of the flathead screw that will be used. The best screws to use are the rather fat #14, #16, #18, or #20. Spindly screws will not hold well in end grain.

☐ Countersink the hole on the underside of cap so that the head of the screw fits flush with the cap.

☐ Insert the required screw in the cap and reassemble the cap and body. When a screw breaks or is damaged it can easily be changed. This differs from some screw chucks in which the screws are brazed in place. Many times chucks of this nature have to be discarded entirely. *Note:* Myford manufactures a wood screw chuck for both the right- and left-hand spindle nose. The backplate can be removed and used as a 2¾-inch faceplate when desired.

The Segmented Wooden Chuck. The segmented wooden chuck is used for faceplate-type turnings that are larger than those turned on the smaller screw chucks. It works well on cups, goblets and other similar turnings. To make segmented wooden chucks:

☐ Fasten the stock to a small faceplate. Be sure the end fastened to the faceplate is flat.

☐ Turn the segmented wooden chuck to the external size.

☐ Insert a multispur bit in the Jacobs chuck. Sizes are available to 2⅛ inches in diameter.

☐ Insert the bit and Jacobs chuck into the tailstock. Advance the bit into the stock to the depth of the segmented parts.

☐ If necessary, enlarge the hole to the desired diameter with a heavy scraping tool.

☐ Set the index pin on the lathe and raise the tool rest to the center line of the turning.

Fig. 3-9A. Myford 3-in-1 combination chuck, backplate and tommy bar.

Fig. 3-9B. Myford 3-in-1 combination chuck, screwplate, clamp ring and face spanner.

☐ Saw across the turning with a fine-tooth saw resting flat on the tool rest.

☐ Set the index pin on the lathe and raise the tool rest to the center line of the turning.

☐ Saw across the turning with a fine-tooth saw resting flat on the tool rest.

☐ Set the index pin for five other cuts and make the cuts. Most lathes have 24 indexing holes so the indexing pin is set at every other hole, making 12 segments in all or six settings of the pin. The saw makes two cuts at each setting.

☐ Purchase, make, or have made a heavy metal ring. Round the internal part of the ring with a file or while turning. The object to be turned is placed in the chuck and the ring is forced on with a mallet. *Note*: If the

turner has a number of extra faceplates, a number of different size segmented chucks can be made. See Fig. 3-12.

The Tapered Key Wooden Chuck. The tapered key wooden chuck is a simple wooden chuck designed to hold pieces of *round stock* all of the same diameter. Very small variations in diameter are allowable as the key takes up the slack. For better holding power in the chuck, it is advisable to make a small, flat spot on the round stock at the key location. To make a tapered key wooden chuck:

☐ Fasten body stock to small faceplate.

☐ Turn body to desired diameter.

☐ Insert a multispur bit in the Jacobs chuck. Sizes are available to 2⅛-inch diameter.

☐ Advance the bit into the stock to desired depth.

Fig. 3-9C. Myford 3-in-1 combination chuck. Collet and clamp ring.

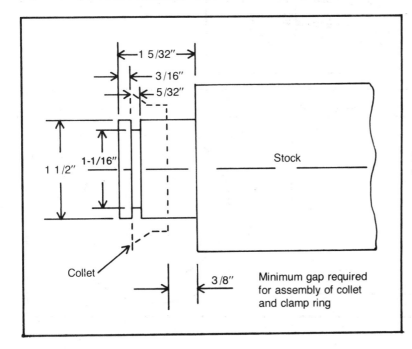

Fig. 3-10. Stock prepared for use with Myford collet chuck.

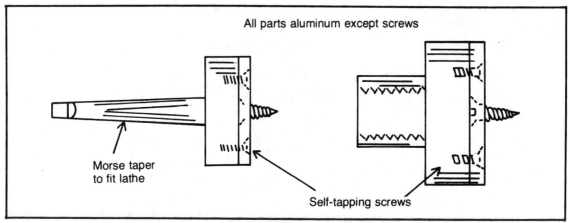

Fig. 3-11. Simple screw chuck.

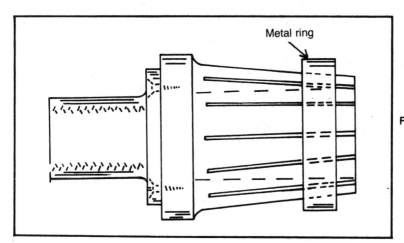

Fig. 3-12. Segmented wooden chuck.

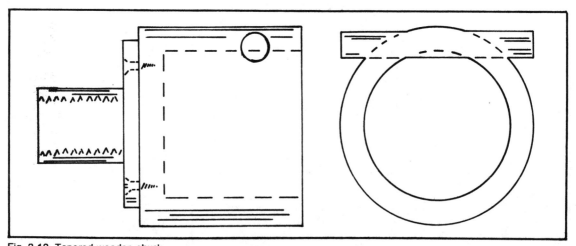

Fig. 3-13. Tapered wooden chuck.

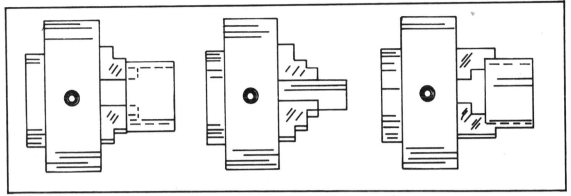

Fig. 3-14. 3-jaw universal chuck.

□ If necessary, enlarge the hole with heavy scraping tools.

□ Bore a hole through the body overlapping the tangent point of internal diameter a small amount. The hole should be about the size of the key about one-third the distance from the large end. See Fig. 3-13.

The Three-Jaw Metal Lathe Chuck. The three-jaw chuck is ordinarily used for metal turning, but it can be used for turning round wood stock. The three-jaw chuck is sometimes called the *universal* chuck. All three jaws move in unison, the same as a Jacobs chuck. Sizes run from 4 inches to 9 inches in diameter; the smaller sizes are used for wood turning. Myford make a 4-inch three-jaw chuck that fits the Myford lathe. See Fig. 3-14.

The Four-Jaw Metal Lathe Chuck. The four-jaw chuck is also known as the *independent* chuck as each of the four jaws work independently of each other. Because of this feature, irregular-shaped pieces of stock can be held in the chuck. Sizes range from 4 inches to 10 inches in diameter. Myford manufacture a 4-inch independent chuck that fits their lathe. See Fig. 3-15.

CENTERS

Centers are used for spindle turning (which differs from faceplate turning). Both the headstock and tailstock require centers for spindle turning. All are fitted with #1 or #2 Morse tapers.

Headstock Centers. Headstock centers are often called live centers, drive centers, or spur centers.

The Four-Spur Center. The four-spur center is considered somewhat superior to the two-spur center because it has more gripping power to rotate the work piece. On softwood, the four-spur center will practically eliminate "tear-out" that takes place when the spur center acts as a drill. The central conical spike should always be longer than the spurs on both the two-spur and

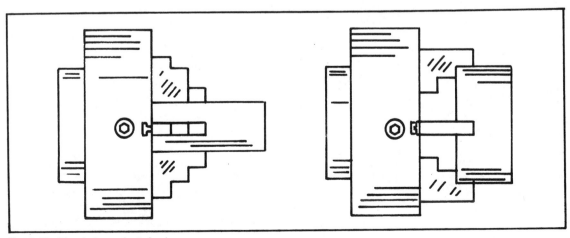

Fig. 3-15. 4-jaw independent chuck.

61

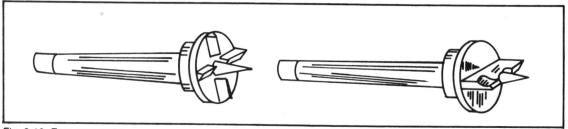

Fig. 3-16. Four-spur and two-spur centers.

four-spur centers. The spurs should be kept sharp and the spike pointed. A fine-tooth file works well for this purpose.

The Two-Spur Center. The two-spur center is sometimes referred to as the chisel center. The two-spur center is easier to manufacture and easier to keep sharpened. If the turner is using hardwoods almost exclusively, the two-spur center will give excellent service. The two-spur center is easier to seat in the end grain of wood. It is best to make saw kerfs about ⅛ of an inch deep across the diagonals on the end of square stock for the spurs to enter. See Figs. 3-16, 3-17, and 3-18.

The Cone Center. Cone centers are generally used for metal lathe turnings, but they are occasionally used for wood turning. The points are usually 60 degrees, but sometimes cone centers with wider angles are used particularly on the softer woods. These centers wear away the wood at a rapid rate, particularly on hard wood,

Fig. 3-17. Two-spur center and headstock of the Myford lathe.

Fig. 3-18. Two-spur center for the Myford lathe.

so the tailstock has to be adjusted at frequent intervals to hold the stock tight. Cone centers are made of both hardened and soft steel.

The Cup Center. The cup center is also known as the ring center. The recessed ring and center spike provide excellent holding power with little wearing of the center. The penetrating power of the center is limited. When the wood starts rubbing the bottom of the recessed ring around the center spike, no further penetration is allowed. The cup center or ring center is the most popular center and is the universal favorite of most wood turners.

The center spike is a separate part of the center, and it is held in place by an Allen set screw. The spike can be advanced as it wears away or needs sharpening, or it can be replaced if necessary. Cup centers are available in both #1 and #2 Mores tapers. See Fig. 3-19.

The Half Center. The half center is ordinarily used for metal turning, but has certain advantages for the wood turner. It permits turning tools more freedom when turning the tailstock end of the turning. The half center is, in essence, a cone center with a portion of the point ground away.

The Revolving Center. The ball-bearing revolving center prevents the burning of wood on the tailstock end of a turning. The revolving center is an absolute necessity if metal spinning is to be done on the lathe. Of course, metal spinning should not be done on the wood-turning lathe unless the headstock bearings will withstand the extra stress and pressure. The purchase of inexpensive revolving centers should be avoided because, in all probability, they will not stand up very long. These centers are usually available with either #1 or #2 Morse tapers. See Fig. 3-20.

LONG BORING TOOLS

The parts of the Myford long boring system are shown in Fig. 3-21. This method of boring is necessary for boring deep and long holes in lamps, musical instruments, and other turned objects.

The boring auger differs drastically from the ordinary twist drill bit. It must have long parallel lips in back of the cutting edge to keep the drill running straight regardless of the grain pattern. Myford supplies two lengths of boring augers: 30 inches and 36 inches long. Other lengths are available from other suppliers. Boring augers are available in diameters from 5/16 of an inch and 3/8 of an inch. Boring guides and control centers are available in the same sizes. If the turning is reversed in the lathe, holes twice the length of the boring augers can be made.

The boring auger is made up of a long tang that fits into a wooden handle. The cutting part is a hollowed-out, parallel-lipped, boring section. The hollowed section is in the uppermost position that allows chips to be cleared out easily. After the parallel, hollowed-out section is advanced to its length, the lathe should be stopped, the chips removed, and the auger advanced for deeper boring.

The support for the boring guide fits into the toolrest saddle. The boring guides are interchangeable for 5/16-inch or 3/8-inch holes. The guides are held securely to prevent loosening or vibrating with a thumbscrew on top

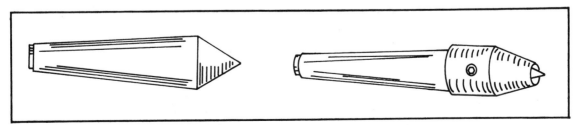

Fig. 3-19. Tailstock centers; cone center, and cup center.

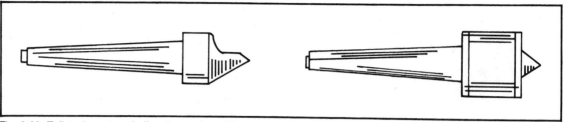

Fig. 3-20. Tailstock centers, half-center, and revolving center.

of the guide. A small turning bar is inserted through a hole in the boring guide to assist in unscrewing and screwing the boring guide from the support. See Fig. 3-21.

STEADY RESTS

Steady rests are a necessity when turning long, slender spindle turnings. Otherwise the pressure of the lathe tool against the turning will cause it to whip and vibrate; this results in a rough and out-of-round turning. In extreme cases the turnings might fly out of the lathe.

There are many styles and designs of steady rests. They range from the very simple to the highly sophisticated engineered metal center rest design for metal turning, but is equally successful as a steady rest for wood turning.

The steady rest must be adjustable to accommodate various size diameters. After the steady rest is securely adjusted to the turning, the tailstock can be removed so that turning can be done on the end of the stock. Of course, in this kind of turning the steady rest must be adjusted nearly to the tailstock end of the work piece.

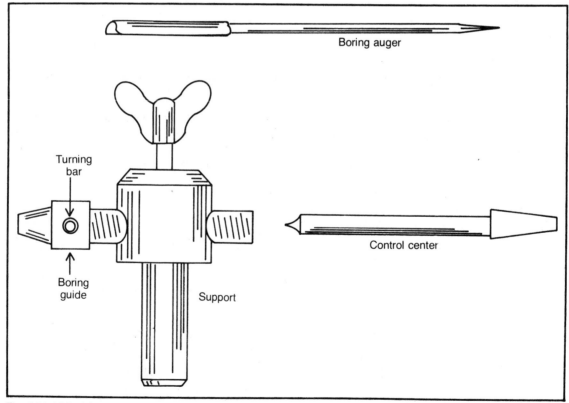

Fig. 3-21. Myford long boring tools.

A little parafin wax rubbed on the ends of the steady rest jaws will prevent burning of the turning.

Homemade Wooden Steady Rest. A steady rest can be redesigned to fit the needs of the user. The C-support is made of 3/4-inch or 13/16-inch stock. Three-quarter inch plywood of birch or fir is ideal. The most crucial measurement is the distance from the center line to the bottom of the C-support. The base should be of 1¼-inch or 1½-inch stock. This design assumes that the base is clamped to lathe bench tip with C-clamps. With a few modifications, the steady rest can be bolted to the tool rest saddle.

The steady rest jaws should be made of ⅜-inch or ½-inch hardwood. Although it is not absolutely necessary, the jaws will move more efficiently if dado cuts about 3/16 of an inch deep are made in the C-support. A little more flexibility is provided if the jaws move in a vertical direction only. In that case, the V-cut in the C-support is not necessary. See Fig. 3-22.

A Simple Wooden Steady Rest. If only occasionally it is necessary to turn longer, slender spindely stock—and the purpose of the rest is to prevent vibration—perhaps a one-jaw rest will perform nearly as well as a three-jaw center rest. This rest can be modified to fasten to the tool rest saddle or to the lathe bench top with C-clamps. See Fig. 3-23.

The Myford Steady Rest. The Myford Steady Rest is complete with saddle, quick nut, stud, tube support, and clamp lever (not shown). It has a 2-inch diameter capacity, with three adjustable bearing pads and hinged cap to facilitate loading and unloading. See Fig. 3-24.

ATTACHMENTS

Disc Sanders for the Myford Lathe. Two disc sanders are available for the Myford lathe: 10-inch diameter and 8 inch diameter. The 10-inch disc sander is attached to the outboard end and the 8 inch sander is attached to the inboard end of the headstock spindle. The 10" disc sander is made up of a plate, a disc, and a sanding table.

The plate is screwed on the left-hand spindle nose and the table is clamped on the bed to the left of the headstock. The table tilts to 45 degrees and can be

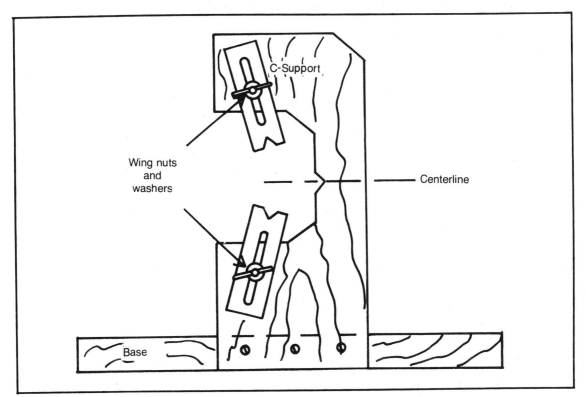

Fig. 3-22. A homemade wooden steady rest.

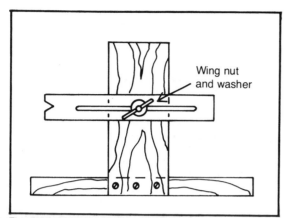
Fig. 3-23. A simple wooden steady rest.

clamped rapidly to any desired angle to give optimum rigidity under all working conditions. The table size is 11 × 6 inches.

The 8-inch disc sander might be supplied as an alternate to the 10-inch sander and is mounted to the right of the headstock. In that position, it will work in conjunction with the bandsaw, grinder or rear turning (outboard) attachments.

The component parts are the same as for the 10-inch sander: plate, disc, and table. A miter gauge groove is machined in both tables. The miter gauge is purchased separately as an accessory.

Homemade Myford Disc Sander. A homemade disc sander can be made for the Myford lathe with little effort. A 10-inch diameter disc is cut out of ½-inch plywood and fastened to the outboard faceplate. The table is about 8 inches long and 4 inches wide. A hole is bored in the underside of the table to accept a dowel that fits the hole in the tool rest saddle. The hole should be bored on a drill press to assure that the table is at right angles to the disc. The only disadvantage of this homemade sander is that the table cannot be adjusted to different angles. See Fig. 3-25.

Bandsaw Attachment The bandsaw attachment for the Myford lathe is mounted to the outboard end of the lathe. It will cut external curves in stock up to 3¾ inches thick. The hinged cover provides complete guarding and the controls are readily accessible for wheel tilting or blade tracking. It has two 10-inch-diameter wheels. The depth of throat is 9¼-inches. The saw is 31 inches high with a table size of 10 × 10 inches.

Grinding Wheel Attachment. The grinding wheel attachment for the Myford lathe is fastened to the outboard end of the lathe so that lathe tools can be ground

while a spindle turning is still held between the centers. A screw-on adapter holds a 6-inch-diameter, 1-inch wide wheel with a 1-inch bore. A guard can be purchased as an extra accessory.

Metal Turning Attachment. By adding a 4-inch-diameter universal three-jaw chuck or a four-jaw independent chuck and a compound rest, light metal work can be accomplished on the Myford lathe.

Short Bed Unit. Where turning between centers is not needed or desired, a Myford short bed unit less tailstock is available for faceplate turning only. This short bed lathe is sometimes known as a bowl lathe.

Mortising Attachments. The Myford mortising attachment will handle hollow square mortising chisels and bits in the following sizes (in inches): 1/4, 5/16, 7/16, and 1/2.

The mortising attachment fastens to the lathe bed. It has a table size of 12 × 3 inches. The screw-operated, vertical-table movement is 1⅞ inches. The lever operated tranverse table movement is 4½ inches. The rack-operated, longitudinal table movement in 3 inches.

A sharpening kit is available for sharpening the hollow-square mortise bits and chisels. It consists of a countersinking tool with five pilots for the five chisel sizes. Included in the kit are 3-inch square and half-round precision files.

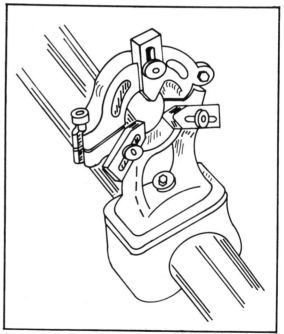
Fig. 3-24. Myford steady rest.

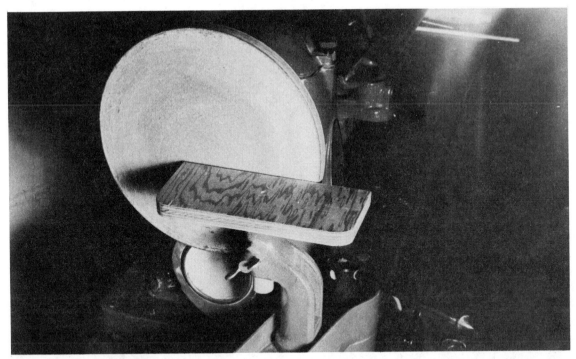

Fig. 3-25. Homemade disc sander.

Fig. 3-26. One-quarter inch faceplate mandrel jig.

Fig. 3-27. Half-inch faceplate mandrel jig.

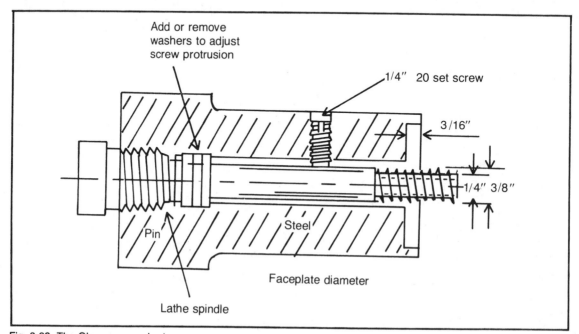

Add or remove washers to adjust screw protrusion

1/4″ 20 set screw

3/16″

1/4″ 3/8″

Pin

Steel

Lathe spindle

Faceplate diameter

Fig. 3-28. The Glaser screw chuck.

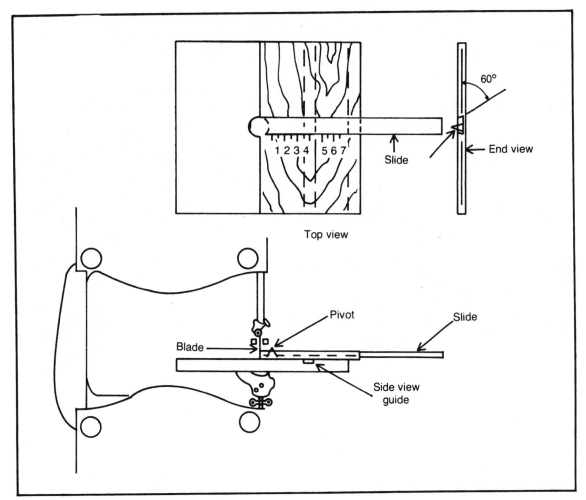

60°

End view

Slide

Top view

Pivot

Slide

Blade

Side view
guide

Fig. 3-29A. Bandsaw circular cutting jig.

Lathe Faceplate Mandrel Jigs. The two mandrel jigs shown (Fig. 3-26, and 3-27) were made to assist in turning wooden wheels for wooden toys, but they can also be used with any circular object that has a ¼-inch-diameter or ½-inch-diameter holes in the center. See Figs. 3-26 and 3-27.

The Glaser Screw Chuck. A simple, yet versatile chuck, has been designed by Jerry Glaser of Playa Del Rey, California, and is manufactured by Turnmaster Corporation of Fountain Valley, California. Turnmaster also makes wood turning chisels and gouges of high-speed steel. The standard Glaser screw chuck has a 1½-inch faceplate diameter. They are available in sizes that fit the Rockwell, Shopsmith, Myford, Arundel, and Hapfor lathes.

The secret of success of this efficient chuck is due to the cylindrical screw (not tapered) and the extremely thin threads. The very thin threads do little harm to the stock and seldom split the wood. They work exceedingly well in end grain. See Fig. 3-28.

HOW TO MAKE A BANDSAW CIRCULAR-CUTTING JIG

The circle cutting jig makes the cutting of round discs for faceplate work an easy one. The jig described as follows is for the Delta-Rockwell 14-inch bandsaw.

The pivot point on the slide can be shifted about 8 inches so that circular discs of 2 inches to 14 inches diameter can be bandsawed. After the position of the pivot point has been established, the slide should be clamped to the jig and to the bandsaw table so that the

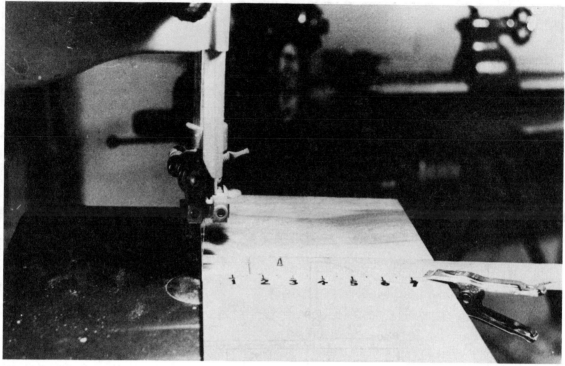

Fig. 3-29B. Bandsaw circular cutting jig.

pivot point and the jig will not change position.

☐ Cut stock (see Table 3-1) for the jig base.

☐ Lay out the guidelines for the slide, 2 inches wide, across the short dimension of the base, equal distance from the two ends.

☐ Set the circular saw at 60 degrees and make two cuts across the plywood, reversing the plywood after making the first cut. The cut should be 5/16 of an inch deep. The remainder of the slot can be cleaned out with the saw or with the dado head. The bottom of the slot should be 2 inches wide.

☐ Cut the stock for the slide slightly over 2 inches wide.

☐ Set the circular saw at 60 degrees and cut the two sides of the slide, reversing the piece after the first cut.

☐ Try out the slide in the slot in the jig base. If too tight, run one edge through the saw removing a small amount of wood or place the slide in the vise and plane the slide until it fits.

☐ Select a flathead screw with a shank diameter approximately equal to the root diameter of the screw if the screw chuck is being used.

Table 3-1. Jig Stock Materials.

Pieces	Description	Size	Material
1	Jig Base	1/2″ × 7″ × 14″	Birch Plywood
1	Slide	5/16″ × 2″ × 15 3/4″	Cherry
1	Guide	3/8″ × 3/4″ × 14″	Cherry
1	Flat Head Bright Screw		

70

Fig. 3-30. Ring master and projects.

☐ Bore a hole through the end of the slide 1 inch back from the end. The diameter of the hole should equal the diameter of the shank of the screw. Countersink the hole on the underside.

☐ Grind or file off the threads of the screw and round off the point.

☐ Insert screw in hole along with epoxy glue.

☐ Cut stock for guide.

☐ Attach the guide to the jig base with glue and brads.

☐ Sand all parts of the jig.

☐ Place the slide in place in the jig base and apply two or three coats of clear spray Deft. Do *not* spray in the slide slot.

☐ Apply paraffin in the bottom of slot and on the guide. See Figs. 3-29A and 3-29B.

THE RING MASTER

The Ring Master is an all-new woodworking machine that is hard to classify. It is neither a lathe nor an accessory, but the author opted to put it under accessories due to its size.

Ring Master will allow the operator to create almost any hollow wooden cylindrical shape up to 12 inches in diameter. That opens a complete new field of discovery in wood working. Simply cut the rings concentrically with the Ring Master, create the shape you prefer by stacking the assortment of rings you've cut, then glue the project, sand, and finish.

It is safe, fun, and inexpensive. A small bowl requires only about thirty-five cents of cabinet grade plywood. The beginner can complete an impressive project the first time. The Ring Master works with both hard and softwoods.

Bowls, dishes, mugs, vases, and lamps are only a few of the projects that can be made with this exciting new machine. The Ring Master is powered by a ½-hp motor. See Fig. 3-30.

Chapter 4

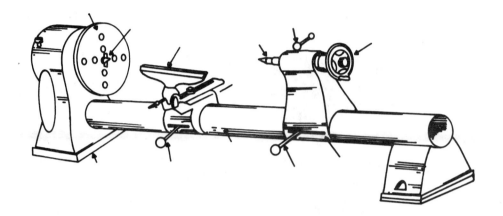

Characteristics and Uses of Wood

ACH LAYER FORMED WITHIN THE TRUNK AND root system of a tree serves a vital purpose in the total development of the organism. The layers found in the trunk and the cutting methods used to obtain them should be of concern to the craftsman. Any wood project depends not only on the skill of the craftsman who fashions the finished product, but also on the quality of the wood itself and the care taken when the wood was harvested.

HOW A TREE GROWS

A tree grows one conical layer on top of another, much the same way as an onion. A tree consists of the trunk, the branches of different sizes, and a root system. The top of the tree is usually referred to as the *crown*.

Growing takes place in two places: at the very tip of the elongated cone, which increase the height of a tree and in the cambium layer, which is between the bark and the wood. This growth contributes to the thickness of a tree.

Ordinarily, the age of a tree can be ascertained by counting the annular rings—spring growth plus summer growth. Usually the summer rings are counted because they are denser, darker, and more pronounced that the spring rings. Trees that grow in the tropics grow con-

tinuously through the year so they do not have well-defined growth (annular) rings. See Fig. 4-1 and 4-2.

Counting the rings on the stump or on the end of a log does not always give the correct age of a tree. If you count the annular rings shown in Fig. 4-2, you get an age of 10 years, not 15. It took the tree between four and five years to reach the stump height. Only but cutting off the tree next to the ground and counting the rings would you get the true age.

The *pith* serves no useful purpose in the tree. Pith is the very center of a tree. It is generally soft and is apt to rot and leave a hollow. Sometimes wild honey bees take advantage of these cavities and deposit their honey there.

The wood that encircles the pith is called the *heartwood*. It is the main portion of the tree trunk and gives it strength and stability. It is no longer in the growing stage and it does not aid in carrying moisture and food to the rest of the tree. The heartwood is generally darker than the sapwood that surround it. The cells in the heartwood are dead and are frequently clogged with dark-colored waste materials that give it some of its characteristic color. Some heartwood turns darker when exposed to the air while other heartwood turns lighter. The spring and summer growth rings are more condensed in the heartwood than in the sapwood.

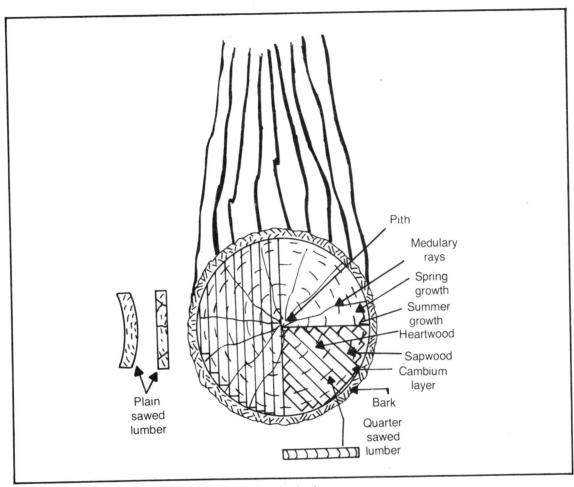

Fig. 4-1. Cross section of a tree showing methods of sawing lumber.

Sapwood is made up of spring growth and summer growth. The spring growth is generally wider than the summer growth because of more favorable growing conditions (moisture, etc.). The summer growth takes place more slowly and is apt to be darker in color and denser in texture (although sapwood in general is lighter in color than heartwood). The sapwood is important as a conductor of food and moisture to the rest of the tree.

The *cambium layer* is between the sapwood and the bark. It is a semiliquid, cohesive substance. The main function of the cambium layer is to create cells that divide. Some of the cells form new wood (sapwood) while others form bark.

IDENTIFICATION OF WOOD CUTS

Each wood has characteristics that differentiate it from all other woods. Color, weight, density, grain configuration, odor, and taste are only a few of these characteristics. Burl walnut, bird's eye maple, and crotch woods are woods with unusual configurations.

Methods of sawing or machining wood can enhance the beauty of the finished product. Wood turned on a veneer lathe and quarter-sawn wood, for example, are quite unusual and attractive.

Quarter sawing of wood is accomplished by cutting a log into four parts, longitudinally, so that the end of the log is in 90-degree, pie-shaped segments. The quarter log is cut in such a manner that the saw cuts are parallel—or nearly so—to the *medullary rays*. Medullary rays conduct sap across the grain in both softwoods and hardwoods by strips of cells that run at right angles to the fibers.

This sawing produces large flakes on the surface of the wood—particularly in oak. Quarter sawing is used with many other woods besides oak to prevent or retard shrinking, twisting, and to prevent small checks from appearing on the surface. Wood cut in this manner will wear much longer than wood cut in other ways.

Plain sawing of wood is the most common way of sawing lumber. There is not as much waste and it is much faster than quarter sawing. Actually, when a log is plain-sawn, two or three pieces in the center of the log (widest pieces) are quarter-sawn in that the saw cuts are parallel to the medullary rays. The outside pieces do not fare as well. When the wood is drying, the tension in these outside pieces is tremendous. In the drying process, the internal forces in the wood apply along the annular rings. The annular rings or growth rings try to contract (that is become a straight line). As a result, the board has a tendency to "cup" to the outside. Naturally, the board the greatest distance from the center of the log will warp the most.

CLASSIFICATIONS OF WOOD

Wood is classified in two categories: *softwoods* and *hardwoods*. Traditionally, softwoods come from evergreens or trees whose leaves do not fall. Trees that shed their leaves annually are called hardwoods. There are certain discrepancies in this method of classification. For example, basswood classified as a hardwood is much softer than some of the pines and firs that are classified as softwoods. Wood is also classified as *open* and *close* grain. Walnut, oak, and mahogany are open grain woods and in the finishing process often require a paste filler. Pine, basswood, birch, maple, cherry, and poplar are only a few examples of close grain woods.

SEASONING WOOD

When a hardwood log is cut in its green stage, it consists of 33⅓ percent to 50 percent free water or sap. The water must be eliminated from the wood before it can be used for furniture or for any wooden object used indoors. *Seasoning* is the term used for the process of removing the water.

The cellular structure of a tree has the capacity for retaining water. The cell cavity and the permeable wall of the cell are the retainers. Wood, in the process of drying, gives up its water first from the cell cavity and then from the cell wall. The cell shrinks after the water escapes from the cell. Because wood is made up of a multitude of cells, it in turn shrinks. On the other hand, if the cell—after it is dry—absorbs moisture the cell will expand

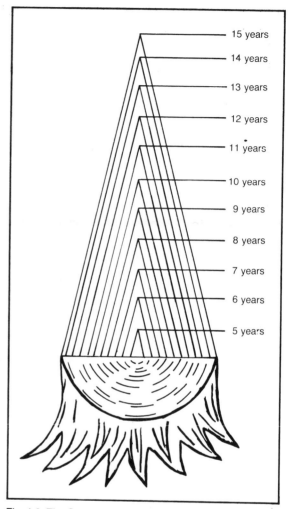

Fig. 4-2. The Cambium layer at different stages of the tree's growth.

(swell). Thus there is both the shrinking and swelling (contraction and expansion) of wood. There are two techniques for eliminating water from wood: *air drying* and *kiln drying*.

AIR DRYING OF WOOD

Air drying is the process of piling lumber in a protected place or in the open with sticks between the boards so that air can circulate around the boards. The evaporation of moisture into the air causes the lumber to dry. Air seasoning provides a minimum moisture content of 15 percent to 18 percent. Air drying is a slow process requiring months or even years with some species of wood.

KILN DRYING OF WOOD

To dry lumber to a point where it can be used for furniture, it must be dried to a moisture content below 12 percent. Dry Kilns are generally the means for obtaining this moisture content.

Dry kilns are huge ovens. Within the kiln, humidity, air circulation, and heat are meticulously controlled and adjusted during the drying process. Lumber is placed on cars (trolleys) with sticks between each layer of lumber and the trolley is pushed into the kiln. Each car or trolley load is called a *bunk*.

WORKING WITH GREEN WOOD

The reader might get the impression that only air-dried or kiln-dried woods are the only woods suitable for woodturning. Such is not the case. Other alternatives follow.

THE PEG TREATMENT OF GREEN WOOD

When green cut wood is allowed to soak in a water solution of *Polyethylene Glycol 1000*, called *PEG* for short, the wood shrinks very little when dried. In addition, the wood swells very little when subjected to high humidity. Unless used with care and properly protected, wood so treated is apt to become slightly sticky at high relative humidities. Polyethylene glycol 1000 has an average molecular of 1000 (from which it gets part of its name).

The time for adequate soaking in the solution of water and PEG depends on the thickness of the stock to be treated. Thick stock might require weeks of soaking. This treatment bulks or fills the cell walls, and that is the reason for its success.

PEG is a nontoxic, noncorrosive, and nonexplosive solution. The treatment has slight effect on color, gluing, or the physical properties. Solutions of water and PEG can be used over and over again by replacing the chemical used up by the repeated soakings. It is recommended that a *hydrometer* be used to make sure that the solution is up to full strength. Different percentages of the PEG and water solution have different specific gravities.

PEG has also been used as a chemical seasoning agent by reducing the checking of green wood during the drying process. Only light treatments of PEG are necessary because high penetration is not required.

The disadvantages of using PEG are its cost, that it can be used only on green wood, and that wood treated with PEG is difficult to finish.

According to R. Bruce Hoadley in his article *PEG for the Woodworker: What You Always Wanted to Know About Polyethylene Glycol 1000* in *Fine Woodworking* magazine Nov/Dec, 1979, a black walnut disc (30 inches in diameter and 3 inches thick) might require $40 worth of PEG.

Supply sources for PEG include Robert M. Albrecht, Constantine and Son, Inc., Craftsman Wood Service Co., Crane Creek Co., Industrial Arts Supply Co., Lemont Specialities, Spielman's Wood Works, and Wilkens-Anderson Co.

GREEN WOOD SOURCES

The chances of finding the right species and sizes of hardwood for turning, especially large bowls, at the local lumberyard are pretty slim. Your best bet in that case is to search for green wood or large timbers in old buildings that are being dismantled.

Quite often it is possible to find what you want close by. The county road commission, the tree surgery companies, the city forestry department, and contractors who are clearing building sites are very good sources of green wood. Sometimes wind storms and blizzards will tear large limbs from trees that will yield sizable turnings.

A visit to sawmills in the vicinity will often pay dividends. Many times short logs, crooked logs, crotches and burls will be discarded because it is not economically feasible to take time and energy to process them into lumber.

Another solution is to cut your own wood if you own or can borrow or rent a chain saw. Sometimes stumps in a farmer's wood lot are available for the asking. The farmer is usually glad to be rid of them. A bonus stump wood produces some of the finest turnings.

Still another solution is to find a tree to your liking and offer to purchase it if it is not on your own land. If you have never felled a tree be sure that you know how or have some one with you who does. Other trees, buildings and the like must be protected. In felling a tree, a horizontal cut is made about one-quarter of the way into the trunk on the side toward which the tree is leaning. A second cut is angled up to the first cut at about 45 degrees. On the opposite side of the tree, make a third cut above the first two cuts. Drive in an iron wedge and the tree will topple. If it does not fall, use the wedge and chain saw alternately until the tree crashes.

Of course, there is a lot of work left to be done in cleaning up the site and in cutting the trunk and limbs into sections. All the ends of usable sections and the stump (if to be used later) should be treated to prevent checking.

Tar, thick paint, grease, hot paraffin, and commercial petroleum products especially designed for this purpose should be applied to the ends of the cut sections.

TURNING GREEN OR SEMISEASONED WOOD

Semiseasoned wood that has been stored in unheated buildings can be used if it is rough turned oversize. For bowls, this means a wall thickness of ¾ to 1 inch. After the bowls have been rough turned, they are removed from the lathe and laid aside from 10 days to 2½ weeks. If checking starts, the rough-turned bowls can be placed in plastic garbage bags to retard the drying-out process.

Green wood is turned in a similar manner, but the wall thickness of a potential bowl should be from 1 to 1½ inches. These rough-turned green bowls are then coated with a furniture paste wax. The bowls are left in an area without heat for about six weeks. They are then moved into a heated area for about four months; after that they have stabilized and are ready to turn.

This might seem like a long, drawn-out process. But when you consider that 4-inch stock of 16/4 stock takes up to four or five years to season, the green turning of wood is not a bad trade off.

BORERS AND BEETLES

Wood infested with wood borers and beetles would at first glance seem to be worthless. But after turning, it might become a work of art and interesting design.

BURLS

Burls are found on many trees and may vary greatly in size. Cutting or harvesting the burls can be taken in any direction as there is no grain direction as is found in other woods. Small defects can be disregarded as they add interest to the turning.

STUMPWOOD

After the stump is sawed off close to the ground, dug up, or pulled up with a tractor or bulldozer, the stump is split and the roots are cut off. In the splitting process, most of the dirt and debris is dislodged. The remainder should be removed with a sharp instrument. Stumpwood makes excellent bowls.

CROTCH WOOD

The crotch is first split down the center following the pith line. Beautifully figured wood is often found in large trees, particularly hardwood trees. Crotch wood cut into veneers, such as mahogany and walnut, converts into beautiful panels and plywood.

SPLATED WOOD

Splated wood is caused by a complex mechanism associated with decay in wood. Although hard to describe, the splating action produces figures and color in wood that are unmatched for its beauty. The process differs from tree to tree and does not occur in all trees. Most woods that are white in color are apt to splate.

Parasites, bacteria and fungi all contribute to the splating process or decaying process, but the wood must be "caught" at the right time before actual rotting takes place. Mineral deposits often cause interesting black or dark colored rings or lines in the wood.

Chapter 5

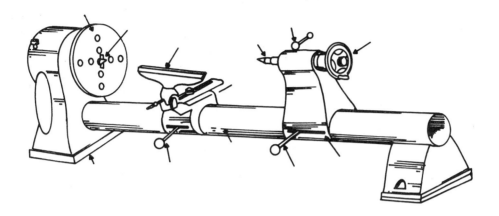

Designing Turned Projects

DESIGNING FOR ARTISTIC QUALITIES IS A very complex and difficult process. What is visually pleasing to one person is not necessarily pleasing to another. There are no rigid rules that one can follow because the visual aspects are often very subtle. The principles of design are often hard to define even after we know what they are. The most often stated guidelines of design are: *proportion, balance, rhythm, color, harmony, center of interest,* and *texture.*

FUNCTIONAL ASPECTS OF DESIGN

In the field of design you often hear the expression "form follows function." The question you should ask is: "Does this piece do well what it is supposed to do?."

The designer's very difficult objective is to achieve elegance, grace, and charm without overstepping the confines of function. The function of an accessory or a piece of furniture must be carefully considered before the process of design can begin.

The turner-designer not only uses wood to advantage, but expeditiously uses ceramics, plastics, marquetry, inlays and ornamental trim to enhance the project. The turner/designer must be acquainted with the tools and equipment used by the woodturner. If he is not

knowledgeable about the capabilities and limitations of tools and machines, he might design a product that is impossible to make or would be uneconomical to construct.

METHODS, PROCESSES, AND OPERATIONS

The basic operations of faceplate, chuck and spindle turning, sanding, finishing, etc., should be understood by the turner/designer. He should be acquainted with, and be able to use, standard woodworking hand tools, and be able to operate auxiliary power woodworking tools (circular saw, bandsaw, drill press) as well as the portable power tools.

CREATIVE PROBLEM SOLVING

What is the problem? What needs to be designed? Let's assume that every summer when you go to your summer cottage that the electric generator konks out. There is a mad scramble to find matches, candles and something in which to place the candles. Care must be taken in the beginning not to name the project needed—only the function of the project. Eventually from this exercise a combination candle storage container, a candle holder and a match recess was developed.

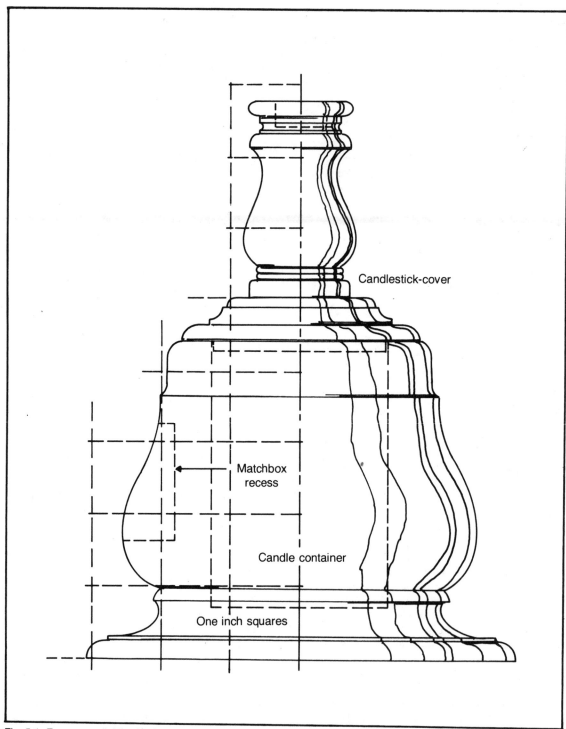

Candlestick-cover

Matchbox recess

Candle container

One inch squares

Fig. 5-1. Emergency lighting device.

What should it do? What should it look like? The process of analysis is a type of brainstorming by the designer. It is highly desirable that many others be brought into the process as well. The following statements might be the outcome:

☐ The project should be difficult to tip over.

☐ The combination cover and candlestick holder should be easily removed.

☐ The candle storage container should be deep enough to hold a standard candle.

☐ The finish should withstand the drippings of hot wax.

☐ It should be structurally sound and, preferably, made of hardwood.

☐ Its cost should be reasonable.

☐ The project should fit into its environment (Early American) and be pleasing in appearance.

Investigation and Tryout

What are some of the possible solutions to the problem? Solutions or partial solutions can be found by doing the following:

☐ Look at similar type accessories in homes and stores.

☐ Study library project books, catalogs, magazines etc.

☐ Sketch ideas as they develop.

☐ Make scale models or make test pieces from inexpensive materials.

☐ Make tentative working drawings.

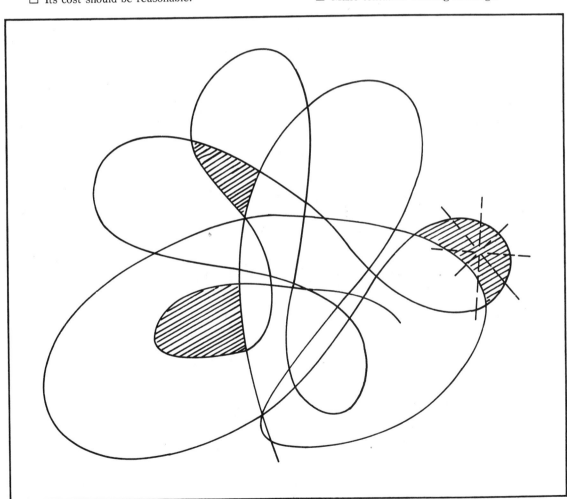

Fig. 5-2. The doodle method.

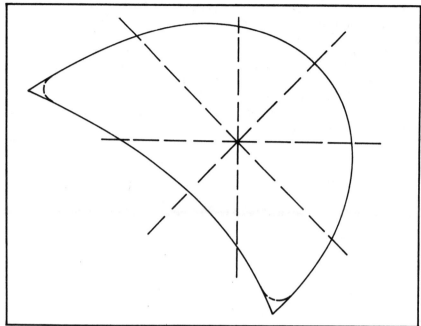

Fig. 5-3. "Doodle" enlarged four times.

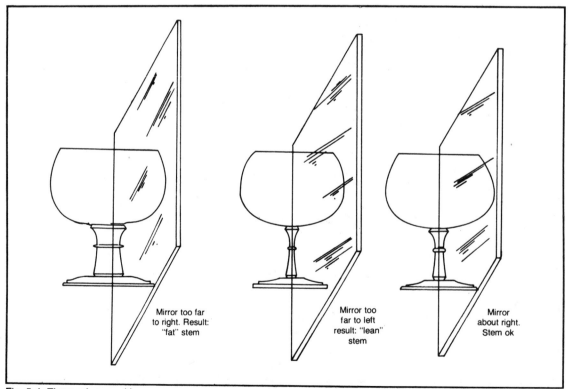

Mirror too far to right. Result: "fat" stem

Mirror too far to left result: "lean" stem

Mirror about right. Stem ok

Fig. 5-4. Three mirror positions.

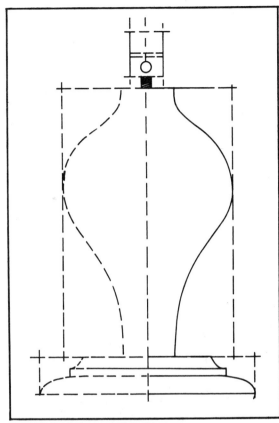

Fig. 5-5. Preliminary sketch of lamp.

☐ Experiment with different materials.
☐ Discuss ideas with other members of the household, other craftsmen, parents, and neighbors.

Evaluation

All the better ideas evolving from investigation and tryout must be carefully evaluated in terms of function and appearance. It is the time for combining ideas. Test pieces or scale models gives the designer a three-dimensional look into the problems relative to size, shape, materials, construction, and finish. Tentative working drawings, pictorial renderings, and material lists can be compiled. The following *construction* questions must be answered.

☐ How do you make it?
☐ What kind of joints are best?
☐ Do you use abrasives and what grades of sandpaper would be right to use?
☐ What tools do you use? Do you have the necessary tools? Are the tools in good condition?

☐ What type of finish would be the most appropriate?

Post Evaluation

Not until the product is complete can the solution be tested and evaluated. Actual use will help provide some basis for evaluation. The designer must be able to answer the following:

☐ Where does the final product (solution) fall short?
☐ What can be done to improve the product?
☐ What do others think about the solution (product)?

The average woodturner would immediately ask the question: "Why do I have to go through all that time and effort to make a project that is only going to be used one month out of the year? But supposing the owner of that cottage also owns a small woodworking plant. If he gets a functional and pleasing project, he might put it on the market. Now how about the time and energy expended? See Fig. 5-1.

DESIGN PRINCIPLES

Proportion. Proportion is the interrelationship between components of a project. A heavy oak table should not be supported by spindly or delicate legs even if those legs are made of the strongest wood in the world. The average woodworker is more apt to make legs of all kinds much too heavy and bulky rather than too slender.

Fig. 5-6. The square.

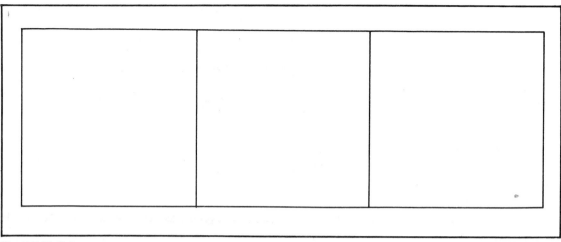

Fig. 5-7. Multiple square.

Balance. Projects that are balanced symmetrically will be balanced. It is possible to obtain balance without symmetry, but this type of balance should be left to the full-time professional designer. It is a subtle arrangement that is hard to achieve. This takes place when completely different components are arranged so that the product appears balanced and is therefore pleasing to the eye. Oriental flower arrangers are masters of this art.

Rhythm. Rhythm is achieved by the use of repeated components or units within a project. A series of coves, beads or Vs on a turning would be a case in point. Inlays, overlays, marquetry, and parquet have reoccurring elements in their design.

Color. Nature has provided wood with many intrin-sic, beautiful colors. These colors should be captured and enhanced by using a transparent finish. There are, however, a few woods that require stain in order to get the desired result. I am very strongly opposed to bleaching woods such as walnut and mahogany. Why destroy the natural beauty of the wood? Inlays, marquetry, and intarsia use naturally colored veneers of different species to achieve amazing results.

Primary colors are seldom used on painted, enameled, or colored lacquer pieces except in small amounts. The primary colors are often mixed with white to form *tints* or mixed with complimentary colors to form *shades* of the color.

Harmony. Harmony is the ability of component

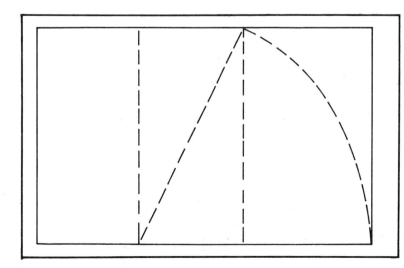

Fig. 5-8. Divine section.

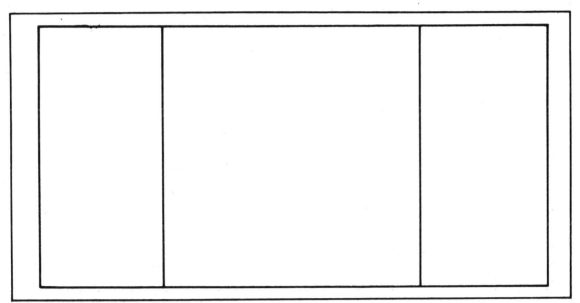

Fig. 5-9. Rectangle divisions.

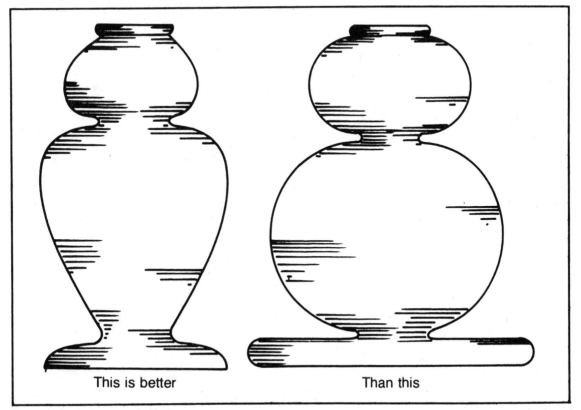

This is better   Than this

Fig. 5-10. Designing curved objects.

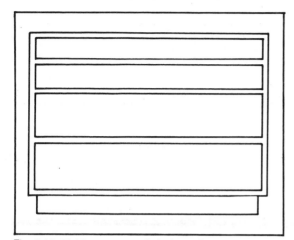

Fig. 5-11. Dividing a rectangle horizontally.

parts to be compatible with each other. A chromium drawer pull would not harmonize with the drawers on a Chippendale chest, and an intricate carving would look out of place on a contemporary table.

Center of Interest. The center of interest is what the eye sees first on a project. It might be a splash of color, a small inlay, a well-done carving or knob, an exotic grained veneer, a piece of hardware, or a small turning.

Texture. Texture has to do, primarily, with the smoothness or roughness of a surface. On furniture, it applies more to the upholstery fabrics than to the wood. Nevertheless, wood does have texture. A small, miniature turning should not be made of oak or ash, but some close-grain wood such as cherry or maple. A high-gloss finish texture is appropriate for the piano, but would be out of place on a Danish contemporary piece of furniture.

DESIGN TECHNIQUES

The Doodle Method. The doodle method (controlled free form) is used in designing bowls, trays, table tops, and other contemporary free-form patterns. An ever-curving, continuous, swirling, sweeping line is drawn on a large sheet of plain, unruled paper. It becomes readily apparent that the drawing will furnish a number of possible forms that can be cross-hatched or darkened to bring them out. See Fig. 5-2.

Select one of the forms for your project. Enlarge the shape selected by drawing a vertical line, horizontal line, and two 45-degree lines through the center of the selected shape.

On a separate piece of paper draw the same set of straight lines. It is then easy to enlarge the shape. If the drawing is to be doubled in size, step off twice the distance with dividers equal to twice the distances of each line of the original on the new drawing. Connect the eight points free hand or with a French curve. The sharp corners can be rounded to soften the design. See Figs. 5-2 and 5-3.

The Mirror Method. The mirror method is used when both sides of a project or component are symmetrical such as salt and pepper shakers or mills, candlesticks, lamp bases, legs, etc. Use of this method is not confined to turnings; it can be used on any project which is identical on each side. The purpose of this method is for you to experiment visually on the relationship between the width of the object before commitment to a final drawing.

Draw the outline of one side of the object on tracing paper. Place the mirror upright—perpendicular to the drawing—beside the drawing on the vertical axis. Move the mirror to the right or left until the right proportion is arrived at.

Draw a vertical line along the lower edge of the mirror as soon as the right position has been established. The lines should extend through the ends of the drawing. This line then becomes the center line of the project. Fold the drawing over on the center line so that the original half of the drawing is on the inside.

Trace the outline of the original half on the reverse side. The pencil graphite will be transferred to the inside opposite the original half and the drawing will be complete when the paper is unfolded.

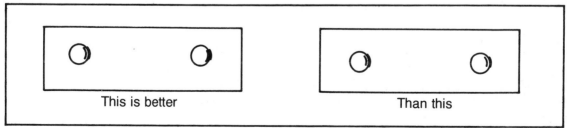

This is better   Than this

Fig. 5-12. Placement of handles and knobs.

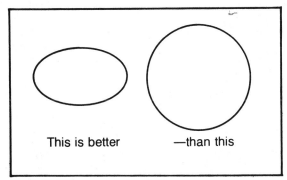

Fig. 5-13. Ellipse versus the circle.

Figure 5-4 shows three positions of the mirror in search of an acceptable design for a turned wood goblet. The one on the right appears to be most appropriate. The one on the left looks much too heavy. The one in the center has a stem much too slender that would be much too fragile in use.

Preliminary Sketches. Sketching is a free-wheeling, brainstorming exercise. Let your mind run wild. There is no need to worry about making mistakes. The designer can make mistakes at this stage without dire consequences. A few more seconds or another sheet of paper is about all that could happen.

Try to visualize what you would like the project to look like when finished. Draw rapidly and do not worry about neat lines, scale, or proportion. It is best to hold the pencil rather loosely some distance back from the point. Block in the object with long strokes, using the elbow as a pivot point. Fingers and wrist motion are used for short lines. After the blocking-in is complete, darken the outline and details. See Fig. 5-5.

GENERAL DESIGN RULES

The *square* (Fig. 5-6) is the least desirable rectangular shape. *Multiple squares* (Fig. 5-7), likewise, are not the most pleasing to the eye and should be avoided. The most satisfying of all rectangular forms is called the *divine section* or *Golden mean rectangle*. The ration of length to width is 1 to 1.618. It can be drawn geometrically by bisecting the square, then drawing a diagonal of half the square, and using the diagonal as a radius to swing an arc that will strike the base of the square extended. See Fig. 5-8.

When dividing a rectangle into parts using vertical lines, it is better to divide the rectangle into odd rather than an even number of parts. The center section is usually larger than the other sections. See Fig. 5-9. *Curves* are more pleasing if the radius or radii are ever-changing, rather than being a portion of a circle. See Fig. 5-10.

In dividing a rectangle by *horizontal* lines (shelves, chest of drawers, etc.), it is more desirable if the drawers or distances between shelves are progressively lower toward the bottom. See Fig. 5-11. *Drawer knobs* and *handles* look more balanced if they are slightly above the center of the drawer. See Fig. 5-12.

CHANGES AND TRENDS IN DESIGN

Design is an ever-changing phenomenon; yet at the same time certain elements remain the same. Certain elements of Egyptian, Greek, and Roman design, particularly in architecture, will always remain as cherished "things of beauty, and a joy forever."

Victorian furniture is a good illustration of the fickleness of the public regarding style. Victorian furniture

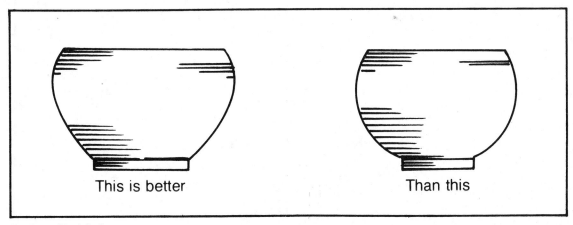

Fig. 5-14. Bowl design.

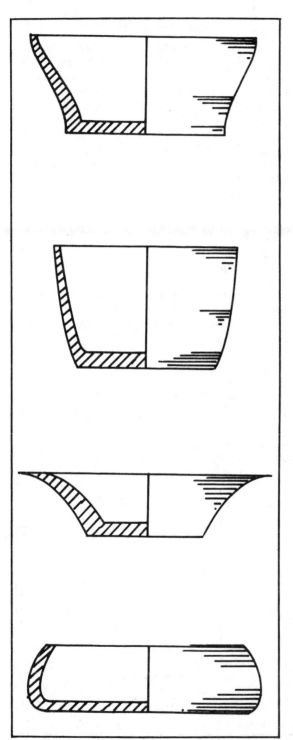

Fig. 5-15A. Traditional bowls.

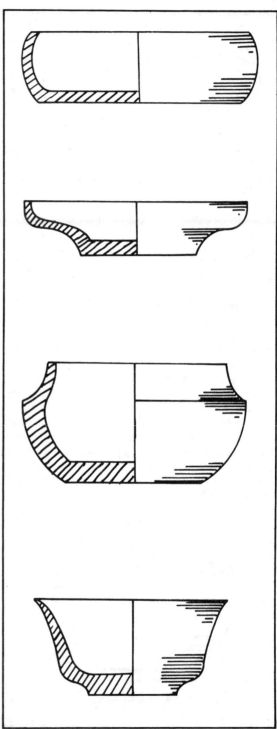

Fig. 5-15B. Traditional bowls.

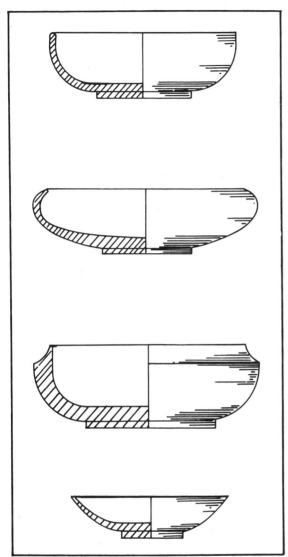

Fig. 5-15C. Traditional bowls.

To define design is a difficult task. What is good design to one person is poor design to another. What is good design today might be poor design tomorrow. Every person has conceptions as to what is beautiful and functional.

Modern and contemporary furniture came into being because it was easier to keep clean, and the scale was more in keeping with our smaller homes and apartments. Contemporary furniture is much plainer. This was primarily due to the advent of the woodworking machine and less emphasis on the hand woodworking skills.

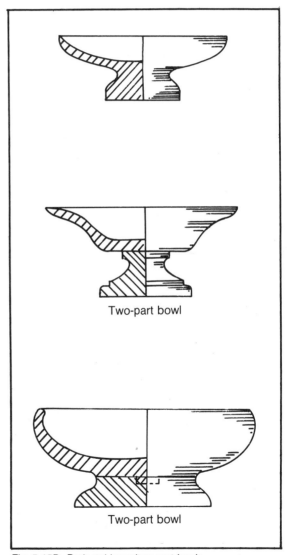

Two-part bowl

Two-part bowl

Fig. 5-15D. Pedestal base/two-part bowls.

had its hayday during the nineteenth century and the first decade of the twentieth century. Between World War I and World War II, many pieces that were not destroyed could be found in attics, barns, unused rooms, in garages, and in second-hand stores. They could be purchased for next to nothing.

But look how things have changed. By the middle '70s Victorian was back in style. Stored pieces were bringing fabulous prices, and many furniture manufacturers geared up to get on the bandwagon. Victorian furniture was moved back into the best homes.

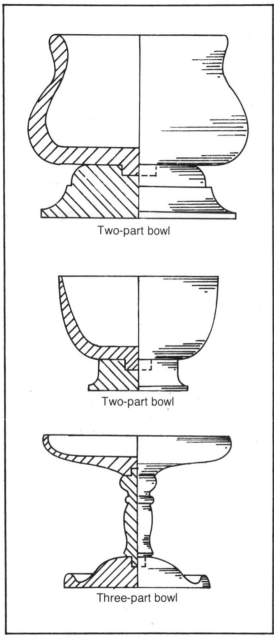

Fig. 5-15E. Pedestal base/two- and three-part bowls.

turner has to reject his own creativity, but must direct his creativity along a different line. Woodturning is a craft where the craftsman has an excellent chance to show his individual talents. The turner must not only keep his ear to the ground relative to his own products, but analyze design—good or bad—in the areas of interior design, architecture, sculpture, and textiles.

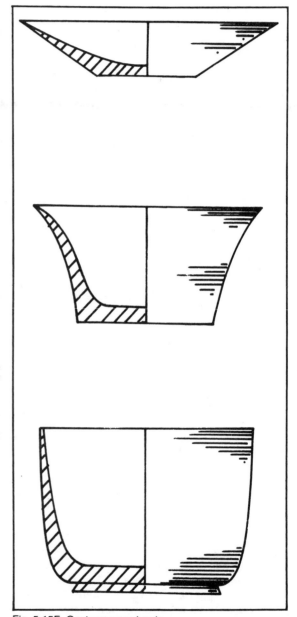

Fig. 5-15F. Contemporary bowls.

The woodturner who offers products for sale must keep his ear to the ground and his eye to the present and potential future trends. He should study accessory and furniture catalogs, visit furniture stores, and spend some time in the library. This does not mean that the wood-

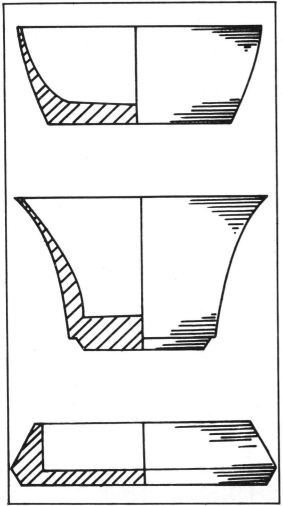

Fig. 5-15G. Contemporary bowls.

Wood presents certain attributes that must be understood. Form should not be forced upon it, but drawn out of its characteristics and the skills necessary to deal with it.

With greater experience comes greater sophistication, and with greater sophistication—mastery. The unsuitable will be discarded, the ugly and uninteresting thrown out. The search thereafter will be for the most structurally sound, the most expressive material, and the most functional and beautiful. In a few words, it will be well designed.

The turner should make every effort to develop his power of discrimination and observation in combining shapes, lines, shadows, colors and texture.

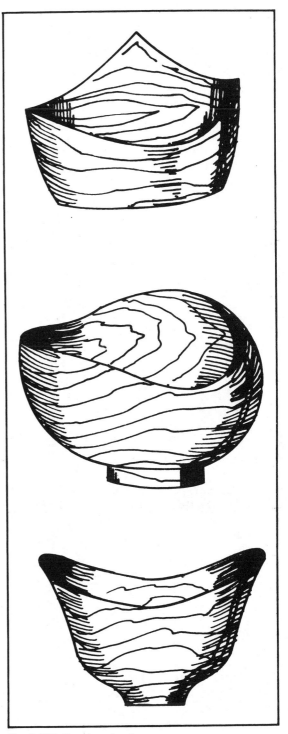

Fig. 5-15H. Free-form bowls.

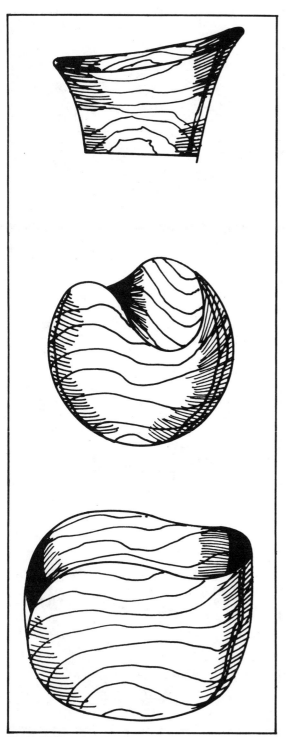

Fig. 5-15I. Free-form bowls.

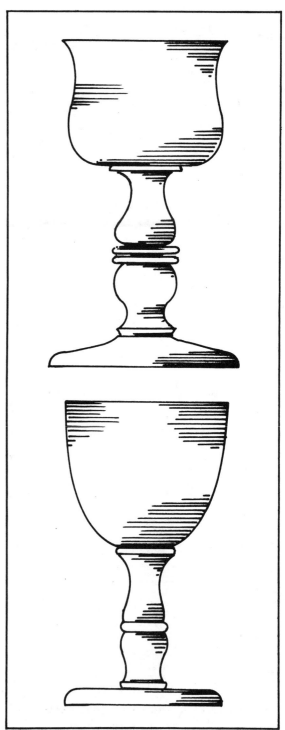

Fig. 5-16A. Goblet designs.

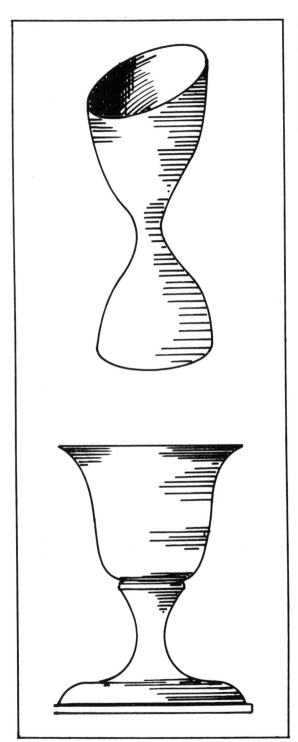

Fig. 5-16B. Goblet designs.

Fig. 5-16C. Goblet designs.

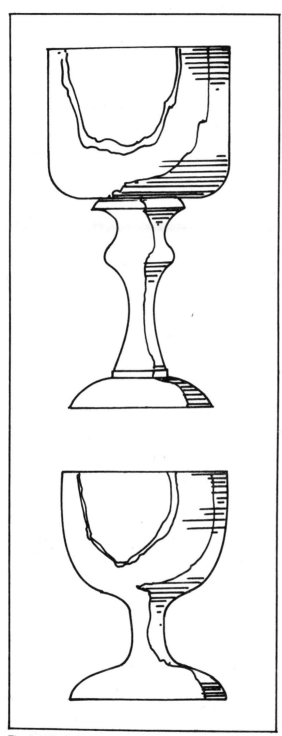

Fig. 5-16D. Goblet designs.

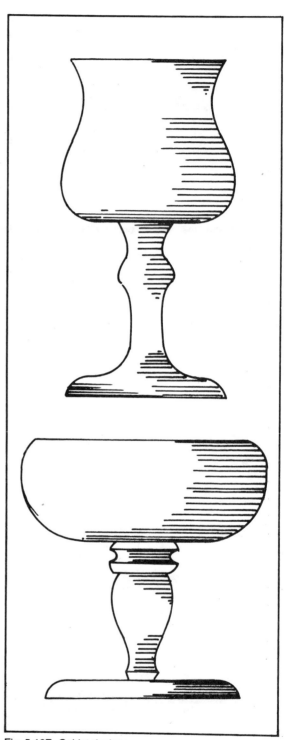

Fig. 5-16E. Goblet designs.

Fig. 5-16F. Goblet designs.

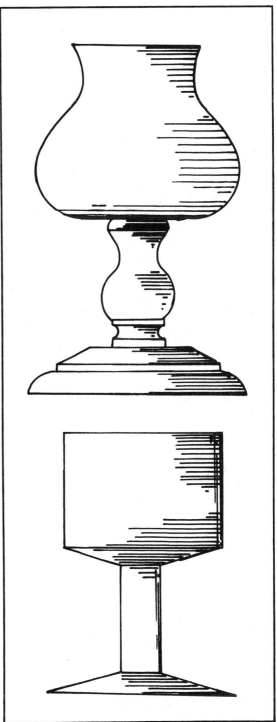

Fig. 5-16G. Goblet designs.

Fig. 5-17A. Egg cup designs.

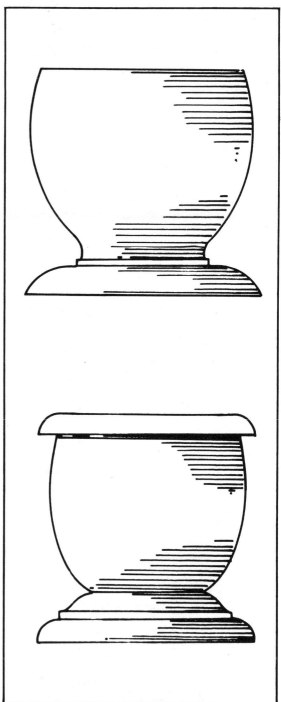

Fig. 5-17B. Egg cup designs.

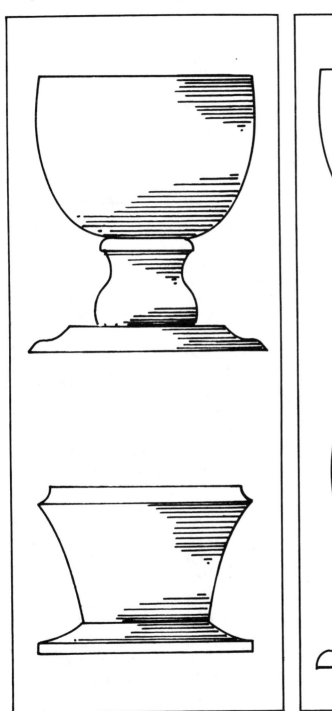

Fig. 5-17C. Egg cup designs.

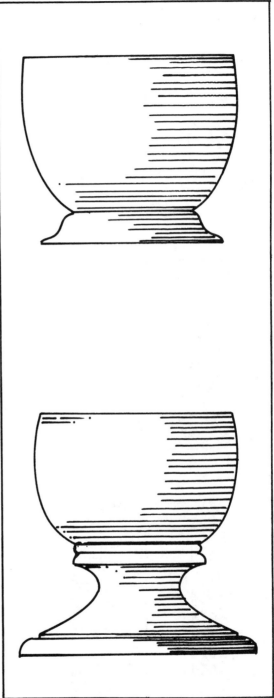

Fig. 5-17D. Egg cup designs.

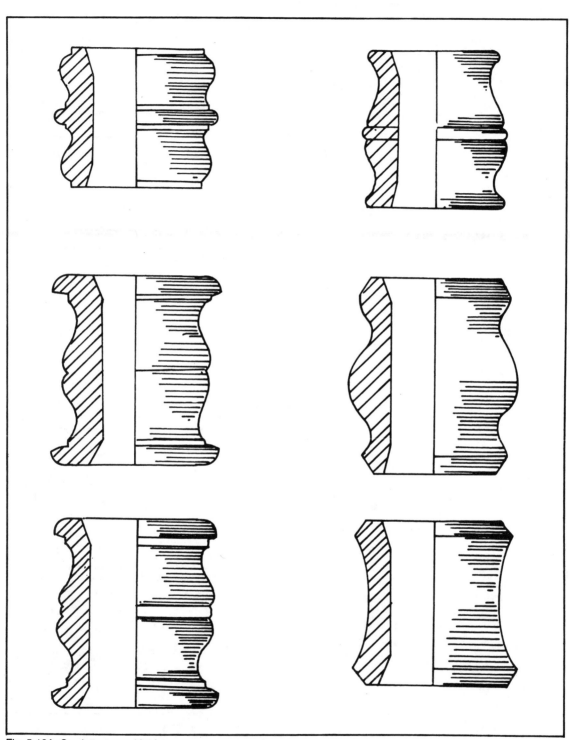

Fig. 5-18A. Serviette or napkin rings.

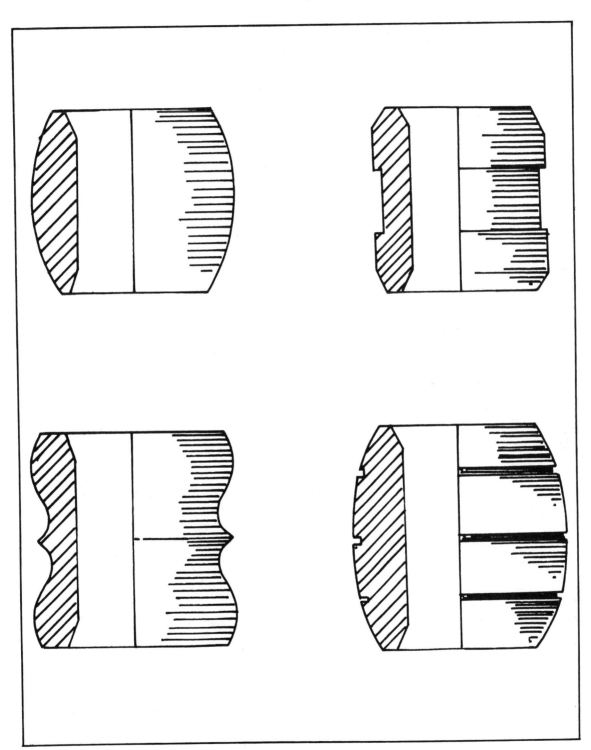

Fig. 5-18B. Serviette or napkin rings.

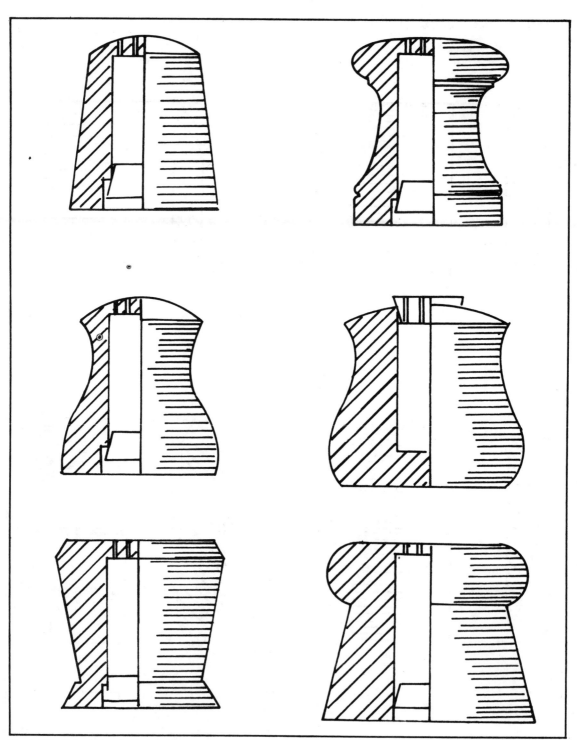

Fig. 5-19A. Salt shaker (cellar) designs.

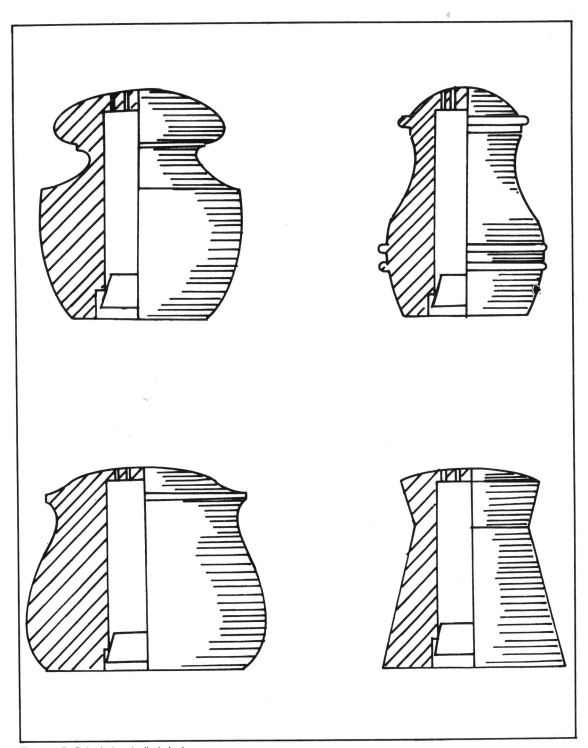

Fig. 5-19B. Salt shaker (cellar) designs.

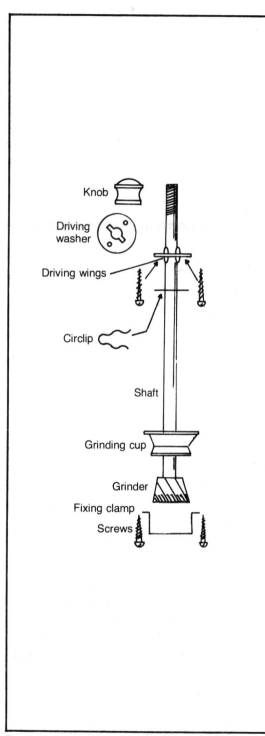

Knob

Driving washer

Driving wings

Circlip

Shaft

Grinding cup

Grinder

Fixing clamp

Screws

Fig. 5-20. Pepper mill mechanisms.

DESIGN APPLICATIONS

In most cases, the ellipse is more desirable than a circle or sphere. See Fig. 5-13. Apply the same principle to the bowl or other faceplate turnings. See Fig. 5-14.

Faceplate and Chuck-Turning Designs. Figures 5-15A through 5-15I show traditionally designed bowls as well as the pedestal base (one- and two-part bowls), contemporary bowl designs and free-form-shaped bowl designs.

Goblet Designs. Goblets require a number of skills and a number of tools (two or three sizes and types of gouges, parting tool, and a large spade, multispur or Forstner bit). Boring a hole for the cavity will save considerable time. See Figs. 5-16A through 5-16G.

Egg Cup Designs. The most important operation on the egg cup is to finish turning the inside with an egg-shaped scraping chisel after the gouge work (¼ inch) is completed. See Figs. 5-17A through 5-17D.

Serviette or Napkin Ring Designs. The combination six-in-one chuck can be used to advantage on the napkin rings. Stock should be turned to fit the collar chuck or split ring. Stock should be long enough for three or four rings. Use a spade, multispur or Forstner to bore the hole in each ring—*one at a time.* The ring is then sanded and cut off before the next hole is bored. The rounding of the inside should be done on a mandrel. See Figs. 5-18A and 5-18B.

Salt Shaker (Cellars) and Pepper Mill Designs. Pepper mills are more difficult to turn than salt shakers because they require two different diameter holes in the interior, and the mill has to be fitted to the pepper mill mechanisms. See Figs. 5-20 through 5-21C. See Chapter 12 for additional information on salt shakers and pepper mills.

CANDLESTICK DESIGNS

Candlestick designs are traditional and contemporary. Large candlesticks are often made in two parts; one is a spindle turning and the other a faceplate turning for the base. See Figs. 5-22A through 5-22G.

Edge Designs. Edge designs are used for a multitude of purposes. See Figs. 5-23 and 5-24.

Baluster and Newel Post Designs. These turnings are used in stair construction. See Figs. 5-25 and 5-26.

Symmetrical Designs. These turnings require a template or contour gauge. See Figs. 5-27A and 5-27B.

Chisel Handle Designs. Chisel handles are ideal spindle turning exercises as the dimensions are not crucial. See Figs. 5-28.

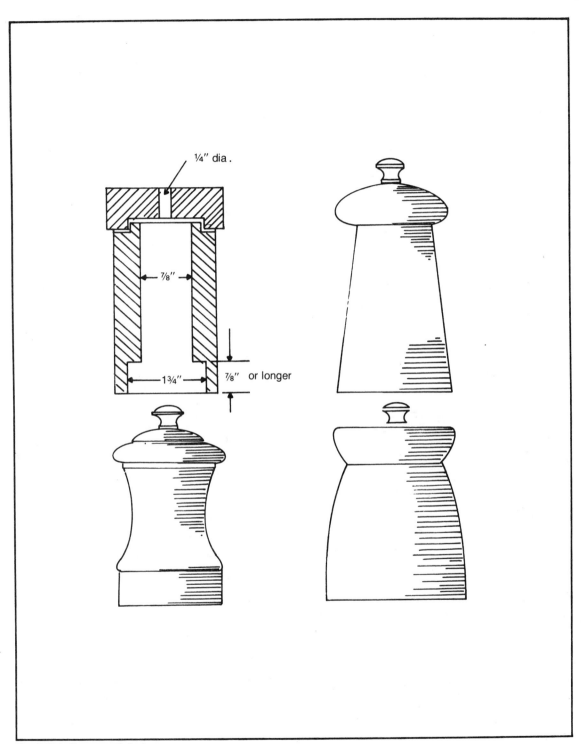

Fig. 5-21A. Pepper mill designs.

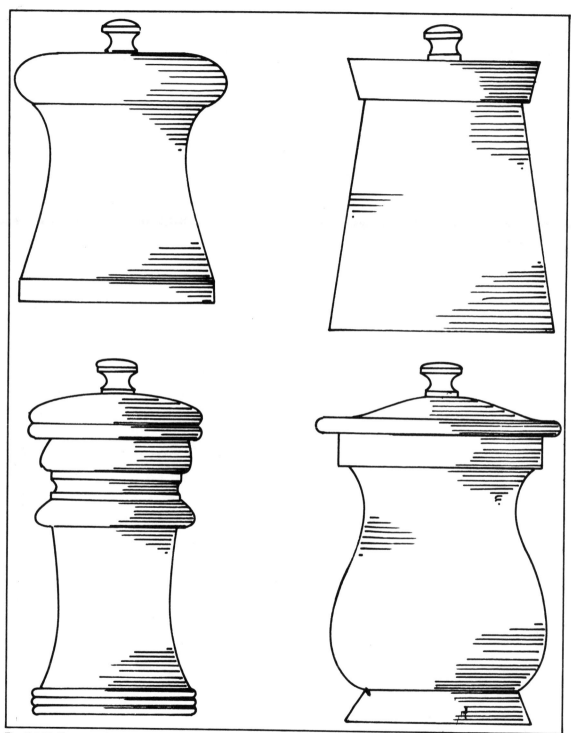

Fig. 5-21B. Pepper mill designs.

Fig. 5-21C. Pepper mill designs.

Fig. 5-22A. Candlestick designs.

Fig. 5-22B. Candlestick designs.

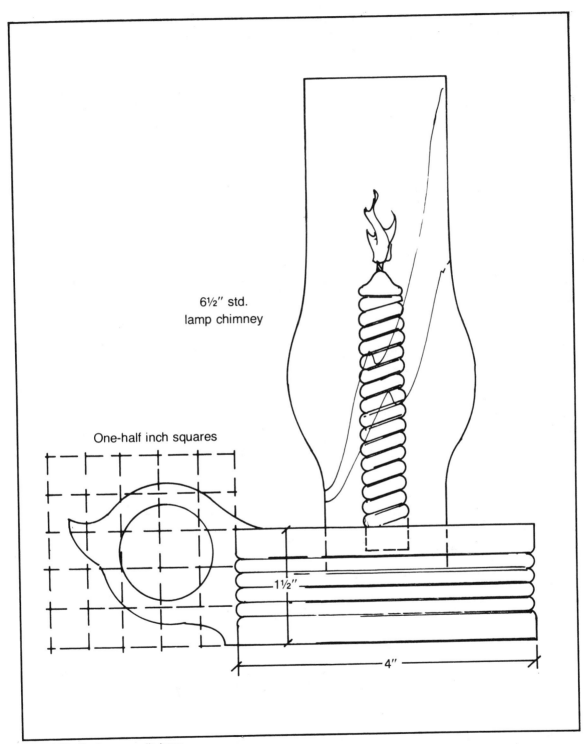

6½″ std.
lamp chimney

One-half inch squares

1½″

4″

Fig. 5-22C. Hurricane candle lamp.

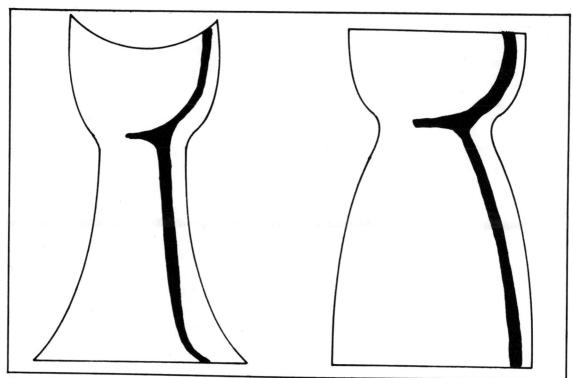

Fig. 5-22D. Candlestick designs.

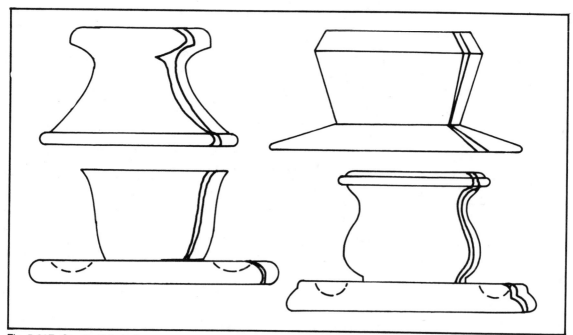

Fig. 5-22E. Candlestick designs.

106

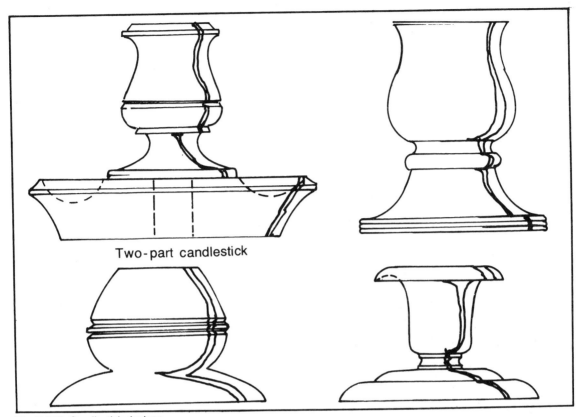

Two-part candlestick

Fig. 5-22F. Candlestick designs.

Fig. 5-22G. Contemporary candlestick designs.

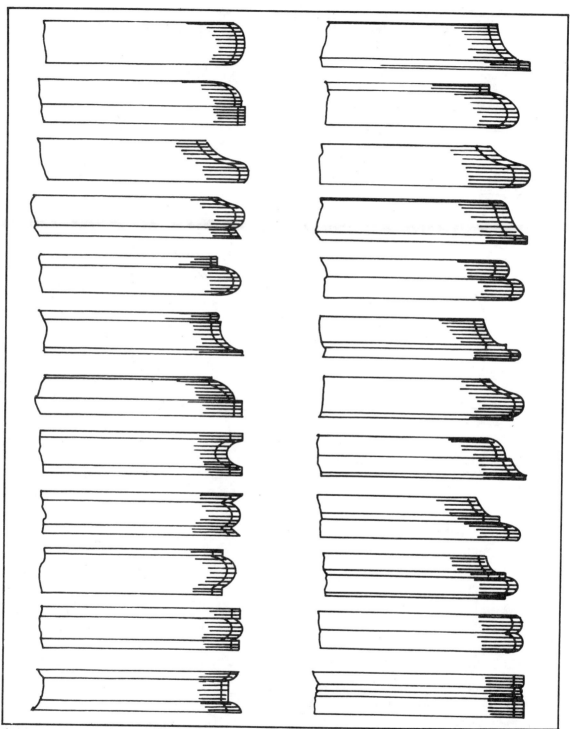

Fig. 5-23. Edge designs for cheese boards, display dome bases, coasters, trophy bases, hourglass stands, etc.

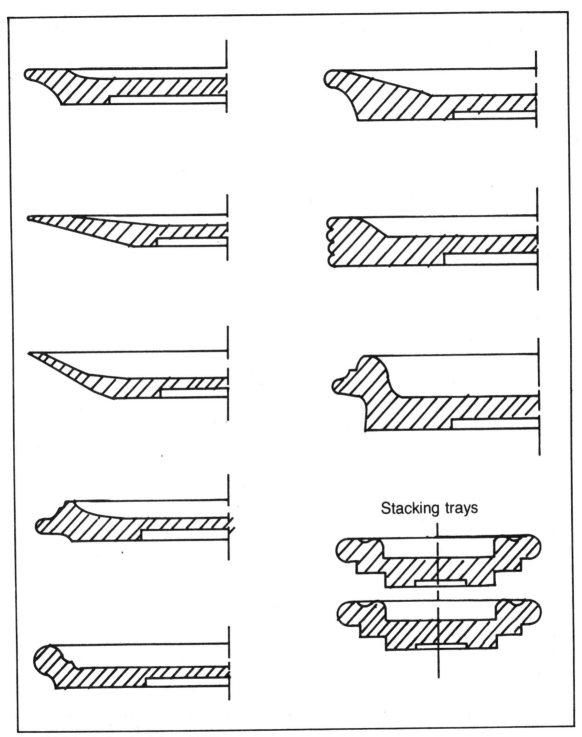

Stacking trays

Fig. 5-24. Edge designs for plates and trays.

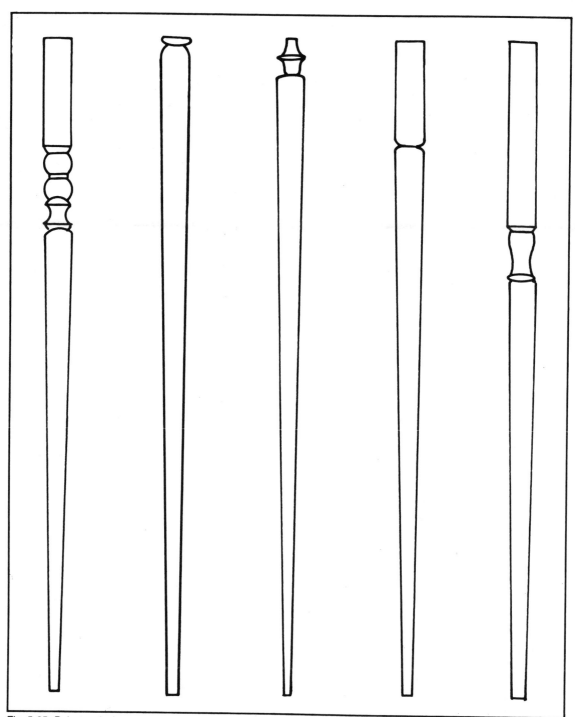

Fig. 5-25. Baluster designs.

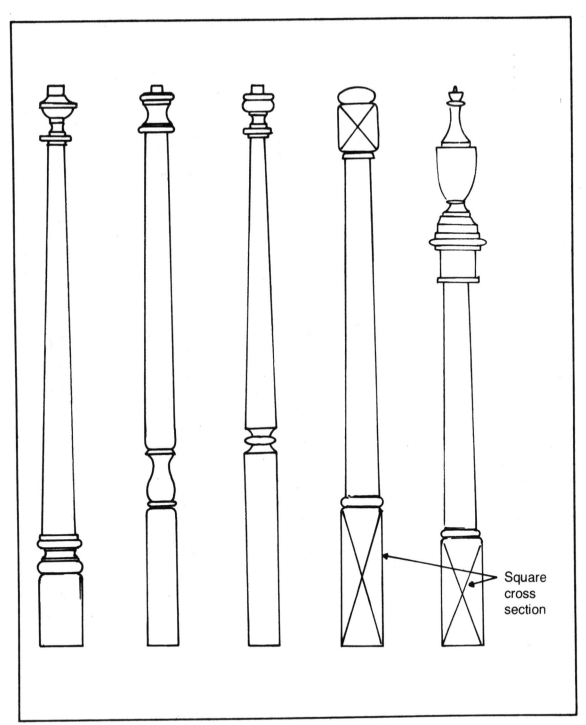

Square
cross
section

Fig. 5-26. Newel post designs.

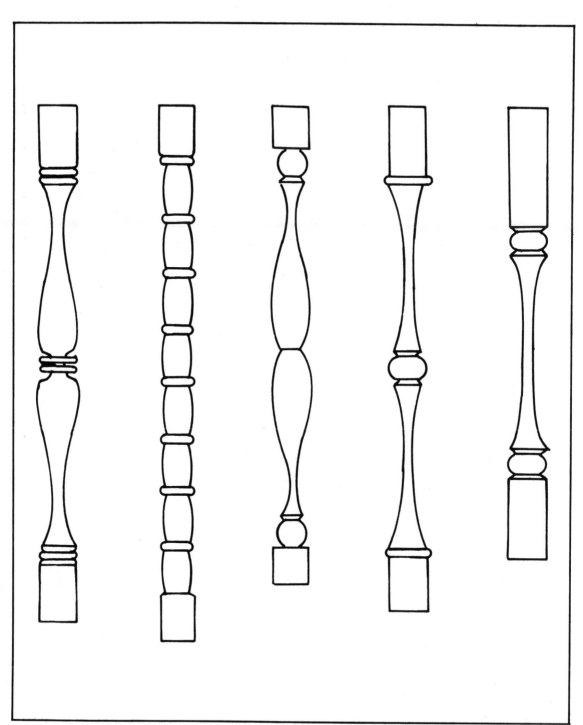

Fig. 5-27A. Symmetrical designs.

112

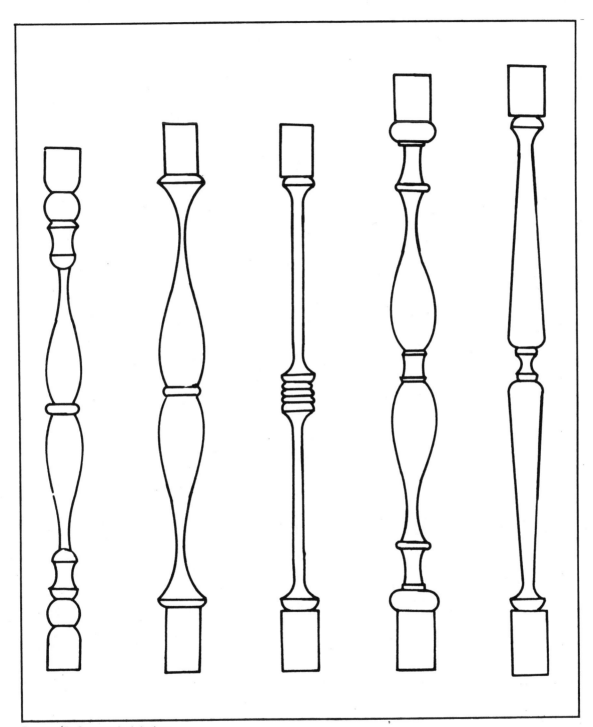

Fig. 5-27B. Symmetrical designs.

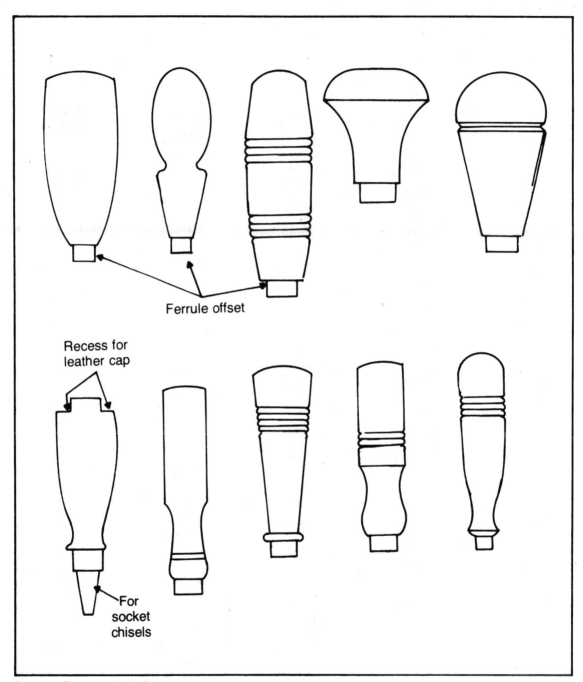

Fig. 5-28. Chisel handle designs.

Ferrule offset

Recess for
leather cap

For
socket
chisels

114

Chapter 6

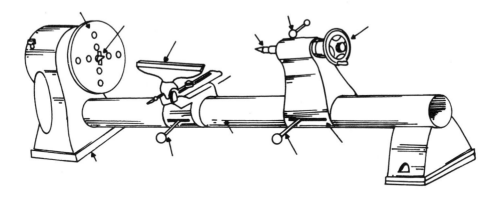

Spindle Turning

THE LATHE IS USED TO PERFORM TWO BASIC OP-erations: *spindle turning,* also known as turning between centers (e.g., a baseball bat), and *faceplate turning* (e.g., a bowl).

PREPARING STOCK

The stock is cut to the required square cross section and to the desired length. In the two practice exercises that follow, two pieces are cut 2 × 2 × 12 inches. Usually pieces of this size can be found in the scrap lumber box. Hardwood is the best for practice purposes, but softwood makes a fair substitute. Hardwoods turn with a crispness not found in the softwoods.

First mark diagonals across corners on the ends of the two pieces of square stock.

Saw two kerfs, about ⅛ of an inch deep, on one end of each piece of stock, following the lines made above.

On the other end of each piece of stock, drill a small hole where the diagonals cross.

Remove the *spur center* (also called the drive center or live center) and the *tailstock center* (also known as the dead center, ring center, tail center) from the lathe. If a ball-bearing revolving center is used, the dead center nomenclature is not apropos.

Place the spur center over the ends of the stock with the saw kerfs. It is best to use a four-prong center if the stock is softwood. Be sure the spurs or prongs engage the kerf. Strike the butt end of the center sharply with a mallet.

File a little registration notch on one of the spurs. With a pencil, mark the kerf on the stock corresponding with the registration notch on the spur. This will prove vitally important if, later on, the stock has to be removed from the lathe. These marks assure that the stock will be reinserted in the lathe at the proper location.

Place the tip of the dead center in the small drilled hole on the other end of the pieces of stock and strike sharply with a mallet.

Place the live and dead centers back in the lathe.

Position the stock in the lathe between centers with the registration marks coinciding. Lock the tailstock and advance the dead center into the stock with the tailstock spindle adjustment wheel. Lock the spindle and turn the stock over by hand, adjust if it is too tight or loose. See Fig. 6-1.

Exercises. On one end of one of the practice pieces, draw a line around the square stock 3 inches from the headstock end (the end with the spur marks) using a try square or combination square. Mark the lines with an extra-black, soft-lead pencil so that the lines can be observed while the lathe is running. See Figs. 6-2 and 6-3.

CUTTING A SHOULDER ADJACENT TO A SQUARE

Place the practice piece with the square end (also known as the pummel) in the lathe. Start up the lathe and three things will be observed: the ghost shadows of the square corners whirling around, the solid core size, and the distinct pencil lines that delineate the square.

The skew is used to mark a V cut on the pencil lines. The skew is placed on its edge on the tool rest with the long point on top. The handle should be held well down. The point of the skew should enter the wood cautiously because the exact corner of the whirling stock is hard to determine. The point enters the wood as the handle is raised and a distinct V is cut as the handle is raised still further.

The V cut is expanded both in depth and width by taking off thin slices from both sides of the V until the round core is reached. When cutting the thin slices on the right side of V, after the point enters the wood, the skew should be tipped to the right so the angle on the skew pushes against the side of the V cut and the angle or bevel follows the point of the skew. The left side of the V is cut in the same fashion. Thrusting the point of the skew directly and straight in should be avoided. That would result in a semiscraping action rather than a true cutting procedure. It also would dull the tool excessively and is very apt to burn the point of the tool.

The procedure described above will leave a slightly rounded corner on the square part. If a straight in, right-angle cut or half V is preferred, then the first cut should be at a right angle, perpendicular to the stock, the second cut is made at an angle, and then alternate straight and angle cuts until the half V is completed.

TURNING STOCK ADJACENT TO THE SQUARE

The wood next to the square must be turned carefully before the rest of the practice piece is turned to the

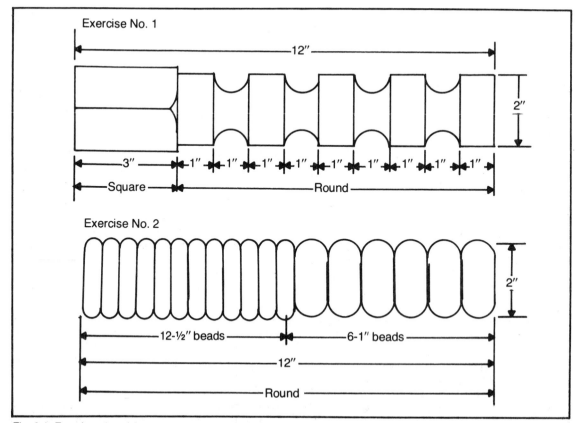

Fig. 6-1. Exercises 1 and 2.

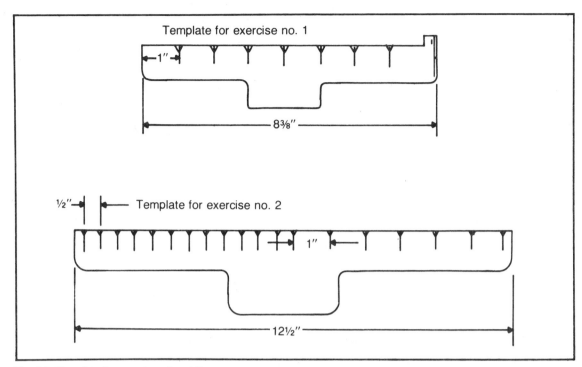

Fig. 6-2. Template for exercises 1 and 2.

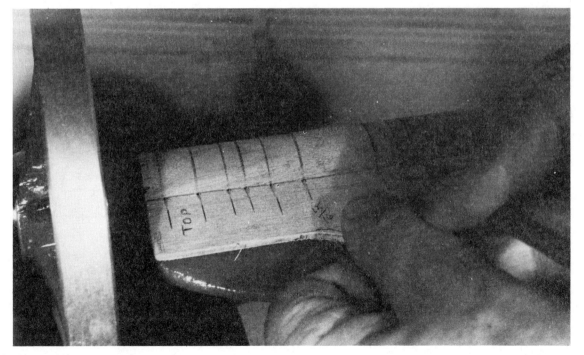

Fig. 6-3. Template in use.

round. A large roughing half-round gouge, with the end ground square across, is used for this purpose. The gouge is placed on its side and the corner is allowed to enter the wood a short distance (about ½ inch from the V). Very little pressure is needed as the gouge moves, almost automatically, until it hits the left side of the V. See Fig. 6-4.

TURNING ROUND STOCK

The roughing gouge is the primary tool for roughing stock down to the round. With the roughing gouge in the same position (flute to the left) as shown in Fig. 6-4, move it so the left or inside corner starts cutting to the right. The gouge is then rolled to the right so that all parts of the cutting edge will be involved. By the time the gouge reaches the end of the turning, it will have made a 180-degree turn with the gouge on its right side with the hollowed-out part of the gouge facing to the right—with the opposite corner doing the cutting. This process is continued until the stock (except the square) is turned to a uniform diameter. The beginner might need calipers and a parting tool before using the gouge to make sure of uniformity. The professional turner uses only his eyes and the "feel" between his fingers.

The surface left by the gouge might be a trifle rough.

At this time, the turner might try his hand at further smoothing with the skew. This is one of the most difficult techniques; the beginner must be patient because miscues are bound to happen. This simply means reducing the diameter of the stock. See Fig. 6-5.

There are two types of chisels used for smoothing: the skew chisel and the squared. The skew chisel is preferred because of the other operations it can perform. I will confine my remarks to the skew.

Wide skews are preferred to narrow ones because only about one-half of the center section is used in skew turning. Narrow skews decrease the cutting edge substantially. That means more mishaps, digs, and scars are apt to occur. Furthermore, the full capacity of the usable half of the skew would be possible only if the skew is held parallel to the stock. The more that the skew is held to the vertical—at right angles to the stock—the narrower will become the cutting surface. Of course, the skew is never held at right angles to the stock for smoothing purposes. The handle is held to the right when turning to the left, and to the left when turning to the right.

The tool rest should be positioned higher than in other turning because the skew turns and rubs the turning close to the top. See Fig. 6-6.

Keep in mind that the skew is not designed to turn

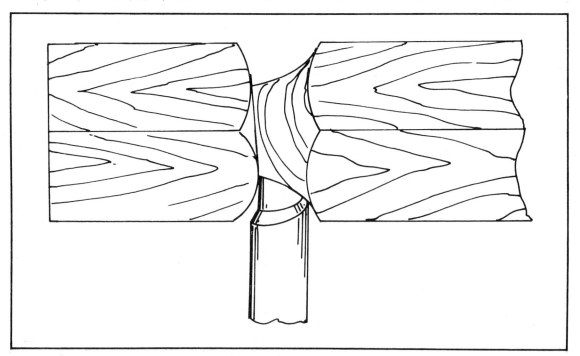

Fig. 6-4. Turning stock adjacent to square.

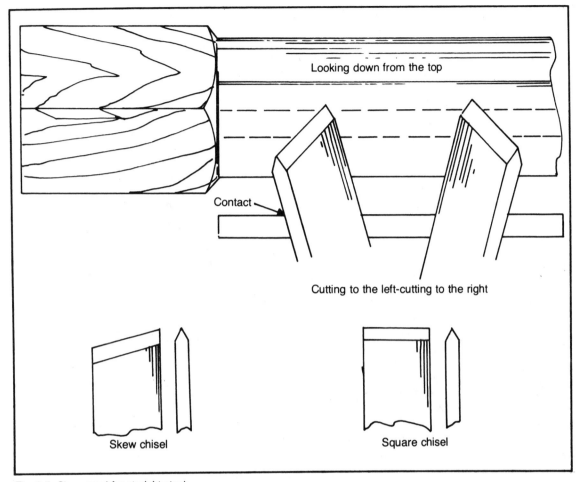

Looking down from the top

Contact

Cutting to the left-cutting to the right

Skew chisel

Square chisel

Fig. 6-5. Skew used for straight stock.

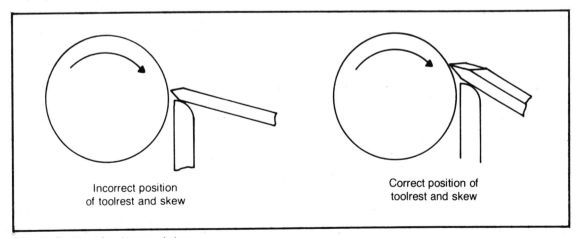

Incorrect position
of toolrest and skew

Correct position of
toolrest and skew

Fig. 6-6. Position of tool rest and skew.

huge quantities of wood, but to turn light, silky shavings leaving a smooth and blemish-free surface that needs little if any sanding. See Fig. 6-7.

Let's use a hypothetical situation. We are skew turning a 2-inch-diameter cylinder with a 1½-inch skew and the skew is held at about 60 degrees. Because only half of the edge of the skew can be used without running into trouble, the position of the skew and width of the cut are crucial. As is shown in Fig. 6-7, we are not able to turn the full ¾ of an inch (½ of 1½ inches), but a strip from ½ inch to 9/16 of an inch wide due to the angle of the skew.

If the skew is moved toward the dotted—that is at a right angle to the cylinder as shown in the drawing—the cutting strip is reduced to about one-half the width or about ¼ inch. The skew must be held very firmly at this angle because any deviation from this position will certainly cause all kinds of trouble.

If the angle of the skew is decreased to less than 60 degrees—that is more parallel to the turning—a wider strip can be turned, but it is apt to be less than a satisfactory surface. Roughness is liable to be the result, and this could defeat the primary function of the skew which is to develop a nice, smooth surface that will require little if any sanding.

When turning toward the left, the left hand is held close to the cutting edge with the knuckles on top and the fingers curled around the skew with the thumb underneath. A portion of the hand rides against the tool rest. The right hand is held low on the end of the handle. When turning a taper, the skew should move downhill; otherwise the tool will be cutting against the grain.

When turning toward the right, the right hand holds the skew point with the left hand on the end of the handle. Of course, this means that the turner has to be somewhat ambidextrous. Whenever posible, the handle of the skew should be held against the body of the turner to provide better stability and control.

Naturally, the skew must be turned up on one edge to obtain the proper cutting position. In this position only one point of the skew rest on the tool rest; this differs from most other turning where the whole width of the tool lies flat on the tool rest. In turning to the left, the left edge of the skew is touching the tool rest and vice versa when turning to the right. This points out another reason why skew turning is more difficult than other turning. With the skew turned up on edge and the hand gripping the skew and riding along the tool rest, a severe pinch of a finger or part of the hand might occur if a miscue happens.

The skew should never be used as a scraper. It only produces fine sawdust instead of shavings, and the sharp edge is dulled very quickly. As with nearly all turning, the bevel of the tool must rub against the turning. When the skew is used as a scraper, this principle has been violated.

The skew, as well as all other lathe tools, should be kept sharp if good performance is expected. The turner who thinks that frequent sharpening of lathe tools is time wasted is laboring under delusions. The time spent will be returned many fold.

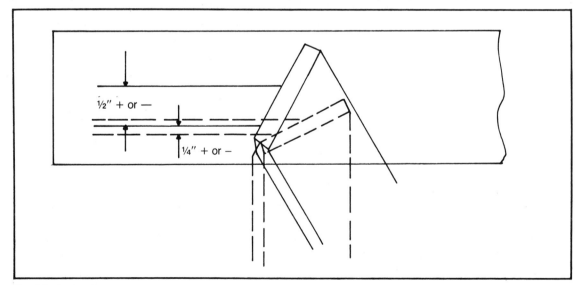

½″ + or −

¼″ + or −

Fig. 6-7. Angle of skew to work.

120

SHARPENING THE SKEW

Mike Darlow, in his article *The Timing of the Skew,* in the Sept/Oct, 1982 issue of the *Fine Woodworking* magazine, gives some fine pointers on sharpening the skew. The following four paragraphs are reprinted from *Fine Woodworking* magazine © 1982 The Taunton Press, Inc., 52 Church Hill Road, Box 355, Newtown, CT 06470.

"An angle of skewness of about 70° is the optimum compromise between retaining a strong long point and providing an adequate clearance. When grinding, hold the cutting edge parallel to the grinding wheel axis, the bevel flat on the wheel, and aim for an angle on each bevel of about 12½°. I find that this sharpening angle works well on all woods, even out native Australian hardwoods (some of which are very hard indeed). The optimum diameter of the grindstone is 8″ to 10″. If smaller, excessive hollow grinding weakens the cutting edge; if larger, the bevel will be rather flat, which makes both grinding and honing more difficult. The grit and composition of the wheel depend on the type of style. For my high-speed steel tools, I use a Norton 19A 60KVBE. Take care to keep the two bevels the same length, so that the cutting edge, when looked at head-on, is centered and parallel to the sides. Then the clearance angle will be the same on both sides.

"There are two misconceptions about sharpening: that the bevel need not be hollow-ground, and that honing is not required after grinding. The bevels need to be hollow-ground so that there is a straight line of sight along the bevel. The turner can then sight along the true cutting edge, the microsharpened bevel, when making cuts with the long point. Although gouges are more easily honed by moving the stone for the skew. Try a shallow tray holding a fine-grade 6″ by 2″ oilstone immersed in kerosene, plus the slips for the gouges, mounted adjacent to the lathe and covered with a lid. Hone the skew with short to-and-fro strokes, and with both the heel and toe of the bevel bearing on the stone. After the bevels have been honed, any burr can be stropped off.

"Some turners do not hone, because the ragged edge straight from the grindstone gives an illusion of sharpness. An unhoned edge, however, scratches the wood surface and does not last. In addition, it is far quicker to rehone than to regrind, and your tools will last much longer.

"A convex bevel is occasionally recommended in the belief that it polishes the cut surface. Actually, the texture of the wood contacted by the bevel is little affected by bevel shape, and the loss of the clear line of sight is a disadvantage."

MAKING AND USING A TEMPLATE

Now that you have turned the two practice pieces to cylinders, except for the square portion on one, it is time to think about laying out the cuts (beads and coves) that are to be made. First make the template for the practice piece with the square end. Templates can be made of any thin wood, but ⅛-inch plywood is the best.

Lay out the template on the wood. The template is for the turned part only and defines four coves 1 inch wide and 1 inch in between. See Figs. 6-1 and 6-2.

Cut the template ¼ inch longer than needed (9¼ inches). This is necessary to provide a V cut in the edge of the template.

Mark off the nine points, 1 inch apart, and carry a line about halfway across the template with a try square. With a sharp knife make a V-shaped cut on the edge of the template at each 1-inch line.

With the template held on the tool rest (Fig. 6-3) using your left hand and with your right hand, allow a sharp-pointed pencil to follow down the V cuts until the pencil lead touches the turning cylinder. Watch that the corners of the square do not hit the template.

Now you can make the template for exercise No. 2, which is a cylinder over its entirety. This exercise concentrates on making beads.

On a piece of thin wood, 12 inches long, mark off twelve ½-inch intervals on the left side and six 1-inch intervals on the right. Cut the Vs as in the first template and mark the intervals on the whirling stock as described earlier. See Fig. 6-8.

Proceed by cutting the 1-inch wide, semicircular coves in the square-end practice piece. Select a ¾-inch halfround, or shallow, spindle-nose gouge. Of course, a 1-inch wide gouge could be used, but it would have to be pushed straight into the cylinder, scraper fashion. That would dull the tool very rapidly.

It is best to use a somewhat narrower gouge than the width of the cove to get the right cutting action from the tool. The gouge was never designed as a scraping tool. For the beginner, who has trouble mastering the cutting tools, a round-nose scraping chisel would be better than trying to use the gouge as a scraper.

When turning coves, the gouge can be thought of as scoop, scooping out a hollow in the wood. The gouge is held on its side with the flute facing the part to be scooped out. The point of the gouge is pressed into the wood on one of the two lines that limit the cove's width. The gouge should be held very firmly because the point, at this stage, will have a strong tendency to move to the side away from the line (opposite the direction of the flute).

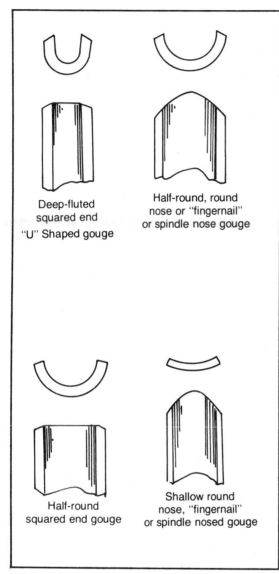

Deep-fluted
squared end
"U" Shaped gouge

Half-round, round
nose or "fingernail"
or spindle nose gouge

Half-round
squared end gouge

Shallow round
nose, "fingernail"
or spindle nosed gouge

Fig. 6-8. Types of gouges.

By moving the handle to the right—if starting the cut on the left of the cove, and vice versa when entering the right side of the cove—the tendency of the tool to misbehave will be lessened. If the beginner has trouble with the initial entry of the gouge, a small V-shaped cut can be made on the limit lines with a skew point. The same procedure can be used if the cove is rather deep. After the initial entry has been successful, and there is no more worry of jumping gouges, the scooping continues with the bevel rubbing all the way down to the bottom of the cove.

When the bottom is reached, the gouge will have turned over on its back with the flute in an upright position. When the bottom has been reached, do not attempt to cut the other half of the cove by cutting up the other side. Withdraw the tool and make an entry cut on the other line. Roll the gouge in the opposite direction. Make as many passes as are necessary to complete the cove. If the diameter of the practice piece at the bottom of the cove is approximately 1 inch, then the cut has been successful. The cove cut should be quite smooth if the gouge has been held in the proper manner, and no sandpaper will be needed.

So far I have mentioned tool rest height very little and there are no fast and hard rules concerning the rest. I mentioned that skew turning required a higher tool rest, and that most turning is done with the toolrest at, or a little below, the center line.

The height of the turner and the height of the lathe greatly affect the height of the tool rest. A tall man working at a low lathe will be working down into the turning rather than straight. That means the tool rest must be higher and the handle of the chisel must be held higher than normal.

The most important thing is that the bevel of the tool (except scraping tools) must be rubbing on the work. As the diameter of spindle turnings are reduced the tool rest must be moved in accordingly. Each turner should experiment with the lathe height and tool rest height until he finds the most comfortable position for him.

TRIMMING ENDS OF PRACTICE EXERCISES

Shoulder cuts and trimming cuts are made perpendicular to the turning itself. The ends of cylinders are apt to be rough and perhaps lopsided as a finishing cut must be made.

There are four tools that may be used for trimming the ends of the cylinders: the parting tool, the parting and beading tool, the skew chisel, and the ordinary ¼-inch chisel. See Fig. 6-9.

The parting tool will do a fair job at trimming the ends and will do it rapidly. Nevertheless, for a clean, ultrasmooth surface the skew is supreme. The first cut is done with the corner of the skew. The corner must be advanced straight in otherwise unwanted rubbing with the side of the chisel will occur and the shoulder will not be square.

For the final cut, after the end diameter has been reduced, the entire bevel of the skew is advanced straight in with the long point down.

By alternating the two cuts described above, the

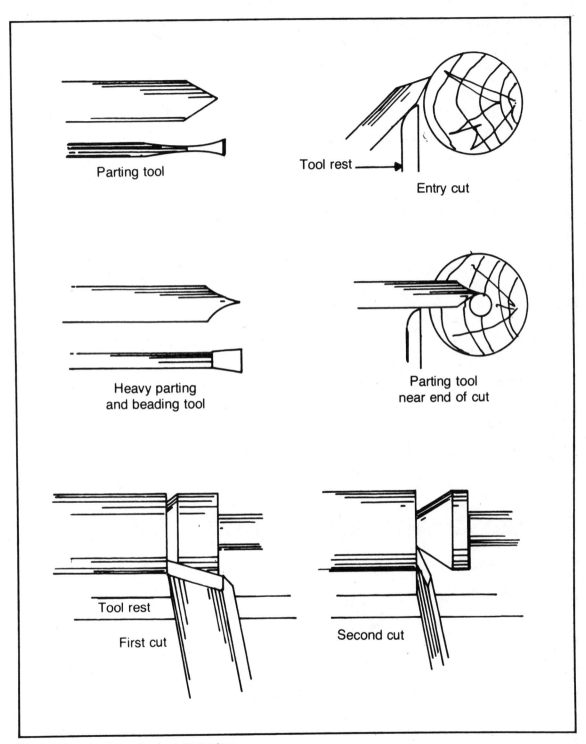

Parting tool

Tool rest

Entry cut

Heavy parting
and beading tool

Parting tool
near end of cut

Tool rest

First cut

Second cut

Fig. 6-9. Trimming the ends of spindle turnings.

first end is cut nearly through. The second end can then be cut entirely through and the revolving piece can be caught in the hand.

The ¼-inch square chisel is used only when a considerable waste portion of the turning is to be cut off. The ¼-inch chisel is very apt to bind because it does not cut clearance as it advanced into the stock. The enlarged end of the parting tool provides clearance. After a ¼-inch chisel has advanced part way into the turning, the turning can be bent forward with hand pressure from the rear of turning. The widened cut allows the ¼-inch chisel to advance to the cut-off position.

After the practice piece, with the square end is completed—and before the ends are cut off—the turner might want to practice the use of abrasives or French polishing on the work piece.

CUTTING BEADS

Beads are often used with turning projects, either singularly or in multiples. Place the turned cylinder in the lathe using the registration marks for reference. The marks delineating the beads have been scribed on the piece earlier.

Half of the cylinder is used to practice turning ½-inch-wide beads, and the other half is used for 1-inch-wide beads. The larger beads present the greater challenge.

Tools used for turning beads are the *skew chisel,* the *parting* and *beading* tool, and the *diamond point* also known as the *spear point.*

THE SKEW CHISEL

The most effective skew is about one-half the width of the bead or a little wider. In other words, the skew used to turn the ½-inch beads should be ¼ or ⅜ of an inch wide, and the one most appropriate for the 1-inch-wide beads would be a ½ or ¾ of an inch skew. Wider skews can be used, but they have the fault of cutting down on visibility while turning. See Fig. 6-10A.

The point of the skew, with the long point down, should be inserted into the revolving stock at the pencil-line locations. All incisions can be cut before proceeding

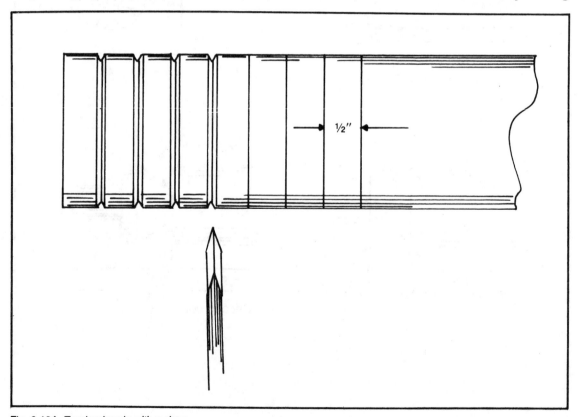

Fig. 6-10A. Turning beads with a skew.

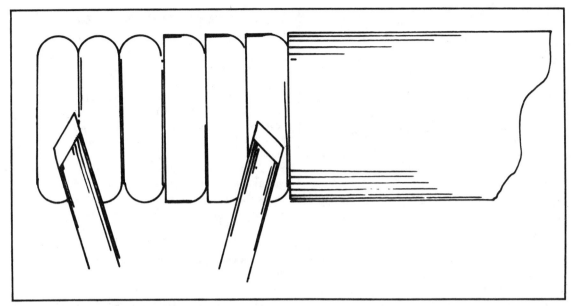

Fig. 6-10B. Turning beads with a skew.

with the rest of the beads. The incisions should not be to the full depth of the bead. As the work progresses in rounding over the bead, the incisions are progressively made deeper. The rounding-over process is alternated with the cutting of deeper incisions until a ½-inch wide semicircular bead is completed. The skew is generally angled slightly in the direction of the cut with the heel of the skew. See Fig. 6-10B.

One-half of the bead is started at the center. One-half of the skew (as in most skew turning) will be cutting the bead at first, but—because the skew is rolled over to a vertical position, with the long point on top—the heel of the skew will proceed down the incision. It will not proceed entirely to the bottom of the incision because of the width of the heel. Therefore, the point of the skew is reinserted in the incision to make it deeper.

As the cut is being made and the skew moves to a more vertical position, the handle of the skew moves to the left and up for a cut to the right and vice versa for the cut to the left. All cuts to the right should be made at the same time, followed by all the cuts to the left at the same time or vice versa, otherwise the turner will be constantly switching hands from the skew blade to the end of the handle.

When cutting to the right, the left hand is held over the skew with a portion of the hand riding on the toolrest. The point where the skew rides on the toolrest is the pivotal point. The right hand holds the end of the handle that should rest against the body. When cutting to the left the hands are reversed.

The skew should be held firmly to prevent the skew from catching on the wood which would ruin the bead. The skew should be sharpened frequently.

The expert or professional turner will make half a bead in one pass of the chisel, but the beginner should be content with making a number of light passes. The heel of the skew is the biggest offender and should be watched carefully, particularly during the first part of the cut.

THE PARTING AND BEADING TOOL

The parting and beading tool is a heavy, nearly square chisel with a squared-off cutting edge. It is usually ¼ to ⅜ of an inch in width, while the ordinary parting tool might be as thin as ⅛ of an inch. The extra weight and stability of this tool reduces the tendency to dig into the wood and vibrating—which is common with the skew.

The bead is formed in a fashion similar to the skew. The bevel of the tool is rested on the top of the bead-to-be and then slowly moved backward with the handle tilted upward until the tool starts cutting.

When the tool starts cutting, the tool is turned over in the direction of the cut. Use your upper hand to hold the tool firmly to the rest. The tool will cut a bead much faster because the tool does not have to be removed from the work to cut the second half of the bead. The entire bead can be cut in one operation.

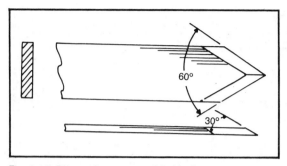

Fig. 6-11. Diamond or spear point chisel.

THE DIAMOND OR SPEAR-POINT CHISEL

If the beginner finds that it is impossible to turn a bead with a skew or parting and beading tool, he might have to resort to a diamond point or spear point chisel. See Fig. 6-11.

It should be kept in mind, however, that the diamond point is *not* a cutting tool but a *scraping* tool. As such, the bevel does not rub on the work, the cutting edge dulls very rapidly, and only sawdust, not shavings, will be the result.

After the initial incision on both sides of the bead with a skew, the diamond point is inserted into the cut and the two half-beads, on either side of the incisions, can be made by rolling the point from side to side.

MAKING THE V CUT

The V cut is probably the easiest to turn. There is little chance of the skew going awry with this cut. See Fig. 6-12.

First the Vs are laid out with a pencil held against the

As a parting tool the sides of the chisel must be hollow ground to provide clearance. The parting and beading tool will not be found in many tool catalogs. It might be necessary for the craftsman to make his own from tool steel or have one made for him by a blacksmith or machinist. The parting and beading tool is considered by many wood turners to be superior to the skew for forming beads.

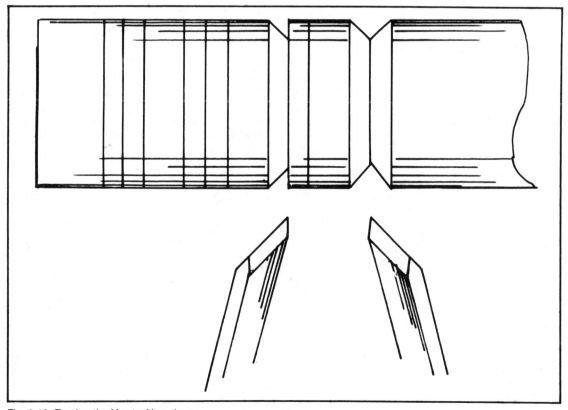

Fig. 6-12. Turning the V cut with a skew.

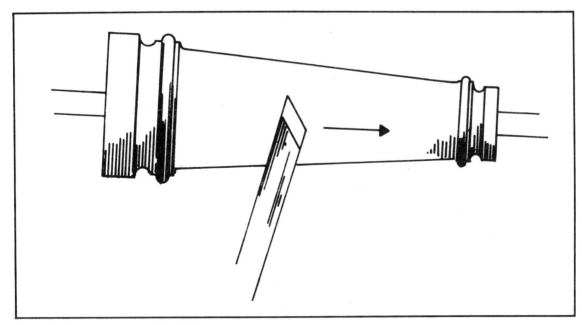

Fig. 6-13. Turning the taper with a skew.

whirling stock. The pencil lines are needed to delineate the V. The two outside lines circumscribe the width of the V, and a third line defines the center. An experienced turner will not need the center line, but it is a great help to the beginner because it indicates where the first cut will start.

The long point of the skew is advanced slowly into the turning with the right edge of the bevel riding against the stock in making the first cut. The handle is held to the left and is gradually lifted to make the cut.

The second cut is made the same way except in reverse. The second cut is more difficult to make as the skew point does not have any support as it enters the wood.

CUTTING A TAPER

Cutting a taper requires the same techniques as used in straight turning of cylinders. The roughing gouge is used for the major cutting with the skew used for finishing cuts. See Fig. 6-13.

The turner should keep in mind which direction of cut is the most comfortable for him. If the turner feels more comfortable turning from the left to the right, then the smaller end of the turning must be toward the tailstock end, and vice versa for those most comfortable turning from right to left.

It must be emphasized again that all turning must be downhill. In other words, the turning is started at the larger part and proceed to the smaller part of the taper.

Any attempt to cut uphill will prove disastrous (in the same manner as trying to plane wood against the grain). Just try sharpening a pencil by starting at the lead and whittling toward the eraser.

Chapter 7

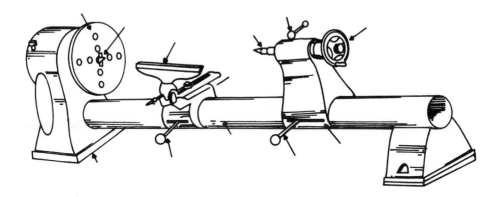

Faceplate and Chuck Turning

BEFORE DELVING INTO THIS CHAPTER, YOU should review Chapter 3. Pay particular attention to Figs. 3-2 through 3-15.

SPICE DRAWER FRONTS

Faceplate turning with a special homemade chisel requires very little skill. Although the directions that follow deal specifically with knobs for a spice cabinet, they can be applied to any construction where recessed knobs are required.

Step No. 1. Determine the size of the knob and the width of the recessed portion. A convenient size for spice drawer fronts is ½ × 2¾ × 4 inches. For this size drawer, the knob diameter should be ¾ of an inch across and the diameter of the recessed portion should be approximately 2 inches. See Fig. 7-1.

Step No. 2. Lay out a cross section of the drawer front through the center of the drawer. The depth of the recess should be 5/16 of an inch (see section A—A in Fig. 7-1).

Step No. 3. Grind a special chisel from an old mill file. Make certain that the clearance is in the underside of the chisel and that the width of the point is not over three-quarters as wide as the recessed portion. See Figs. 7-2 and 7-3.

Step No. 4. Make a faceplate jig for turning. Turn a 6-inch diameter piece of stock, about 1 inch thick, on the faceplate. Lay out and cut on the bandsaw or jigsaw the special chuck or jig to hold the spice drawer front. Fasten this to the turned 1-inch piece with countersunk, flathead screws. Be sure that the recessed chuck is centered. Drive two small, sharpened brads into the bottom of the recess to keep the drawer front from shifting in the jig. See Fig. 7-4.

Step No. 5. Make a marking tool. The tool shown in Fig. 7-5 will mark a recess 2 inches in diameter and a knob ¾ of an inch in diameter. The spurs are made by driving small brads into the handle and sharpening the brads to a point with a file.

Step No. 6. Mark the drawer front recesses. Place the drawer front blank in the recess in the faceplate jig. Strike firmly with a soft mallet so that the sharp brads will penetrate into the back of the blank. In this position, the blank will not fly out of the lathe or shift around in the jig and the exact center will be maintained.

Turn on the lathe and place the tool rest about one-half inch from the blank. With the piece turning, the exact center will be easily observed. Place the marking tool on the toolrest with the center pin about ⅛ of an inch from the turning blank. The two other pins will then be to

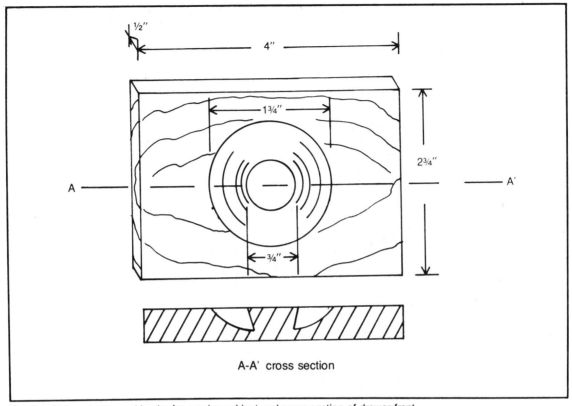

Fig. 7-1. Sizing of recessed knobs for a spice cabinet and cross section of drawer front.

the *left* of the center. Push the marking tool toward the blank until the center pin penetrates the center of the blank and the other two pins scribe circles on the blank. These circles define the recessed portion.

Step No. 7. Cut the recessed portion. With the lathe still running, insert the special chisel into the space on the blank between the two scribed circles and move the chisel slowly back and forth until the scribed circles are reached. See Fig. 7-6.

Step No. 8. Sand and remove the blank. Sand the recess with coarse sandpaper and finish sanding with #2-0 or #3-0 sandpaper. Remove the drawer front from the faceplate jig by using the cutout portions for finger insertion and easy pull out. See Fig. 7-7.

PRELIMINARIES

Faceplate turning presents problems not inherent in spindle turning. The grain of the wood in faceplate turning generally runs across the diameter of the workpiece. The grain in spindle turning runs longitudinally with the workpiece, thus presenting little difficulty except in large

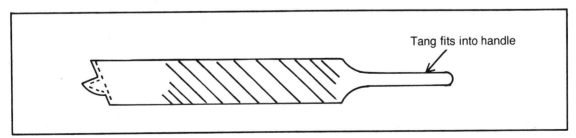

Fig. 7-2. Special chisel for spice cabinet drawer fronts.

Fig. 7-3. Special chisel and spice cabinet drawer front.

diameter spindle turnings. In faceplate turning, the cutting tool is encountering both end grain and side grain.

Bowls are the most common faceplate turnings. It is best to start with bowls of small diameter (5 or 6 inches) and shallow (not over 2 inches deep). The same techniques are used with large bowls. The only difference is that a small bowl is ruined during the learning process; the loss of expensive wood is minimized. Once

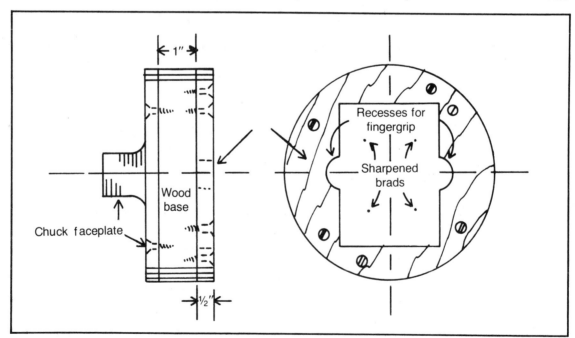

Fig. 7-4. Faceplate jig for holding and turning recessed knobs.

130

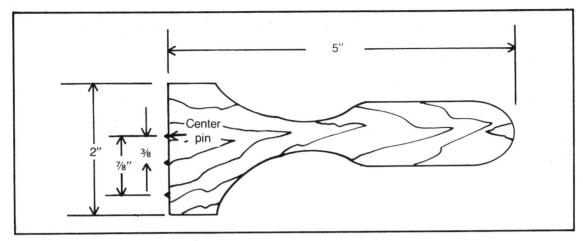

Fig. 7-5. Marking tool to locate the recess and knob diameters.

the turner has turned a number of small bowls without fear, he can go to the larger bowls with confidence. The alternating grain pattern of the larger diameter bowl, however, might prove troublesome.

If green wood is available, it should be used. It is inexpensive, and the long ribbons of shavings will peel off with ease, giving the turner a greater sense of achievement and satisfaction.

The serious bowl or faceplate turner should, early in the game, acquire a bandsaw that will handle 3-inch hardwood stock. It should be adequately powered with a ½- or ¾-hp motor, and the table should be capable of tilting to at least 45 degrees. The rollers and guides should be of hardened steel and should be closely inspected before purchase.

The wheels should be at least 12 inches in diameter. The smaller, wheeled bandsaws might be adequate for cutting bowl blanks, but the problems of broken bandsaw blades, due to fatigue in passing over the smaller wheels, will eventually become an expensive and frustrating nuisance.

The bandsaw blade should have medium or coarse spacing of teeth. There is little need of a fine-tooth blade because the surface is eliminated when turning takes place. The skip-tooth blade is by far the best for rough bandsawing. The only thing against this blade is that it cannot be resharpened. The craftsman should keep in mind that the narrower blades will cut smaller bowl blanks than wider blades.

Gouges and Scrapers

Gouges and scrapers are the tools most often used in faceplate turning; the parting tool is used occasionally to start a cut on the interior of a bowl. The "long and strong" variety of gouges and chisels is considered by most turners to be the most efficient. See Chapter 2 for a detailed description and use of these tools.

Faceplates

Faceplates are of different diameters and are pierced by countersunk holes to provide for short, squat, flathead screws that hold the workpiece or the base for the workpiece. The closer the screw shank size is to the size of the hole, the more secure it will hold the workpiece.

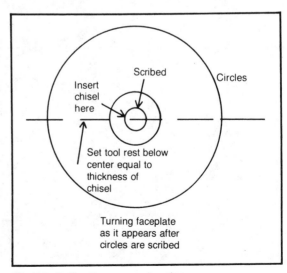

Fig. 7-6. Cutting the recessed portion.

Any project that is turned from the headstock end only, without benefit of the tailstock, is usually referred to as faceplate turning. Chucks and other devices might be used to hold the wood.

The standard faceplates for both the inboard and outboard ends of the headstock spindle for the Myford lathe are identical except that threads are reversed in direction. This ensures safety by exerting pressure against the faceplate, thus tightening the faceplate against the spindle avoiding a dangerous spin-off of the faceplate and work.

Both faceplates for the Myford lathe are 6 inches in diameter and each have eight countersunk holes. See Chapter 1.

Chucks

There are many kinds of chucks; each is used in a little different way. The simple screw chuck is used as a small faceplate. It is simple to use on small projects because there is only one centered screw to be concerned about.

Chapter 3 gives instruction for making a screw chuck. It is important that the simple screw chuck, which in essence is a screw center faceplate, be as large in diameter as possible to adequately support the base of the turning without danger of the tools hitting the faceplate. The serious turner, who does considerable faceplate and chuck work, will have a number of screw chucks of different sizes made or he will make them himself.

PROCEDURES

☐ Select stock. For large turnings, it will probably be necessary to glue up stock. Be sure that joints are straight and true and pieces are securely clamped together.

☐ Swing a circle ¼ to ⅜ of an inch larger than the finished turning with a compass or dividers.

☐ Cut off the waste stock by bandsawing on the scribed line just made.

☐ Fasten the work piece to the faceplate or screw center. If the screw center faceplate is used, remember

Fig. 7-7. Spice drawer cabinet.

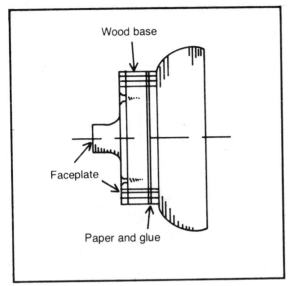

Fig. 7-8. Paper chuck.

Table 7-1. Roughing Cuts.

Diameter of Work Piece	Speed
Under 2″	800-1200 rpm
2″ to 4″	550-900 rpm
4″ to 6″	500-850 rpm
6″ to 8″	400-550 rpm
8″ to 10″	250-425 rpm
Over 10″	175-275 rpm

bowls must be turned in the outboard position, which sometimes requires a special stand for the tool rest.

☐ Make templates for the interior and exterior of turning. They should be of thin wood, hardboard, Masonite or thin plywood.

☐ Set the tool rest just below center across the edge of the workpiece and true up the edge until the piece is perfectly round. Start at a slow speed to prevent vibration.

☐ Move the tool rest across the face of the workpiece and smooth the face.

☐ Move the tool rest back to the edge and turn the outside to the preferred shape. Use a template to check the work.

☐ Turn the inside to the desired shape. Use a template to check the work.

☐ Sand and finish if the finish is applied while the piece is turning in the lathe.

☐ Remove the workpiece from the faceplate.

Lathe speeds for roughing cuts are shown in Table 7-1. The speeds are only guidelines and they would only be applicable to lathes with variable speed controls. Most lathes have three- and four-step pulleys. In general,

that it has only one screw holding the workpiece. It is important that the screw center faceplate be as large in diameter as possible to adequately support the base turning, without danger of the tools hitting the faceplate. If there is any danger of a lathe tool hitting the faceplate, it is best to fasten a piece of scrap stock to the workpiece. Make sure that the correct faceplate has been selected. The *outboard* and *inboard* faceplates have different threads.

☐ Attach the work piece and faceplate to the headstock spindle. If the workpiece and faceplate are attached to the inboard spindle, the spur (live) center must be removed from the spindle. Of necessity, large

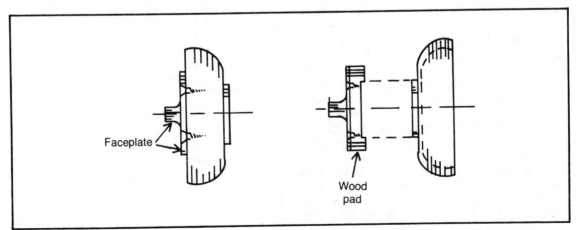

Fig. 7-9. Wood chuck.

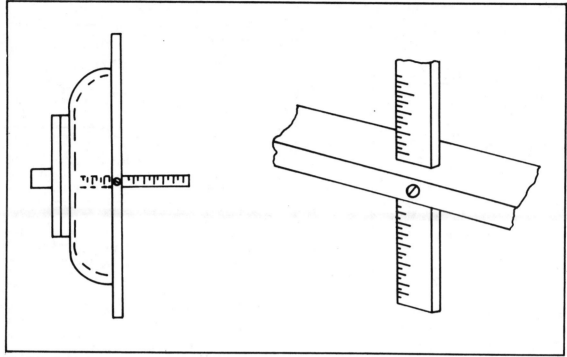

Fig. 7-10. Depth jig.

roughing is done at slower speeds as well as turning of large diameter. Care should be taken, especially with larger diameters, because excessive speeds can be dangerous to the turner and detrimental to the lathe. The Myford lathe has four speeds ranging from 700 to 2850 rpm with a 1425 rpm motor.

Speeds indicated in rpm (revolutions per minute) have little meaning when applied to a given diameter as the work is being turned. One part of the turning might have a large diameter and another part of the turning a small diameter. What is important is not the rpms but the speed of the work going by the chisel—designated in feet per minute. It is next to impossible for the turner to work out a meaningful formula for all situations. The turner might better be guided by his own intuition and experience. Of course, excessive speeds will burn and dull tools while speeds too slow will result in a poor surface. In general, lathe speeds are not a crucial factor in providing fine turnings.

The greatest moment of concern occurs before the stock is turned to a cylindrical shape. One way to reduce this problem with faceplate turnings is to bandsaw the stock a trifle oversize. Trouble is more apt to occur when you are trying to turn square stock.

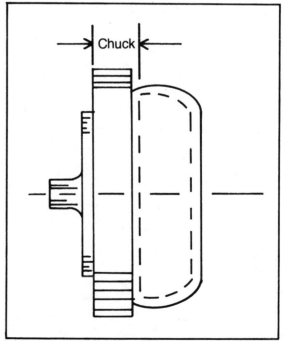

Fig. 7-11. Interior stepped chuck.

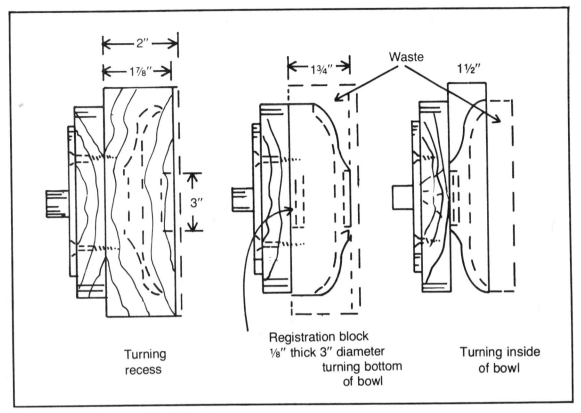

Fig. 7-12. Chuck for recessed bottom bowls.

HOMEMADE CHUCKS

The Paper Chuck. One way of eliminating screw holes in the bottom of bowls or similar projects is to use a paper chuck. Glue is applied to both sides of a piece of paper and placed between the workpiece and the base piece. A sharp knife or chisel is used to separate the wood base from the bowl or other project. See Fig. 7-8.

The Wood Chuck. Another way of eliminating screw holes is to use a wood pad with a recess cut in it to hold the base of a bowl or similar turning. The base or bottom of the bowl is turned first on the faceplate. The pad is then fastened to the faceplate and the recess is cut in it to the exact size of the bowl. The sides of the recess should be slightly tapered. See Fig. 7-9.

The Depth Jig. A depth jig will be necessary for measuring the depth of faceplate turnings while they are being turned. First, a shaft of hardwood stock about 1 × ½ inch in cross section and somewhat longer than the anticipated diameter of the faceplate work should be cut.

Second, cut a hole in the center of the shaft about 3/16 of an inch wide and ¾ of an inch long.

Third, cut a piece of hardwood—maple or birch is fine—about 6 inches to 8 inches long that will slide, rather snuggly, into the hole made in the shaft. Put a coat of white shellac on the depth rod and scribe 1-, ½-, ¼-, and ⅛-inch divisions on both sides of the depth rod. With a ruling pen, fill in the scribed with black India ink. When the ink is dry, apply another coat of white shellac.

Fourth, bore a hole in the edge of the shaft that will intercept the depth rod hole, and insert a round-head screw that will hold the depth rod in place. See Fig. 7-10.

The Interior Stepped Chuck. The interior stepped chuck is not used to any great extent, but it might be found advantageous for bowls with fairly thick walls that are turned at right angles on the inside edges. The force of the turning tool will keep pressure on the bowl so that it will not jar loose from the chuck. Of course, the part of the chuck that fits the interior of the bowl must be a close, snug fit. This jig works well with flat-bottom bowls that do not have a recessed base. Of course, the interior is turned first in the conventional manner. The bowls should be removed from the chuck from time to time to

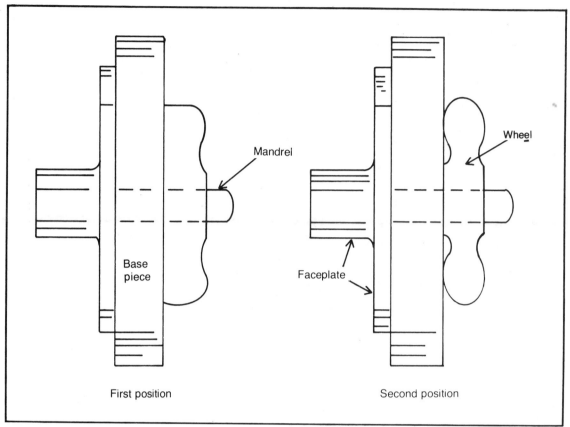

Fig. 7-13. Mandrel chuck.

check on wall thickness. See Fig. 7-11.

Chuck for Recessed Bottom Bowls. Recessed bottom bowls are fairly easy to turn provided that care is taken in turning preliminary holes and the recess to exact dimensions. The turner should predetermine the exact diameter of the recess. It makes it easier if some whole number of inches is used for the diameter of the recess (2, 3, 4 inches, etc.). Three inches has been chosen for the bowl shown in Fig. 7-12.

Mandrel Chucks. Projects with uniform hole of a specific size can be turned on a mandrel chuck. A base piece, somewhat larger than the diameter of the circular piece, is fastened to the faceplate. A hole the same size as the mandrel is bored into the base piece and the mandrel, usually a birch dowel, is glued into the hole. Be sure that the mandrel dowel runs straight and true before the glue dries. Short, sharp pointed brads are driven into the basepiece if there is danger of slippage. The illustration used is a 3-inch diameter wheel used on wooden toys. See Fig. 7-13.

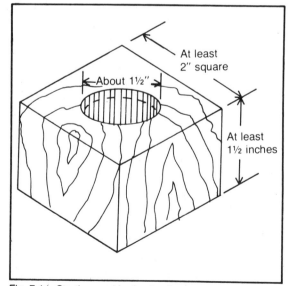

Fig. 7-14. Starting napkin ring turning.

136

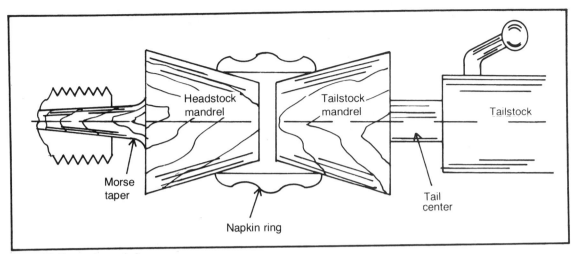

Fig. 7-15. Tapered mandrels.

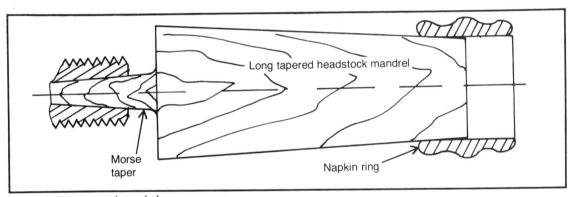

Fig. 7-16. Long tapered mandrel.

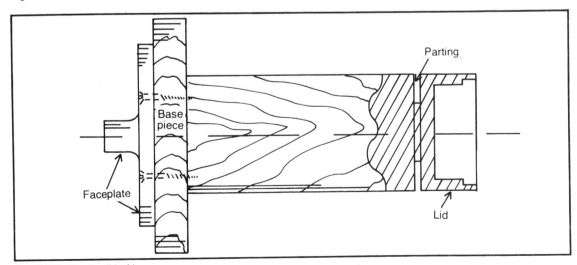

Fig. 7-17A. Turning lid of box.

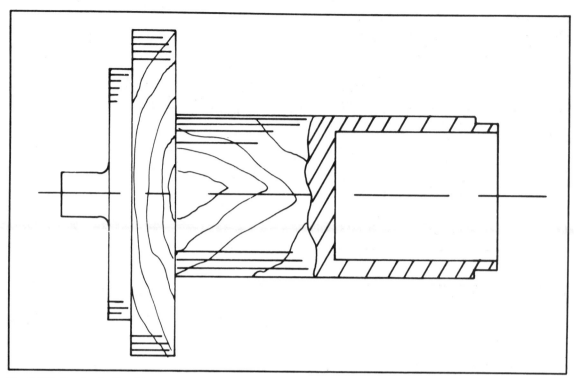

Fig. 7-17B. Turning inside of box.

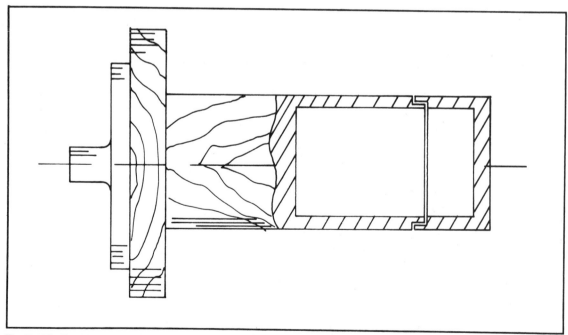

Fig. 7-17C. Finish turning and sanding box and lid.

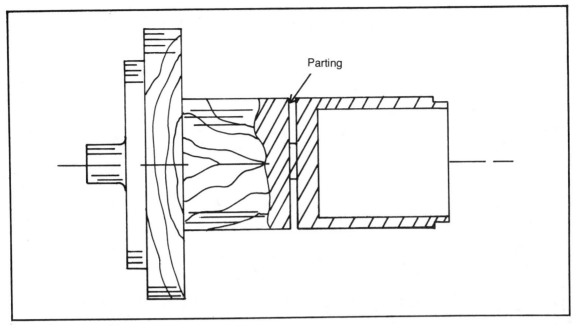

Fig. 7-17D. Cutting off box.

Chucks for Turning Napkin or Serviette Rings. First, bore a hole approximately 1½″ diameter through a piece of hardwood stock 1½ to 1¾ inches long and at least 2 inches in cross section. See Fig. 7-14.

Second, make a tapered mandrel fitted with a Morse taper to fit into the headstock spindle and another tapered piece for the tailstock. See Fig. 7-15.

Third, place the blank between the two tapered pieces and tighten by advancing the tailstock center. Do not tighten too tight as the ring blank is apt to split when the finished size is approached.

Fourth, turn the ring to the preferred size. Follow by shaping and sanding the outside.

Fifth, make a long tapered mandrel, with a Morse taper, that will extend about two-thirds of the way through the ring.

Sixth, smooth up the inside of the ring as far as possible, and round up gently toward the end so that the napkin will enter smoothly. Sand the interior. Reverse ends and do the same on the second end.

Seventh, finish with carnauba wax or French polish in the lathe or remove and finish in the conventional manner (stain, shellac, varnish, lacquer, or polyurethane). See Fig. 7-16.

Rabbeted Chuck for Turning Boxes and Containers. The inside of the lid to the box is turned after the cylinder has been turned to the round. It is then sanded and cut off with a skew or parting tool. See Fig. 7-17A.

Turn the inside of the box. See Fig. 7-17B.

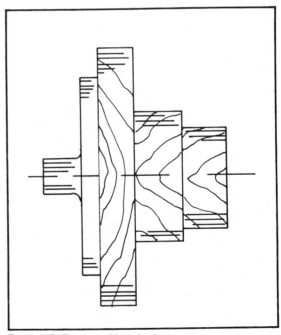

Fig. 7-17E. Turning rabbet chuck.

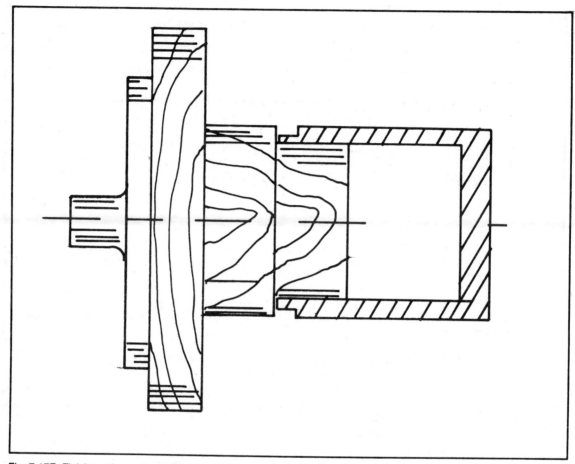

Fig. 7-17F. Finish turning and sanding bottom of box.

Place the cover on the box, finish turning, and sand the exterior of the box and the lid. See Fig. 7-17C.

Remove the cover and cut off the box with parting chisel. See Fig. 7-17D.

Turn the rabbet chuck from the remaining stock on the faceplate. See Fig. 7-17E.

Place the box on the rabbet chuck. Finish turning the bottom of the box and then sand. See Fig. 7-17F.

Chucks for Mass Production of Short Turnings. If a number of turnings are to be made of the same cross section (1½″ × 1½″, 2″ × 2″, etc.) a square chuck can greatly accelerate the process. A wooden disc is turned about the size of the faceplate. The disc is removed from the faceplate and a diameter is marked through the center. Another diameter is marked through the center at right angles to the first.

Scribe a circle in the center of the disc with a com-

pass or dividers equal to the diagonal across the squared stock that is to be used. Connect the points where the circle intersects the two diameters that are at right angles to each other. Saw out the square with a saber saw or jigsaw at a small angle so that the part that will be next to the faceplate will be slightly smaller than the outside opening.

Round stock or large dowel stock can be turned in a round chuck. After the disc is turned, a hole, the size of the round stock to be turned, is bored or turned almost through the disc. Drill two holes at 180 degrees to each other, and at right angles to the grain of the wood, to accommodate two long, flathead screws. Countersink the screw holes fairly deep so that there is no danger of damaging clothes or injuring hands. The screws clamp the round stock in place so that there is no danger of slippage. See Fig. 7-19.

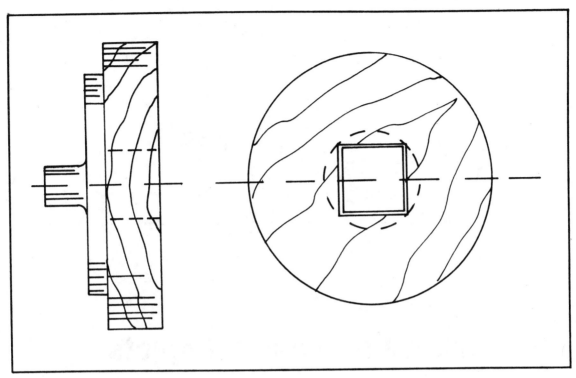

Fig. 7-18. Square chuck.

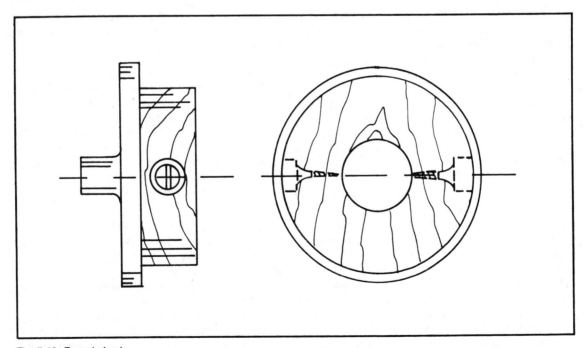

Fig. 7-19. Round chuck.

Chapter 8

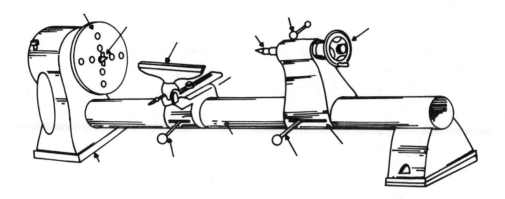

Finishing Turned Objects

ALL TOOL TURNING SHOULD BE DONE BEFORE sanding is attempted. Sandpaper is never used as a method of removing wood—only as a smoothing device—and that very sparingly. Never attempt to turn wood after sanding is completed because the abrasive particles from the sandpaper left on the surface and in the pores of the wood will rapidly dull the cutting edges of lathe tools. Use the finest grade of sandpaper that will do the job. Coarser-grade sandpaper will cause rings in the wood that will be very hard to remove. If rings show up in the sanding process, stop the lathe and sand lengthwise of the project by hand.

If it is found necessary to use coarse sandpaper, further sanding should be done with successive grades of finer sandpaper. Generally, sandpaper works better on spindle work if cut into narrow strips (1 to 1½ inches wide). For sanding beads and coves, the sandpaper can be folded lengthwise. A full sheet of sandpaper can be folded into a pad for faceplate work. The sandpaper should be kept in motion at all times to prevent clogging.

Flint sandpaper should never be used for sanding turned objects, and today it is seldom used for any kind of sanding. Although first costs are minimal, in the long run it is uneconomical because of its short life.

Garnet sandpaper, of reddish color, is excellent sandpaper and is well adapted to lathe work.

Aluminum oxide paper, a man-made abrasive, will last longer and will cut faster than either flint or garnet paper.

Silicon carbide, the hardest and the sharpest of the abrasives, is purplish-black in color. It is used in wet-or-dry abrasive papers that are primarily used in sanding finishes. It is never used on bare wood.

Weights of abrasive papers are designated by the letters A, C, D, and E. The A weight papers are the lightest and E is the heaviest grade. Papers of A weight are the most appropriate for sanding wood turnings (although C weight is used occasionally).

SANDPAPER GRITS

Sandpaper grits range from Coarse to Very Fine. Table 8-1 lists the different grits. Usually a 2/0-100 or 3/0-120 grits followed by 4/0-150 or 5/0-180 are sufficient for the coarser grained woods. For final sanding on fine grained woods 6/0-220 or 7/0-240 work well.

When sanding with the finer grits over a prolonged period a face mask dust protector should be worn.

David Ward gives some tips on sanding and finishing

Table 8-1. Sandpaper Grits.

	Old Classification	New Classification
Coarse	½	60
	0	80
	2/0	100
	3/0	120
	4/0	150
Fine	5/0	180
	6/0	220
	7/0	240
	8/0	280
Very Fine	9/0	320
	10/0	400
		500
		600

in his article *Sanding and Finishing on the Lathe* in the Jul/Aug, 1981 issue of *Fine Woodworking* magazine. The following three paragraphs are reprinted from *Fine Woodworking* magazine © 1982 The Taunton Press, Inc., 52 Church Hill Road, Box 355, Newtown, CT 06470.

"Once the piece is adequately sanded I use a finishing process that is a takeoff on French polishing. The ingredients are similar and so are the results, but the method of application is much different. The turning is first soaked in raw linseed oil. This brings out the color of the wood better than any other oil or mixture I've tried. After a few minutes, wipe off the excess oil and apply liberally a mixture of about twenty five parts of orange or white shellac and one part of raw linseed oil. The oil lubricates the finish when it is being buffed. Too little oil will cause the surface to drag, while too much will not permit the shellac to heat up enough. The proportions may need adjusting for specific application.

"After the shellac-and-oil mixture has dried for two to ten minutes, depending on how porous the wood is, run the lathe at a fairly high speed. Step to one side before doing so, however, to avoid a shower. Then hold a pad of folded soft cotton cloth firmly against the turning. Most of the excess shellac will be quickly removed, leaving a clear surface on the work. The surface must be burnished with increasing pressure until the finish ceases to migrate, as observed in the glare of a light. At this point any shellac remaining on the wood has been driven into the wood by heat and pressure.

"I usually apply a final coat of clear shoe polish for extra luster and durability. The result is a hard surface finish that does not coat the wood with plastic—a penetrating finish that will not dull with time and takes minutes rather than hours to complete. The finish works well on most hardwoods."

REPAIRS

After the first coarse sanding, the turning should be inspected for cracks, holes, blemishes, and dents. These defects should be corrected before continuing with the sanding.

One of the least expensive of hole fillers is the sanding dust, from the piece being worked on, mixed with a little glue to a putty-like consistency and forced into the hole with a putty knife or patching knife. The hole filler should be left a little higher than the depression. After it is thoroughly dry and hard, sanding with fine abrasives can continue.

If the hole is perfectly round, a small tapered peg, with a small amount of glue, can be driven into the hole. After the glue is dry and hard, the peg is cut off slightly above the surface and then sanded down level with the surface.

Plastic Wood comes in different colors and can be used to fill holes. As it has a tendency to shrink, it should be piled up above the surface of the wood. When it is dry, it can be sanded flush with the surface. Plastic Wood, a commercial product, is also made of fine sandings; the sandings are mixed with lacquer rather than glue.

Stick shellac and stick lacquer are also used to repair holes and depressions, but they are more apt to be used after the project is partially or completely finished. They are available in many wood colors and shades. Stick shellac and stick lacquer are "burned" into the wood by using an electric burning-in knife or a knife heated over an alcohol lamp. Expert furniture finishing specialists prefer the alcohol lamp.

There are many other pastes, compounds, and putties that can be used to fill holes. Each has its own individual characteristics and the craftsman should be selective in his choice for best results.

Repairing Dents. Dents are the result of crushed wood fibers. If the fibers are returned to their original position, the dent will disappear. Repairing small dents requires only a sharp needle and some hot water. Dip the needle in the water and prick, very lightly, the surface of the dent. The hot water will cause the fibers to swell and expand. After the repair spot is completely dry, the surface can be sanded and the dent will have disappeared.

Repairing large dents require the point of an electric iron or soldering iron and a dampened cloth. The dampened cloth is placed over the dent and the hot iron is applied to the cloth directly over the dent. Only the deepest dents will resist this treatment.

LACQUER SEALER

Lacquer sealer or sanding sealer is especially valuable in

finishing turnings because it does not clog the sandpaper. Lacquer sealer is a mixture of lacquer (cellulose) and a chalky like substance (sterate) that, when dry, sands to a powdery substance. It works well on bare wood or over stain. No other finish will be necessary if two or three coats are used and if it is followed by a good furniture wax or polish.

Clear spray Deft, from an aerosol can, is a good finish because it is a combination of lacquer and lacquer sealer. It dries very rapidly and is convenient to use.

The craftsman can make his own lacquer sealer by adding French chalk or talcum powder to an equal amount of lacquer.

After the lacquer sealer is thoroughly dry and sanded, very lightly, with very fine sandpaper, 8/0 or 9/0, it is rubbed with #0000 steel wool.

LACQUER

Lacquer should be applied only with a spray gun or aerosol can because brushing will leave a streaked and ridged surface. Lacquer works best over lacquer sealer and fairly well over shellac, but should never be used over varnish, polyurethane, or other similar material.

FRENCH POLISH

French polish is a high-quality finish. It is rather difficult to apply, particularly to flat surfaces, because the pad or rubber has to be kept in motion at all times. If the rubber is stopped on the surface, it will take some time and a lot of effort to remove the defect.

Because turnings are moving, French polish is ideal to use on lathe projects.

The most important aspects of French polishing are the ingredients used. Use only the highest quality of denatured alcohol, linseed oil, and white shellac. Orange shellac can be used on some woods to advantage if the color is compatible. The three ingredients should be kept in separate containers within easy reach of the turner.

For spindle turnings, a soft cotton cloth, about 16 inches long and about 6 inches wide, is folded twice longitudinally making a rag 1½ inches wide by 16 inches long. Shellac is applied to the center portion and worked into all layers of the cloth.

Apply a small amount of linseed oil to the same area and work it into the layers of the cloth.

Turn on the lathe and apply the cloth to the turning very carefully. If the cloth has a tendency to grap the turning, add more linseed oil to the cloth. Eventually the cloth will dry out and harden. At that time apply more shellac and alcohol to the cloth. Considerable pressure

should be applied in order to "burn" the shellac and oil to the surface of the wood.

After applying the initial coat, set the turning aside for one or two days, at which time a second coat is applied. Again let dry for at least 24 hours and "spirit out" the residue oil with a cloth moistened lightly with denatured alcohol. Hold lightly against the turning and it should leave a highly polished surface.

For faceplate turnings and long, rather straight spindle turnings with no coves or beads, it is best to use a French polishing pad. The pad consists of a conical-shaped central core of cloth or cotton waste placed in the center of a piece of cloth about 7 inches square and the corners brought up over the core.

The pad is then immersed in very thin shellac: about 3 parts of alcohol to 1 part of 4-pound cut shellac. By pushing the pad against the bottom of the shellac container a few times, the shellac will completely saturate the pad. When removed from the container, the pad should be squeezed to prevent dripping of the shellac. Place a couple of drops of linseed oil on the pad and hold against the revolving project. Spirit out in the same fashion as with spindle turnings.

POLYURETHANE

Although one of the best of all finishes for turned projects, polyurethane is not a popular finish because it requires considerable time to dry, and the finishing should be done in a dust-free environment.

After a number of coats have been applied, allowed to dry, sanded with very fine sandpaper, and rubbed with #0000 steel wool, the craftsman has a project that is nearly fool-proof. It does not change color and it is resistant to foods, moisture, alcohol, and grime. Many craftsmen would rather have their finish *in* the wood rather than *on top* of the wood. Others prefer a dull or semigloss finish over a high-gloss finish.

Polyurethane has a life span greater than varnish or lacquer. United Gilsonite Laboratories, Scranton, PA 18501, manufactures five polyurethane finishes, under the name ZAR, ranging from a dull flat to a high gloss.

VARNISH FINISHES

Varnishes and shellac were once the mainstays of clear finishes on wood, but in more recent history lacquers and synthetics (polyesters, polyurethanes, epoxies, etc.) have taken over.

The major drawback with varnishes is their slow drying time. An environment free of dust must be provided. Varnishes cover well and are fairly easy to apply.

They are resistant to moisture and are hard, durable, and tough.

Shellac is often used as a sealer coat under varnish. And for that it is well suited. Nevertheless, 4-pound cut shellac should be thinned substantially.

Generally, three or four coats of varnish are sufficient. After the final coat is allowed to dry at least two days, the surface can be rubbed with pumice stone and water for an eggshell gloss or rubbed with rottenstone and oil for a high-gloss or "piano" finish.

Varnish should not be shaken or stirred before using. Such a disturbance will cause very small bubbles in the varnish, and when they dry on the surface the bubbles will cause small pits to appear.

When applying varnish to a turned project, use as few strokes of the brush as possible. The varnish should be flowed on with a full brush. On spindle turnings, brush around the circumference first—followed by a few quick strokes longitudinally.

Varnish stains should be avoided. If a stain is necessary, it should be applied before the varnish as a separate operation (usually under a coat of shellac).

OIL FINISHES

Penetrating oil finishes are a godsend for the home craftsman. Dust problems are eliminated and you do not have to worry about special finishing facilities. Brushes and spray equipment are not needed (which eliminates another problem).

Many wipe-on and penetrating finishes are synthetic chemical ingredients that not only penetrate the surface, but actually combine chemically with the wood. They combine to form a substance with a different molecular weight; this is known as *Polymerization.*

Watco Danish oil is a popular penetrating polymerizing oil finish particularly adapted to contemporary and Scandinavian furniture. It *primes, hardens, seals, finishes,* and protects in one simple application. It completely and deeply penetrates with its five-in-one action, and then changes from a liquid into a permanent solid inside the wood, not on it.

Watco Danish oil is available in natural, medium, and dark and black walnut colors. It is designed for new wood, but can be used on old wood if the old finish is completely removed. It works best on hardwoods (walnut, teak, rosewood, maple, cherry, and birch), but can be used on softwoods such as knotty pine, cedar, redwood, etc.

Watco Danish oil finish will not gum out in warm weather, aand it will not chip, peel, or wear away. Be-

cause of its sealing action, it lessens warping, swelling, splintering, and checking.

Sealacell by General Finishes, Box 14363, Milwaukee WI 53214, provides a 1-2-3 process of penetrating wood finishes. Sealacell #1 is the first process. The application of Varnowax #2 is the second process, and the third process involves the application of Royal Finish #3.

John Harra Wood and Supply Company markets a DPS (deep penetrating sealer) that penetrates deeply, seals, stabilizes, and applies easily. It retards the movement of moisture from inside and outside by lining the cellular wall and sealing these cells via a chemical (polymerization) process. Polymerization is complete in 72 hours. The result is a dry, clear, nontoxic, waterproof, long-lasting finish. DPS penetrates ¼ of an inch deep on end grain and up to ⅛ of an inch on surface grain.

DPS can be applied by rag, brush, spray, or by dipping. It enhances the wood's natural color and can be mixed with any oil based stain. Varnish, shellac, lacquer, enamels or polyurethane may be applied over DPS.

Penofin oil finish is applied to wood that has been sanded with 180 grit or finer and wiped clean. All surfaces are soaked with Penofin oil. Penofin oil is applied to dry areas as they appear for a period of 30 minutes. Penofin oil is reapplied to all surfaces; allow an additional 15 minutes for penetration.

Wipe off any excess oil remaining on the surface with a soft dry cloth. Oiled surfaces should be wiped dry within 45 minutes of initial application to avoid surface buildup and tackiness. These conditions can be removed by rubbing affected area with fine steel wool lubricated with fresh Penofin oil. Wipe dry immediately. When the surface feels dry, additional coats of Penofin oil can be applied to enhance the finish. Wipe dry as before. Allow finished wood to dry at least 12 hours before putting to use. Penofin oil can be applied with fine steel wool, brush, spray, cloth, or by dipping. Penofin oil should not be thinned.

Minwax (Minwax Co., Clinton, NJ 07014) is a penetrating sealer anad wax, often combined with a stain, that is applied only to surfaces completely free of other finishes. The penetrating material should be used only on raw wood or over itself. No primer or sealer should be used. Two coats are recommended.

Minwax should be mixed thoroughly and the first coat is applied with a brush or cloth. It is allowed to penetrate 5 to 15 minutes, removing excess with a clean cloth.

After 12 hours, a second coat can be applied in the

same manner. Twenty-four hours after the second coat is applied, a paste finishing wax can be applied and polished.

If a harder finish is preferred, Minwax's antique oil finish or polyurethane can be used instead of paste wax. Minwax is available in mahogany, walnut, maple, oak, and pine colors.

Mineral oil is sometimes used on containers and bowls designed to hold food. Vegetable oils are to be avoided as they are apt to become rancid.

WAXES

In general, waxes are used primarily on turnings as a quick and easy finish. The surfaces are often too soft and are apt to pick up dirt and grime. Some waxes, or mixture of waxes are better than others. Eye protection should always be used when applying wax to turning projects as the heated wax sometimes flies off.

Carnauba Wax. Carnauba wax, from the wax palm tree of Brazil, is probably the most widely used wax. It is a favorite of some woodturners because it is relatively inexpensive, it can be applied quickly, and it produces high gloss. It does, however, take considerable time and effort to apply it correctly.

Remember that carnauba wax finish is not a permanent finish. It should not be used on projects that are handled to any extent.

The major objective is to apply the wax in thin coats, that is easier said than done. After it is applied direct from the block or from pieces held in a cloth against the turning piece, a clean cloth is used to smooth out the wax.

The wax will roll up in gummy rings if too much pressure is used with the cloth because the wax will turn hot and melt. If not enough pressure is exerted, the wax will be transformed into a cream-colored mess and the high gloss you are seeking will not appear.

Some turners have much better luck with carnauba wax if a sanding sealer is applied to the turning before the wax is applied. If a block or lump of carnauba wax is applied directly to the turning piece, the turner must be sure that a large area of the wax is held against the turning. The sharp, dense edge or corners could cause defects in the surface.

Beeswax. Beeswax, by itself, is a rather poor finish, because it is hard to achieve a gloss or polish with

it. Nevertheless, it can be used as a fairly good, easy and quick wood filler. Beeswax should seldom be used alone, but it can be used as a base for other finishes. A beeswax finish is apt to be flat, dull, or mottled.

Cobbler's Wax. Some turners prefer cobbler's wax to beeswax because it is somewhat harder.

Parafin Wax. Parafin wax can be fine to rub on drawer guides of sticking drawers or on the tips of tailstock centers to prevent the burning of wood at the tailstock end. As a finish for turned projects, it should be avoided.

Wax Mixture. The best wax for finishing turnings is a mixture. The ingredients most often mentioned are carnauba wax, beeswax, and top-grade turpentine. Break up at least twice as much beeswax as carnauba wax and place both in a double boiler or an empty glue pot. Add turpentine to partially cover the wax and heat until completely melted. Pour the melted wax into suitable containers that are tapered on the sides so that the wax can be extracted without difficulty. The wax can be applied directly to the revolving wood.

A cloth is used to spread the wax and force it into the pores of the wood. Final polishing is accomplished by using higher rotating speed.

APPLYING A WAX FINISH

☐ Apply the wax evenly, with no attempt to polish to a gloss. It is sometimes advisable to do this with the work stationary as the revolving piece is apt to remove too much wax.

☐ The initial coat should be left on from 15 to 20 minutes. It is then buffed with a cloth until a semishine starts to appear.

☐ The first buffing is done with the project revolving, followed by hand buffing longitudinally while the lathe is turned off.

☐ Let the work stand from 20 to 30 minutes and apply more wax and polish again.

☐ Continue to apply wax and buff until a good polish is obtained. It is better to apply a number of very thin coats of wax than one heavy coat.

There are a number of good finishing compounds available under different trade names. It is important to follow explicitly the directions on the can or bottle.

Chapter 9

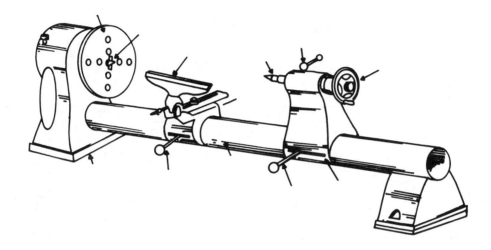

Lathe Duplicating

WITH A WOOD-TURNING DUPLICATOR, MULTIple turnings, exactly alike, can be turned with ease. A few of the systems and devices are described as follows.

TURN-O-CARVE TOOL

One of the simplest wood-turning duplicators is manufactured by the Turn-O-Carve Tool Company. The Turn-O-Carve A-Base Wood Turning Duplicator Model 101-7200-A (Fig. 9-1) is cast from Almag, a basic type of aluminum alloy that is used in the manufacture of high quality tools, aircraft and race car parts. It has a high tensile strength that far exceeds that of similar alloys.

There are no moving parts to oil or wear out. Simply line up the high-quality tool steel chisel to the lathe center by raising or lowering it in the tool post to the preferred position. It is then secured in place by tightening the screws provided. The duplicator is now ready for immediate use without ever adjusting it again on the lathe. The only requirement is the sharpening of the turning chisel when needed (something that need not be done very often). The tool steel chisel is of an exact gauged hardness for long, heavy-duty turning. Prior to heat treating, each chisel is hand ground to close proxim-

ity to the finished stage. After hardening, it is again hand ground to the finished stage retaining its full hardness.

In operation, the duplicator is placed on the lathe ways or plate and is gently slid in the desired direction as the turning chisel is gently brought to bear against the rotating work blank being turned. If the contours of the flat template or original turnings are shallow, a straight back-and-forth movement of the duplicator is all that is required. Where deep contours are involved, the contours are followed with the chisel and tracer.

By using extension brackets, the duplicator can be used on lathes with an approximate 18-inch swing. A plate (Fig. 9-2) is at all times required for the reproduction of faceplate work. The Craftsman single tube lathe also requires the use of a plate for all duplicating work.

The duplicator will operate on 6-inch to 12-inch swing wood or metal turning lathes without the use of extension brackets. It will handle any length spindle turning that the lathe will permit.

Figure 9-2 shows a top view of the plate for the Craftsman single-tube lathe. This plate is so designed that the headstock on this lathe can be moved without the removal of the plate. The plate is screwed down on top of the support clamp of the Craftsman lathe with a 5/16-inch

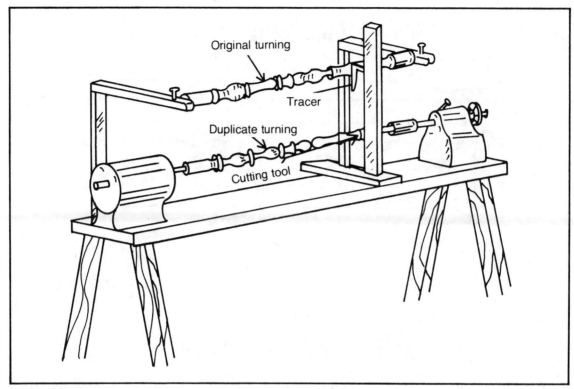

Fig. 9-1. Simplified drawing of the Turn-O-Carve woodturning duplicator.

18-inch flathead steel screw. The material used is ¾-inch plywood or pressed board. If the plywood is covered with Formica, so much the better.

Turn-O-Carve also manufactures a ball bearing steady rest to use with slender spindle turnings. They also manufacture Morse taper extension adapters that permits the operator to extend the lathe headstock spindle and tailstock quill hole several inches.

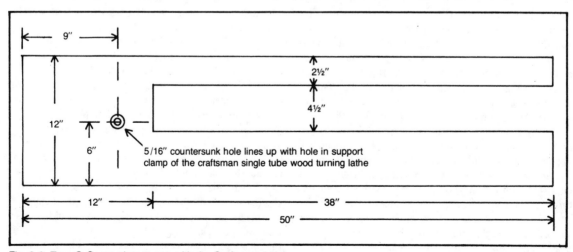

Fig. 9-2. Turn-O-Carve plate to use with the Craftsman lathe.

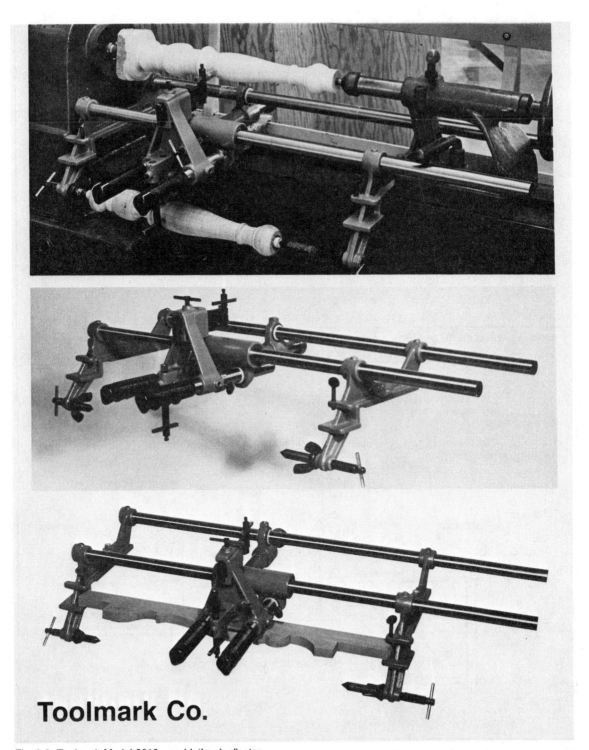

Toolmark Co.

Fig. 9-3. Toolmark Model 3010 wood lathe duplicator.

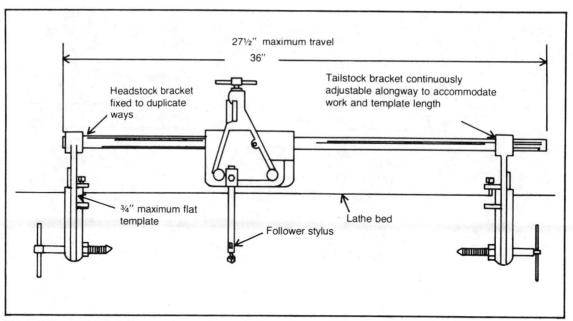

Fig. 9-4. Front view of the Toolmark Model 3010 wood lathe duplicator.

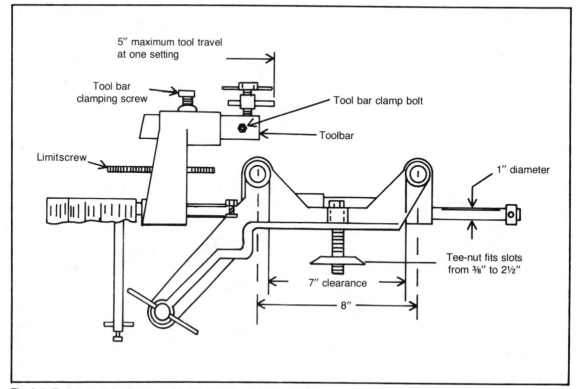

Fig. 9-5. End view of the Toolmark Model 3010 wood lathe duplicator.

Fig. 9-6. Toolmark Model 520B wood lathe duplicator.

On a 12-inch swing lathe, 10-inch diameter turnings can be turned if the lathe is of the flatbed type. Only 9-inch diameter turnings may be turned if the ¾-inch-thick plate is used.

Four radii sizes (in inches) of chisel and tracer sets are available: 1/16, 1/8, 3/16, and 1/4. The smaller the radius of the chisel and tracer the closer the operator can make corner cuts on the duplicate turnings.

TOOLMARK

The Toolmark Company manufactures the Model 3010 wood lathe duplicator that will make identical wood turnings from round originals or from flat templates. It is of rugged construction with two 1 inch diameter, hardened, ground steel ways. It has a versatile mounting method that adopts to almost any lathe. Adjustable stabilizer bushings are installed in both the lateral and transverse directions to minimize deflections. An adjust-

able tool holder accommodates limited vertical tool positioning and right- or left-hand shoulder cuts. It has linear ball bushings with bronze and felt wipers for main-load bearings. The operating control hand grips are located away from the cutting area for safety. See Figs. 9-3, 9-4, and 9-5.

The Toolmark Model 520B Wood Lathe Duplicator is a rugged, versatile tool that enables the lathe operator to make one-of-a-kind wood turnings or to make identical copies from either round or flat patterns.

A versatile mounting method for the slide table and pattern holder brackets is adaptable to most any flat way type of lathe bed. Special modifications are required to accommodate tubular or other types of beds.

A hand-held duplicator slides on a flat work surface with complete two dimensional and angular freedom. This allows right- or left-hand shoulder cuts, limited undercuts or straight-on cuts. The main tool post can be readily shortened to accommodate larger increment vertical height adjustments.

The Duplicator has a cast-iron tool frame and is equipped with a high-speed tool steel cutter bit. The follower stylus has a fully adjustable roller for most duplicating operations and a wedge point stylus for the fine duplicate work. The operating control hand grip has a clear safety shield and is located away from the cutter bit for maximum operator safety.

A Quick-Latch clamp enables the operator to position the table to any desired location along the cutting axis of the work piece. The 16-inch table provides a very adequate cutting surface. Moving the table to accommodate long work pieces is quick and easy to do. See Fig. 9-6.

The Toolmark Model 101B U-Tool Woodshaver contains a U-shaped blade made of high-speed hardened steel that shaves instead of scraping wood to the desired shape. It functions much like the skew wood turning chisel. See Fig. 9-7. Here are the procedures for mounting and using the U-Tool.

☐ Loosen the tool bar clamp bolt and remove the old-style tool (if applicable). Loosen the bolt and remove the stylus assembly (see the front view of the duplicator).

☐ Screw the U-Tool into the tool bar and adjust to get the cutting edge at the lathe center height, perpendicular to the lathe axis and then tighten the clamp bolt.

☐ Slight adjustments above or below the center might be better depending on the kind of wood.

☐ Loosen the tool bar clamping screw.

☐ Install the new stylus assembly, provided with the U-Tool, into the frame. Adjust the stylus and the cross slide assembly until the stylus tip is at the pattern center line. Tighten the stylus bolt.

☐ Maintaining the stylus tip at the pattern center, move the tool bar until the cutting lip of the U-Tool is at the lathe center. Tighten the tool bar clamping screw.

☐ Mount the pattern and the workpiece onto the duplicator and lathe.

☐ Using the limit screw to regulate cut depth, rough the work piece down to the diameter that is approximately ⅛-inch larger than the largest diameter on the pattern.

☐ Using the largest pattern diameter as a refer-

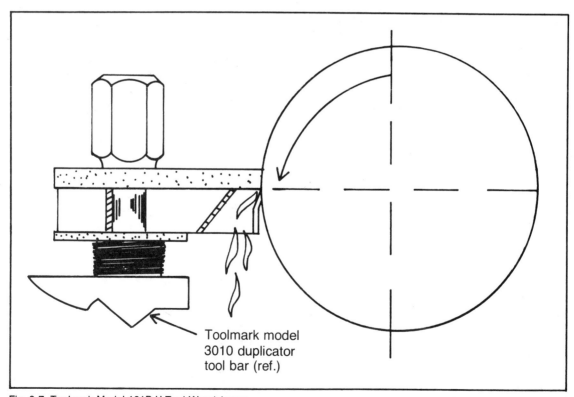

Toolmark model
3010 duplicator
tool bar (ref.)

Fig. 9-7. Toolmark Model 101B U-Tool Woodshaver.

Fig. 9-8. Rockwell wood-turning duplicator.

ence, carefully begin turning the corresponding area on the work until the two diameters are equal. Use calipers to make measurements. Additional adjustments of the tool bar and stylus might be necessary during this step.

☐ When the 1:1 ratio of the largest diameter has been established, make sure that all clamping screws and bolts are tight, and then begin duplicating the pattern. The pattern rather than the limit screw will now control cut depth.

Parameters such as turning speed, depth of cut, rate of lateral cutting movements, etc., are largely influenced by the operator's choice of material and complexity of the turning. It is important to leave ⅛″ oversize on the work to give yourself the ability to "fine tune" the duplicator adjustments. The initial time taken to achieve a good 1:1 ratio of pattern to work will result in accurate reproductions. Once the ratio has been set, any number of reproductions can be made from the same pattern. The U-Tool can be used with both models of the Toolmark Wood Lathe Duplicators.

ROCKWELL

The Rockwell Wood Turning Duplicator will make safe, accurate duplicate turnings up to 4 inches in diameter and 28½ inches long. The cutting tool is a standard cutting tool bit, ¼ × ¼ inch ground to shape. The Rockwell Duplicator can be used on lathes other than Rockwell's.

By avoiding mistakes, there will be few, if any, discarded turnings. Complicated turnings (balusters, table legs, chair legs, lamps, ball bats, lamps) can be perfectly turned. See Fig. 9-8.

SEARS ROEBUCK AND CO

The Copy Crafter by Sears not only copies spindle turnings but faceplate turnings as well. All that is necessary is to follow the outline of the original turning or template. The cutting tool (high-speed tool steel) duplicates the workpiece, which helps eliminate costly mistakes and wasted wood. The Copy Crafter does not interfere with normal lathe operation. Spindle turnings can be made up to 2½ inches in diameter and 36 inches long and can be duplicated from original turnings or up to 6 inches in diameter and 36 inches long from a template.

Shallow faceplate turnings up to 8 inches in diameter can be duplicated from a template. The high-speed tool steel bit gives a shear-type cut and does not scrape the turning. The Copy Crafter, made of cast iron and steel, is 36½ × 11 × 3¼ inches.

Accessories include instructions for using stone for sharpening the bit, and hardware.

HAPFO DUPLICATING ATTACHMENTS

International Woodworking Equipment Corporation manufactures two copying attachments: the KA-TS3 and the KA-90. The KA-TS3 offers particular advantages for copying thin parts such as stair and chair struts and other difficult shapes. The unit is driven by means of a stranded steel cable with the the the aid of a large handwheel. It has a maximum coping length of approximately 35½ inches.

Long, thin workpieces have a tendency to spring and vibrate during the turning operation; this problem is costly and dangerous. When such delicate pieces (length of 10 times the smallest diameter) are encountered, the KA-TS3 enables the turner to steady the workpiece with a backrest. The KA-TS3's adjustable steel backrest (adjustable for each diameter from 13/16 to 2⅜ inches) fits into a ball bearing ring. By means of the adjustable backrest insert, the wood is supported in front of the two cutting tools for copying. With the KA-TS3, there is no danger of vibration and the workpiece can be finished in one working pass. Of course, the KA-TS3 attachment handles conventional thicknesses with ease, but its particular advantage is for copying thin parts and other difficult shapes.

This attachment is particularly suited for the HAPFO Wood-Turning Lathe AHDK125. The attachment is installed at the factory, and cannot be added at a later date.

The KA-90 copying attachment is simple in operation and use. The KA-90 can be set up to turn a specific part in a very short time, and can virtually pay for itself in producing even a few pieces. The copying attachment can be used for both longitudinal spindle turning and transverse turning.

The KA-90 can safely turn diameters as small as 1¾ inches when the full copying length of approximately 37 inches is used.

The copying tool moves forward by means of a roller chain. Installation of the KA-90 is accomplished by placing the attachment on the lathe bed and bolting it into position.

Chapter 10

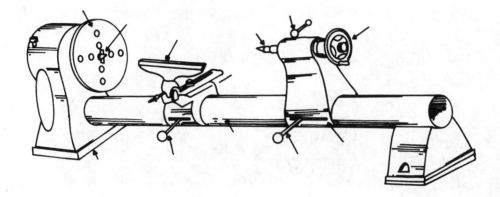

Miniature Wood Turning

THE DREMEL LATHE (FIG. 10-1) IS A LIGHT-weight, efficient mini lathe. It is the first successful attempt to provide a power woodturning tool at a reasonable price. There are other small lathes that are primarily designed for metal turning and can be adapted to wood turning, but the prices are almost prohibitive for all but the most affluent miniaturist.

The lathe turns at 3450 rpm and will handle turnings up to 6 inches in length and 1½ inches in diameter. In addition, faceplate work can be done on the lathe.

This lathe is just the ticket for turning legs for chairs, sofas, tables, beds and other parts such as bed posts, turned ornaments, newel posts, and small, round-top tabletops. After using the lathe for many hours, I could find only two minor faults, and these are greatly outweighed by its many excellent features. The constant-speed motor runs a bit too fast for 1½-inch diameter stock and a trifle too slow for stock ¼ inch in diameter and under. One other criticism has to do with the four lathe turning tools (60-degree chisel, 30-degree chisel, round-nose chisel, and parting chisel). The handles are much too short. The turning tool handles can be increased by either of two methods.

Method No. 1. Turn an extra length of handle and splice into the existing handle. A quarter-inch dowel that is at least one-half inch long should be turned on the end of the extra length. This dowel will fit into a quarter-inch hole drilled in the end of the original handle.

Method No. 2. Turn a completely new handle about twice the length of the original. Remove the existing handle and replace it with the longer handle. The lathe should be mounted to the board a little longer than the lathe (with a "lip" fastened to the board at a right with screws). This makes the lathe a portable tool because it can be stored when not in use. When needed for turning, the "lip" is inserted into the bench vise and tightened securely. This removes any tendency for vibrations to occur.

SIMULATED TURNINGS

Some craftsmen use only files—particularly needle files—instead of lathe tools to shape turning stock on the small lathe. This is about the only way there is to shape stock 3/16 inches in diameter or less. Less breakage and more control can be obtained with needle files. Very little pressure has to be exerted to remove excess wood.

There are other craftsmen who put the stock in a drill press or portable electric drill to shape the work with needle files, emery boards and sandpaper.

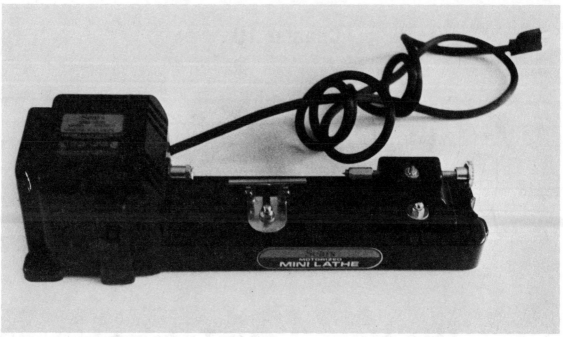

Fig. 10-1. Dremel Moto-Lathe.

There is at least one professional miniaturist who does turning and shaping of irregular shapes, such as Queen Anne legs, by holding the pieces against various sizes and shapes of grinding wheels. The results are amazing.

Others whittle the rough shape with craft knives, such as X-Acto knives, and then finish the simulated turning with needle files, emery boards, and sandpaper.

HOW TO MAKE A DISC SANDER

☐ Purchase a few extra faceplates for the lathe. These faceplates can be used for many practical purposes.

☐ Scribe a circle on ½-inch or ¾-inch scrap stock with a compass with a 1 1/16-inch radius.

☐ Cut the circle on a bandsaw or jigsaw. The disc should be approximately 2⅛ inch in diameter after sawing.

☐ Attach the disc to the faceplate with four FHB (flathead bright) wood screws.

☐ Attach the faceplate and disc to the lathe. Turn the disc to 2 inches in diameter.

☐ Remove the faceplate and disc from the lathe. Place the disc on the reverse side of sandpaper and trace around the edge with a pencil. Cut out the sandpaper disc with an old pair of shears. Mount the sandpaper disc to the wood disc with rubber cement.

HOW TO MAKE A CYLINDRICAL SANDER

☐ Cut a 1-inch-diameter birch dowel to 6 inches in length.

☐ Place the center marks in each end of the dowel. Cut shallow saw kerfs in the end of the dowel that goes against the driving (spur) center. The saw cuts are made at right angles to each other so that the four spurs on the driving center will fit into the saw kerfs. Insert the piece in the lathe.

☐ Mark out three, 2-inch intervals on the edge of a piece of scrap stock. Resting the scrap piece on the tool rest, ⅛-inch from the revolving stock, mark the three sections of the cylinder with a pencil held against the rotating piece.

☐ Turn the three sections. If the centering is done correctly, only a small amount of wood will have to be turned from the 1-inch diameter section.

☐ Set the calipers for a ¾-inch diameter and turn the remaining 4 inches to ¾ of an inch in diameter. Hold the calipers in the right hand and the parting tool in the left hand when cutting to the proper depth. Check constantly so as not to cut too deep.

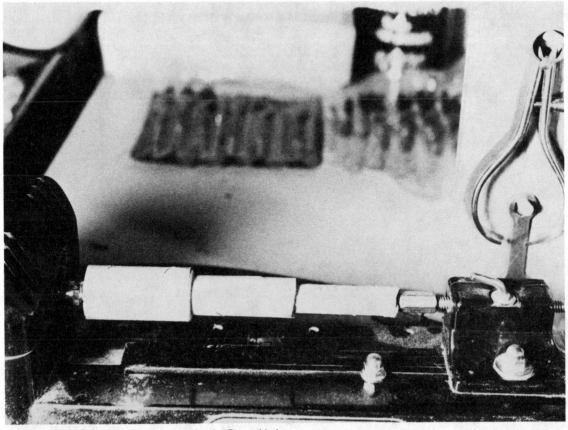

Fig. 10-2. Homemade cylindrical sander for the Dremel lathe.

☐ Mark again the section to be turned to a ½-inch diameter with the marking stick. Reset the calipers to ½-inch and finish turning the cylinder.

☐ Leave the cylinder in the lathe and attach sandpaper strips to the cylinder with rubber cement.

Narrow strips are spiralled around the cylinder. See Fig. 10-2.

WILLIAM AND MARY TEA TABLE AND MULTIPLE TURNINGS

A William and Mary tea table is used here to illustrate the

Table 10-1. Tea Table Materials.

Pieces	Description	Size	Material
1	Top	3/32″ × 2 1/2″ × 3″	Walnut
2	Front and Back Skirts	3/32″ × 7/16″ × 2 3/4″	Walnut
2	End Skirts	3/32″ × 7/16″ × 2 1/4″	Walnut
4	Legs	3/16″ × 3/16″ × 2 13/32″	Walnut
2	Front and Back Stretchers	3/16″ × 3/16″ × 2 3/16″	Walnut
2	End Stretchers	3/16″ × 3/16″ × 2 3/16″	Walnut

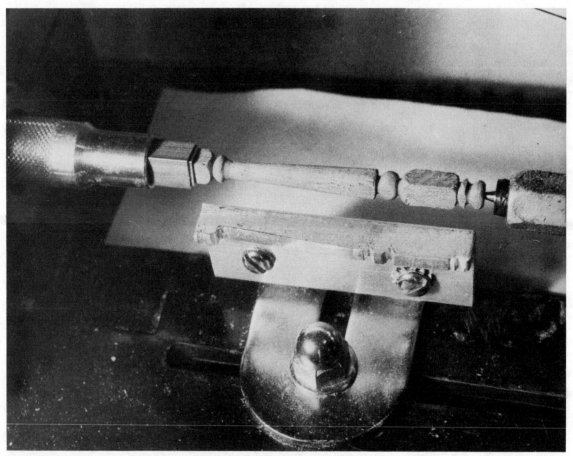

Fig. 10-3. Bell Yankee Chucker, leg-turning and special profile tool rest for multiple turnings.

process of multiple turnings on a miniature lathe. William and Mary is the first distinct period of any note in America. This English and Dutch inspired furniture was adapted to city and urban living, although American cabinet makers and designers took some liberties with the original design.

William and Mary furniture, circa 1690-1720, was the first attempt by the English to develop a slender and light kind of furniture. Some pieces were made taller to fit into the houses with higher ceilings. In fact, some bed posts were twice the height of a person.

Walnut was the most popular material and maple was a close second. There are many distinguishing characteristics of William and Mary pieces. Turnip-shaped feet, trumpet-turned legs, acorn-drop decorations, teardrop pulls, serpentine cross-stretchers, scalloped skirts and rails, "double bottle" legs on gateleg tables, and butterfly drop leaf tables are a few. Some legs were spiral turned.

Keep in mind that when full-size pieces are miniaturized, it is often necessary to eliminate certain small details and reduce or simplify larger elements. See Table 10-1.

Top

☐ Cut a piece to size in the circular saw.

☐ Cut a 1/32-×-1/32 rabbet on all four sides to simulate molding.

☐ Sand with 100-2/0 sandpaper. Roll over the edges of the table top and sand the rabbet.

Scalloped Skirts

☐ Cut the four skirts (front, back, and ends) to size.

☐ Miter both ends of the four pieces to 45 degrees.

☐ Trace a scallop design on tracing paper and transfer to self-adhesive paper. Make two patterns for the front and back and two for the ends.

Fig. 10-4. Chisel adapted to multiple turnings.

☐ Apply the self-adhesive paper patterns to the longer faces of the four skirt parts.

☐ Cut scallop designs with the jigsaw. Eliminate irregularities with needle files.

☐ Sand all surfaces with 100-2/0 or 120-3/0 sandpaper.

Legs

☐ Cut 3/16″ square strips for legs. These strips should be about 1/128″ undersize to allow the leg stock to insert easily into the Bell Yankee Chucker. The Bell Yankee Chucker can be used for turning both square and round stock. See Fig. 10-3.

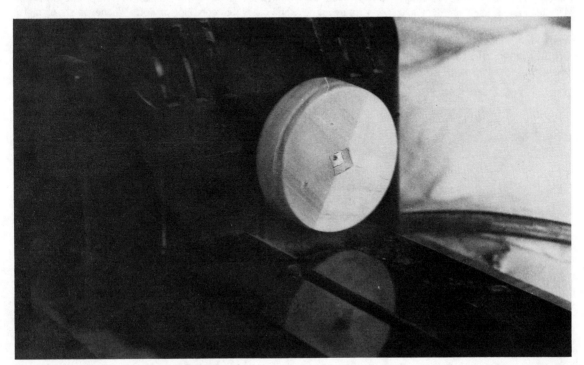

Fig. 10-5. Homemade jig for turning square stock.

□ Cut legs at least 2⅞ inches long. This allows ⅞ of an inch of square stock to be inserted in the 3/16-inch sleeve of the Bell Yankee Chucker. Do not cut to the length given in Table 10-1 until after turning takes place.

□ Thread the Bell Yankee Chucker on the drive shaft of the Dremel Moto-Lathe. Remove the 1/16-inch, 3/16-inch, 1/8-inch, and 5/32-inch sleeves from the chucker.

□ Insert one of the leg parts into the sleeve and advance the tailstock to hold the other end.

□ Mark a piece of cardboard, about ¾ × 2½ inches in size, the location of the square parts and the incised cuts.

□ Mark the square part while the leg is stationary in the lathe.

□ Turn the other parts of the leg until they are round. While the lathe is running, hold the cardboard next to the turning piece and mark the incised parts (beads, concave cuts, V cuts, etc.), with a pencil point. Never use a scale or rule.

□ Start the cuts with the 30-degree chisel and do the final shaping with the needle files.

□ Sand the straight parts with emery boards. Sand the beads, concave cuts, and V cuts with a piece of 120-3/0 sandpaper. *Note:* The leg of the William and Mary tea table is used as a demonstration turning in the section on how to make multiple turnings on the Dremel-Moto-Lathe.

□ The stretchers are made in the same fashion as the legs.

□ Glue the four parts of the skirt together with Sobo glue. Be sure the corners are square. Use clamps or rubber bands to hold together until the glue sets.

□ Glue the skirt assembly to the underside of the top. Make sure margins are equal and that the skirt is properly centered.

□ Place glue on the two faces of the upper square parts of leg and insert in the inside corner formed by the skirts. Clamp with small X-Acto clamps until glue is set.

□ Cut stretchers to fit openings between the legs. Glue in place and clamp with rubber bands.

□ Sand the entire table with 220-6/0 sandpaper.

□ Apply five or six coats of clear spray Deft finish to the table. If walnut paste filler is used three coats of Deft are enough. After each coat of Deft sand lightly with 240-7/9 or 280-8/0 sandpaper. Rub the entire piece with #0000 steel wool after the final coat.

□ Apply two coats of paste wax and buff to a gloss or semigloss.

MULTIPLE TURNINGS ON THE DREMEL LATHE

The leg of the William and Mary Tea Table is used here as a demonstration turning. Remember that the principles applied here can be used in making any spindle turning in multiples. For making only one or two turnings, the effort and time expended in making the special profile lathe rest and other jigs does not pay off. Whenever six or more duplicate turnings are needed, however, the extra effort will save considerable time and energy.

MAKE A SPECIAL PROFILE LATHE TOOL REST

□ Trace the profile (one-half of the turned part) of

Fig. 10-6. Multiple legs for William and Mary tea table.

Fig. 10-7. Completed William and Mary Tea Table.

the leg (longitudinally) on tracing paper.

☐ Transfer to a piece of self-adhesive paper from 3/16 to ¼ inch wide.

☐ Cut a piece of right-angle aluminum stock (⅛ × ¾ × ¾ inches) 2⅛ inches long with a hacksaw. Remove the burr with a file.

☐ Press the self-adhesive paper pattern on the *inside* corner of the aluminum stock and press down. The profile of the leg is to the outside edge away from the corner. The pattern must be placed on the inside so that the aluminum stock lies flat on the jigsaw while the profile is being cut.

☐ Cut the profile on the jigsaw with a fine tooth blade. Remove self-adhesive paper when completed.

☐ Smooth the profile contour and remove irregularities with regular and needle files followed with emery cloth. There can be no rough spots on the edges of the profile tool rest.

☐ Take off the top part of the regular tool rest. Using the two holes as a pattern, drill two holes in the aluminum profile tool rest on the part of the right angle that is perpendicular to the profile. Replace the top part of the regular tool rest with the profile tool rest. See Fig. 10-3.

ADAPT A CHISEL FOR MULTIPLE TURNINGS

☐ Select the round nose chisel that comes with the Dremel Moto-Lathe. Grind and whet the point so that it is slightly narrower.

☐ Cut a piece of ⅛-inch-thick aluminum stock 3/16 of an inch wide and 1 1/16 inches long. Sharpen the point

to about the same angle at the sides of the chisel. Round over the end slightly.

☐ Clamp the piece of aluminum to the underside of the chisel blade. The piece of aluminum will act as a follower as it rides against the profile rest in turning the leg spindles. It will follow the contour of the profile toolrest and prevent the chisel from cutting too deeply into the wood. See Fig. 10-4.

CHISEL ADAPTED TO MULTIPLE TURNINGS

Although the Bell Yankee Chucker commercial jig can be used in this example, enterprising craftsmen might want to make a homemade jig for turning square stock.

☐ Fasten a piece of ⅜-inch stock to the Dremel Moto-Lathe with FHB (flathead bright) screws.

☐ Turn the piece to 1¾ inches in diameter.

☐ Mark the center while the lathe is running.

☐ Drive a short brad into the center. Cut off the head, leaving about 1/16 of an inch protruding. Sharpen to a sharp with a file while the lathe is running.

☐ Cut two semicircles, 3/16 of an inch thick, on the jigsaw. Cut to 1¾ inches diameter. Cut one-half of a 3/16-inch square out of both segments on the radius line and in the exact center.

☐ Attach these semicircles to the first ⅜-inch turning with small brads. Do not glue. The square hole might become worn or loose and the segments would have to be replaced. The segments should be made of hardwood.

☐ Continue turning multiple legs either with the homemade jig or with the Bell Yankee Chucker. See Figs. 10-5, 10-6, and 10-7.

Chapter 11

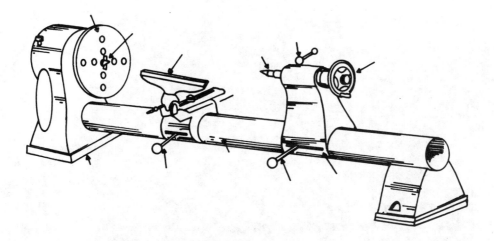

Industrial Mass Production of Turnings

THE AUTOMATIC LATHE, SOMETIMES KNOWN AS the shaping lathe, is quite different in design and function from other production lathes. It is widely used in many furniture industries because of its versatility. Other lathes produce only round turnings, but the automatic lathe can shape in addition to round, square, hexagonal, octagonal and many other shapes. Both centers of the automatic lathe are powered by a separate motor which turn the centers at the same slow speed.

The arbor, with the cutterheads attached, is driven by a powerful, high-speed motor. Each cutterhead is fitted with two or three or up to six or more knives that are secured in such a fashion as to produce a shearing cut. This assures smooth surfaces that require a minimum of sanding.

A separate knife marking fixture is necessary to mark the knives. A pattern is fastened to the fixture and the pointer that follows the contour inscribes the profile on the knives. The knives are carefully ground to the marked outlines and precisely balanced before being attached to the arbor.

The head and tailstock carriage, with the stock between the two centers, is advanced very slowly toward the high-speed cutters while the stock is revolving very

slowly. The stock is pushed against the cutterhead by a hand lever.

When turnings, other than round are desired, special castings (square, hexagonal, octagonal, etc.,) of the same shape are attached to the headstock. This specially shaped casting rides against a guide on the arbor that moves the carriage forward or away from the cutterhead knives.

THE MATTISON LATHE

The automatic lathe and the Mattison lathe are considered synonymous. The words are virtually interchangeable. Quality performances are traditional with the Mattison. Through the years, Mattison has earned a position of leadership in the woodworking industry and its lathes are used throughout the world.

Both the Model 66 and the Model 69 Mattison lathes are available as manually or fully automatically operated lathes. On both the Model 66 and 69 lathes, the actuation of the tailstock and carriage, the steady rest, and the hopper-feeding units are fully automatic. Once the operator loads the hopper, such operations as centering the piece, engaging the knives, and ejecting the finished turnings are performed automatically. Cycling of the feed

Fig. 11-1. The Mattison Model No. 66 manually fed woodturning lathe.

can be adjusted to any production rate that the particular stock or kind of turning permits. Minimum supervision is required. This allows the operator more time to inspect stock for defects while loading several machines. See Figs. 11-1, 11-2, and 11-3.

The Model No. 66 applies to Mattison lathes having a capacity to make turnings up to 30 inches long. The Model No. 69 is manufactured in two sizes: 42 inches and 54 inches. Both the No. 66 and the No. 69 are available in manually operated and fully automatic models. Extended hopper feed capacity of the Model 69 (54-inch machine) allows a full 54 inches of turning to be accomplished in an automatic mode. An extension of the hopper feed and carriage to handle 60-inch-long stock is offered as an option.

The entire hopper-feeding unit is hinged and can be swung away from the front of the machine without dis-

turbing setup adjustments. This gives the operator unobstructed access to the cutterheads for whetting, touching up, or setting knives.

The automatic hole-boring unit broadens the scope of operations because both boring and turning are combined in one machine. The boring unit can be mounted in the center for front side drilling or mounted at a 45-degree angle for corner drilling.

Boring units are mounted on bases with lateral and transverse adjustments. Swiveling arrangement provide for front-side boring up to 20 degrees either side of center. Two or more units may be operated simultaneously. Units are completely automatic and they can drill as fast as the lathe can handle turnings. The sequence of operations is interlocked with the lathe carriage. Stock is clamped while the boring is accomplished, and then unloaded by air cylinders. To ensure that the turning will be concentric with the holes, the turning operation can be located from the bored holes. A manual cycle mode is provided for making setups.

Accessories required for turning include a knife-marking machine, setting-up box, even-balance scales, and balancing ways.

GOODSPEED PRODUCTION LATHE

Goodspeed Machine Company manufactures full hy-draulic hopper-fed, back-knife lathe, semiautomatic, and variety lathes. The Goodspeed Model FH-30 Full Hy-draulic Hopper-Fed Knife Lathe has a turning rate of up to 600 pieces per hour, depending on size and shape. With a 10 hp headspindle drive and a 2 hp hydraulic drive, it will turn 1-inch to 3-inch squares or dowels with lengths from 9 inches through 30 inches long. Spindle speeds vary from 2250 to 4625 rpm. See Fig. 11-4.

The Goodspeed Model BV Hollow-Spindle Variety

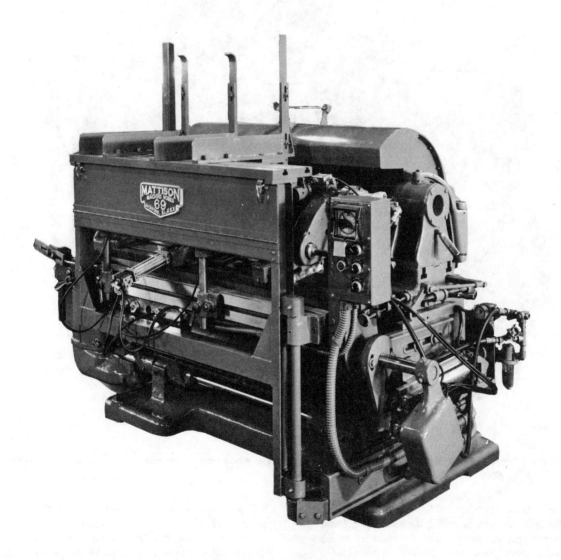

Fig. 11-2. The Mattison Model 69 fully automatic lathe with hopper feed.

165

Fig. 11-3. The Mattison Model 66 Wood-Turning lathe with two boring units, one unit is for boring a hole in the end of the turning and one for boring a hole in the side.

Lathe is manufactured in 24-inch and 36-inch sizes. The BV is designed for producing a variety of small-diameter wooden parts at high production rates, such as golf tees, balls, plugs, beads, etc. It is a combination air- and cam-operated machine that allows one operator to tend as many as six machines. Dowel stock is hopper fed through a hollow type of spindle using a rapid opening and closing type of chuck for driving the dowel stock for turning.

Parts are formed by using top tooling and end tooling (which includes drilling) or a combination of both with all tooling, including cutoff, cam driven mechanically to maintain exact timing and duplication of parts. Air-dried

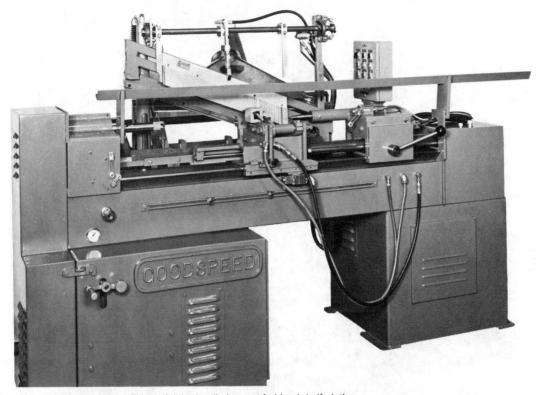

Fig. 11-4. Goodspeed Model FH-30, full hydraulic hopper-fed back-knife lathe.

Fig. 11-5. Goodspeed Model BV-24 hollow spindle variety lathe.

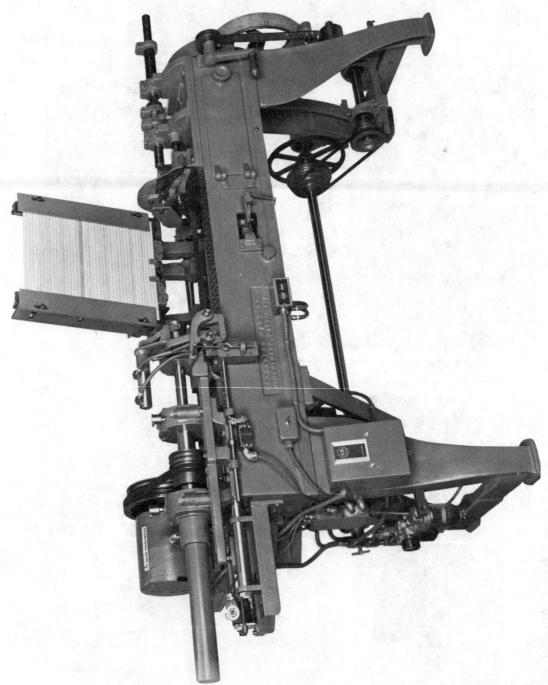

Fig. 11-6. Goodspeed Model SV-11 lathe.

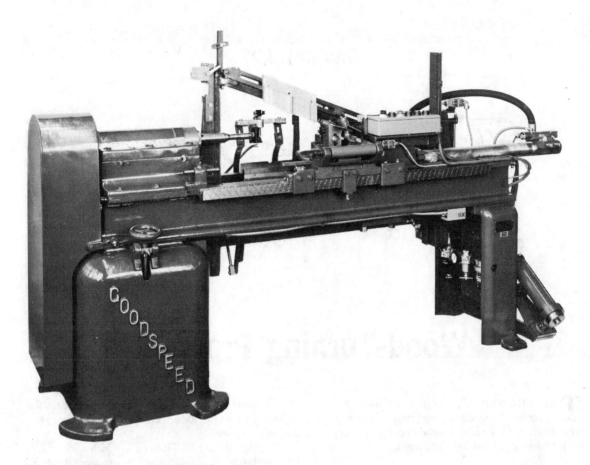

Fig. 11-7. Goodspeed semiautomatic lathe.

white birch (12 percent to 15 percent moisture content) is ideally suited for this machine while maple and beech or species of similar density give good results. All tooling is completely adjustable for location and timing. A manual clutch engaging handle along with a cam shaft hand wheel allow complete operator control of machine for setup or automatic operation. See Fig. 11-5, 11-6, and 11-7. This lathe will produce 1½-inch-diameter and 3-inch-long turnings very rapidly.

Goodspeed also makes a double or triple-trim saw, a hopper-fed, trim, chuck, and boring machine, and an air-operated, deep-hole boring machine.

DIEHL MACHINES

Diehl Automatic Hydraulic Lathes come in two sizes: the TL41 (has a stock capacity of 4 × 4 × 30 inches) and the TL42 (has a stock capacity of 4 × 4 × 44 inches). The TL41 is powered by a 15-hp motor and the TL42 is powered by a 20-hp motor. Diehl lathes shape the product round, square, polygonal, and irregular shapes.

Diehl's dual hopper option enables the TL41 or TL42 to turn two separate pieces—different shapes—simultaneously. In fact, the unit handles different size blanks, different lengths, finished to different sizes, and different patterns—automatically, at the same time. In practice, it doubles the capacities of the equipment. To turn stock beyond 44 inches in length, extensions are available in 72, 96, and 120 inches.

Chapter 12

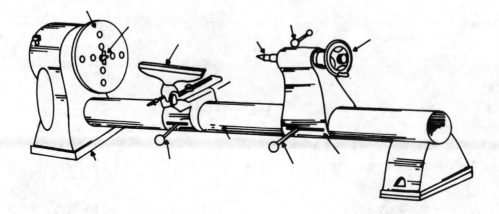

Wood-Turning Projects

THIS CHAPTER CONTAINS STEP-BY-STEP IN-
structions for wood-turning projects. Some of the projects are for beginning woodworkers and others are for advanced woodworking enthusiasts.

DISPLAY DOME BASE

Woodcraft Corporation provides glass for a display dome. The display dome can be used to show off Hummels, miniatures, knickknacks, small dolls, small flower arrangements, small scupltured carvings, and other miniature items.

Hardwood should be used because the base should be heavy enough to ensure stability. I chose mahogany. The turner should wear a face shield while turning and a face mask while sanding on the lathe. See Figs. 12-1 through 12-9.

☐ Cut a 6-inch square block 1⅛ inches thick.

☐ Cut a circle, 5½ inches in diameter, with the bandsaw circular cutting jig attached to the bandsaw table. See Chapter 3.

☐ Fasten the blank to the faceplate or attach to a screw chuck. I used the Myford screw chuck.

☐ At a fairly slow speed, turn the blank down to a 5¼-inch diameter with the gouge.

☐ Move the toolrest and straighten the face to a flat surface if it needs it. When completely round, the speed can be increased.

☐ Turn the 3 13/16-inch cut, ⅛ inch wide, with a parting chisel. This provides a ledge on which the dome sits.

☐ Set the calipers at 4⅝ inches and make the second, straight-sided cut, just above the bead at the bottom of the base, with the parting tool.

☐ Set the calipers at 4 3/16 inches and establish the outer edges of the ledge with a parting chisel. This also establishes the upper dimension of the cove (concave) portion.

☐ With a round-nose chisel make the cove cut. The chisel should be sharpened to a fine edge and the wire edge turned over with a burnisher. This scraping tool should be held with the handle rather high and the scraping edge rather low. If small, silky shavings are not produced, the chisel has not been sharpened correctly. The cove is approximately ½ inch wide.

☐ Turn the bottom bead, ⅜ of an inch wide, with the skew or diamond point chisel.

☐ Sand the display dome base. Use medium-grit abrasive paper followed by fine sandpaper while the base is turning in the lathe.

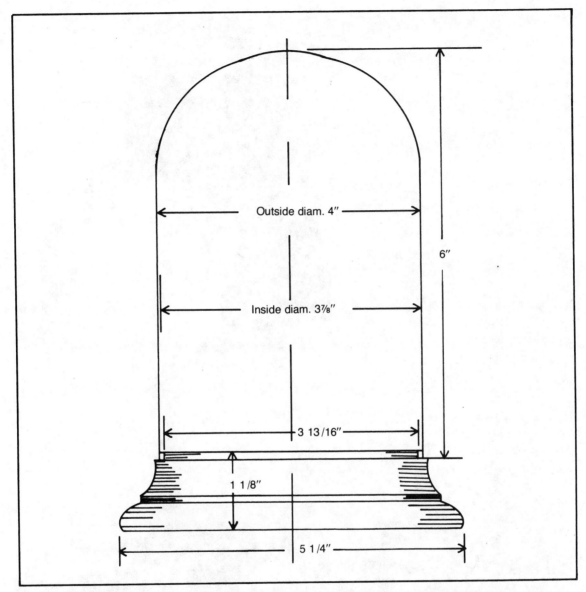

Outside diam. 4″

6″

Inside diam. 3⅞″

3 13/16″

1 1/8″

5 1/4″

Fig. 12-1. Display dome.

☐ Apply a liberal amount of Watco Danish (Natural) oil with a brush or cloth. Allow it to penetrate for 30 minutes, adding fresh Watco oil to areas that may absorb the oil faster.

☐ Reapply Watco oil, allowing an additional 15 minutes of penetration. Then wipe completely dry.

☐ After 24 hours, for added luster, apply a small amount of Watco oil using it as a lubricant while wet-sanding all surfaces lightly with #600 Wet-O-Dry

sandpaper. After 10 minutes, wipe clean and dry and polish with a soft cloth.

☐ For close-grained woods, the above is all that is necessary. Nevertheless, I applied one coat of clear spray Deft because the grain in the mahogany was still showing. If a filler had been used on the mahogany before the Watco oil, the coat of Deft would not have been necessary.

Note: Watco Danish Oil is one of many penetrating

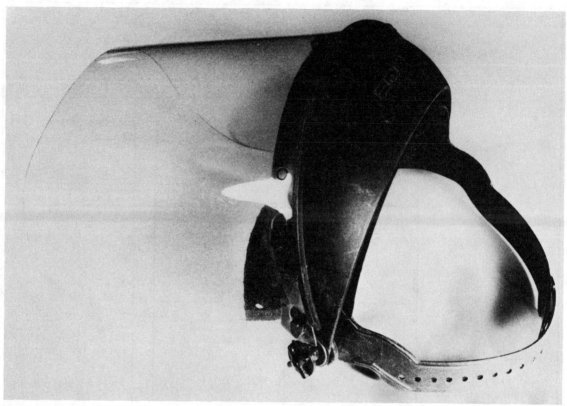

Fig. 12-2. Face shield.

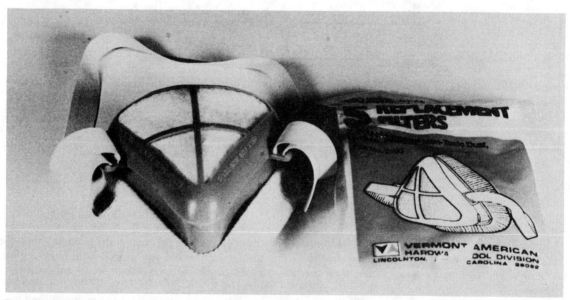

Fig. 12-3. Face mask.

172

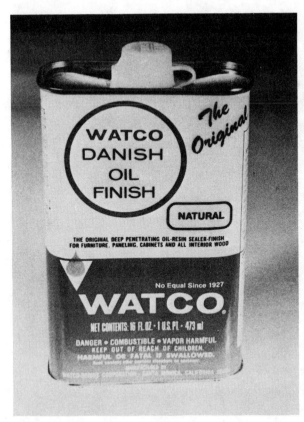

Fig. 12-4. Watco danish oil finish.

finishes that are ideal for the home craftsmen. You do not have to worry about special finishing facilities and dust problems are eliminated. Brushes and spray equipment are not needed. Many wipe-on and penetrating finishes are synthetic chemical ingredients that not only penetrate the surface, but actually combine chemically with the wood. They do not react chemically, but combine to form a substance with a different molecular weight known as polymerization.

☐ After the Deft is thoroughly dry, place the base back on the lathe and hold some #0000 steel wool against the base while it is revolving.

☐ Apply a thin coat of paste furniture wax while the lathe is stationary. After about 10 minutes, polish the base by holding a soft cloth against the base while it is revolving.

THREE-MINUTE HOURGLASS

The glass/sand element of the three-minute hourglass, hand-blown in Europe to Woodcraft's specifications, is one of a number of hourglasses available from Woodcraft. In addition to the three-minute glass/sand element, there is a 10-minute and also a 1-hour element. In addition, there is a giant hourglass element with a height of 20 inches.

Mounting tips at each end allows the glass to be mounted between the base and top of the hourglass. The top, bottom, and supporting spindles can be turned of any suitable hardwood. I chose cherry because of its fine grain, excellent turning qualities, and because it does not need a filler. See Table 12-1.

☐ Make full-size drawing of the hourglass. It is not necessary to follow the suggested design. See Fig. 12-10.

☐ Make a template to assist in turning the three spindles. See Fig. 12-11.

☐ Cut two blanks for the top and bottom ½ × 3¾ × 3¾ inches.

☐ Draw diagonals across the face of the two blanks.

☐ Mark the centers where the diagonals cross with an awl or center punch.

☐ Bore holes where the diagonals cross with a drill the diameter of the root diameter of the screw of the Myford screw chuck. Bore the holes ⅜ of an inch deep.

☐ Cut the circles (top and bottom) on the bandsaw circle cutting jig about 3⅝ inches in diameter. The pin of the jig will fit into the holes bored in the previous step.

☐ Attach the circular blanks (one at a time) to the Myford screw chuck already mounted to the lathe.

☐ Turn the top and bottom to the design selected. I used the miniature lathe tools that accompany the Dremel lathe for turning the design, as well as parts of the design of the spindles.

☐ Sand the edge and face, first with medium sandpaper then with fine abrasive.

☐ Remove the circles from the Myford screw chuck.

☐ On the sides with the center holes, lay out centers, 120 degrees apart, ⅜ of an inch from the edges.

☐ Bore ¼-inch holes, ¼ of an inch deep, at the centers established in the previous step.

☐ At the center hole bored to attach the circle to the Myford screw chuck, countersink a hole about ¼ of an

Table 12-1. Hourglass Materials.

Pieces	Description	Size	Material
1	Glass/Sand Element	2″ diameter × 5″	Sand/Glass
2	Top and Bottom	½″ × 3½″ diameter	Cherry
3	Supporting Spindles	½″ × ½″ × 5″	Cherry

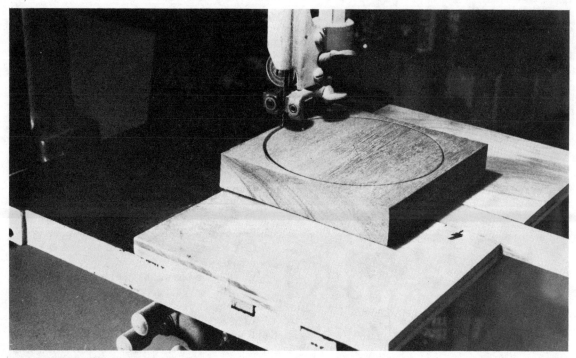

Fig. 12-5. Blank for display of a dome base being cut on the bandsaw circle-cutting jig.

Fig. 12-6. Blank of a display dome base attached to a Myford lathe screw chuck.

174

Fig. 12-7. Display dome base finished.

inch deep into which the tips of the hourglass will eventually be inserted when the hourglass is assembled.

☐ Cut the stock for the three supporting spindles.

☐ Draw diagonals across the ends of the three pieces.

☐ On one end of each piece, cut a saw kerf about ⅛ of an inch deep on the diagonals.

☐ On the other ends, bore a hole, about ⅛ inch deep, about ⅛ inch in diameter, where the diagonals cross.

☐ Drive the live center of the lathe into the end with the saw kerf and insert the live center and spindle blank into the lathe.

☐ The tailstock center is advanced until the tip of the center enters the hole at the other end of the spindle.

☐ Turn the stock to the round with a spindle-turning (fingernail) gouge.

☐ With a pencil sharpened to a long point, establish the major dimensions by holding the pencil point against the revolving stock opposite the corresponding points on the template.

☐ With the parting tool and the Dremel round-nose chisel, turn the diameters at the points established in the previous step.

☐ Turn the major parts of the spindle with a small, spindle-turning gouge.

☐ Turn the minor parts of the spindle with the small Dremel lathe tools. See Fig. 12-12.

☐ Sand the spindles with emery boards and narrow strips of sandpaper while the lathe is turning.

☐ Grab a handful of cherry shavings under the lathe and hold them against the turning spindle. It will burnish the surface to a hard, shiny finish.

☐ Assemble and glue the top, bottom, spindles, and glass/sand element. See Fig. 12-13.

☐ Wrap a cylindrical piece of facial tissue such as Kleenex around the sand/glass element to protect it against the clear spray Deft.

☐ Spray on two or three coats of clear spray Deft.

☐ Remove the protective Kleenex.

175

Fig. 12-8. Display dome.

□ With a small brush, apply Deft to the unfinished areas at the ends of the glass.

□ When the finish is thoroughly dry, rub the wood with #0000 steel wool.

□ Apply furniture wax to the wood parts and polish. See Fig. 12-14.

CHEESE BOARD AND DOME

A cheese board and dome is a fairly simple and easy faceplate project. It can be turned of any hardwood; I choose birch.

Woodcraft is the supplier of the glass dome. They also market a smaller (4¾-inch outside diameter and 5 inches high) glass dome. These clear glass domes offer a distinctive and elegant way to serve snacks and cheese. The cracker rim provides a means of stacking small party crackers.

The portion of the board under the dome where the cheese is cut must be finished with a nontoxic finish. The area can be rubbed with paraffin or, better yet, covered with a suitable ceramic tile of the proper size.

□ Cut a piece of square stock, ¾ × 9 7/16 × 9 7/16 inches.

□ Cut the piece to a circle on the bandsaw circle cutting jig. In the absence of a circle cutting jig, mark the stock with a compass or dividers before sawing.

□ Attach the circular stock to the outboard faceplate. The board is too large to turn in the inboard faceplate and the Myford screw chuck cannot be used on the outboard end of the lathe.

□ Turn the rim to 9 5/16 of an inch with a gouge.

□ Mark and cut the recessed groove into which the dome sits with a parting tool to a depth of approximately ⅛ inch.

□ Turn the curved portions on the top and bottom at a slow speed with a well-sharpened gouge. I used a "long and strong" gouge, See Fig. 12-16.

□ Follow up with a round-nose scraper tool to eliminate any ridges.

□ Remove the tool rest and sand, first with medium grit then with a fine grit abrasive. Use a face mask or respirator to combat dust when sanding.

Fig. 12-9. Display dome with ceramic bird.

176

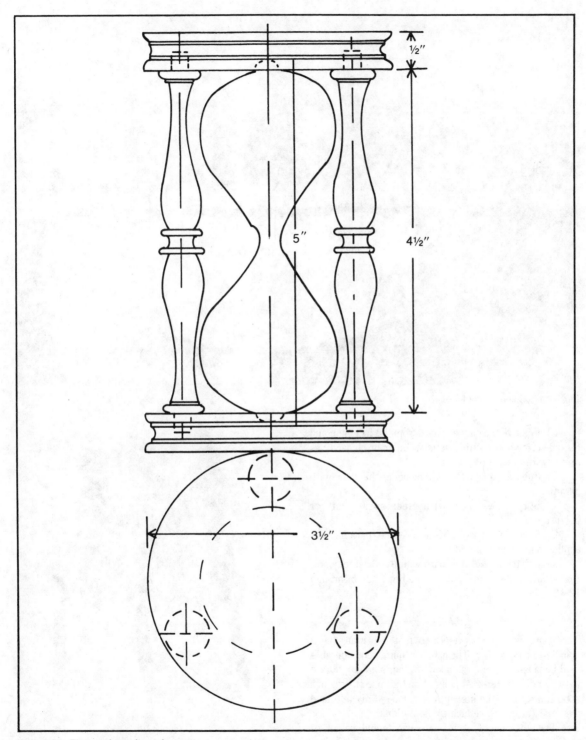

Fig. 12-10. Three-minute hourglass.

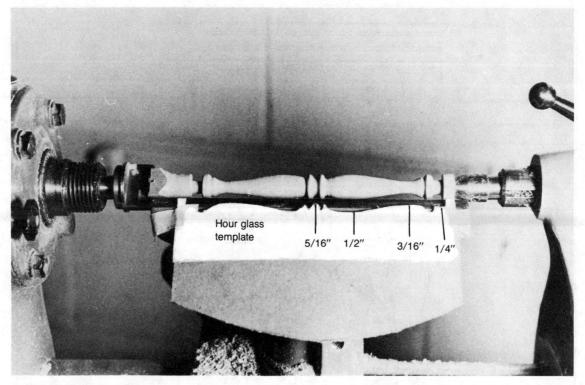

Hour glass template

5/16" 1/2" 3/16" 1/4"

Fig. 12-11. Spindle template.

☐ Remove the cheese board from the faceplate and fill the screw holes with Plastic Wood or birch sandings mixed with glue.

☐ Rub the portion that will be under the dome with paraffin.

☐ Spray the board with clear spray Deft or polyurethane.

☐ Scrape off the finish where the paraffin was applied and reapply paraffin.

☐ Rub the rest of the board with #0000 steel wool. Apply furniture wax and polish. See Figs. 12-15 through 12-18.

GAVEL

The gavel is a good project to test the craftsman's spindle-turning ability. The handle requires considerable skill because the long, slender turning is apt to vibrate between the centers. Although I did not use it, this is a good time to use the steady rest. I looped my left hand over the turning to reduce the vibrations.

The selection of birch for the handle and walnut for the head presents an interesting study in contrasts be-

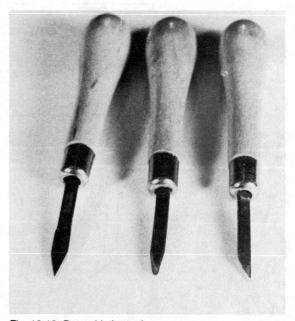

Fig. 12-12. Dremel lathe tools.

178

Fig. 12-13. Three-minute hourglass before assembly.

Fig. 12-14. Completed three-minute hourglass.

tween light-colored and dark-colored wood. See Table 12-2.

Gavel Head

□ Cut the gavel head in the rough to about 2½ × 2½ × 4 inches to allow for waste. Check the wood for knots, splits, or other defects before sawing. See Fig. 12-19.

Gavel

□ Draw diagonals across both ends of the walnut block.

□ Make saw kerfs about ⅛ inch deep on one end. This end will be placed against the live center.

□ Drill ⅛-inch holes about ⅜ of an inch deep at the point where the diagonals intersect on both ends of the block.

□ Remove the live center from the lathe and drive the spurs into the saw kerfs with a mallet.

□ Place the live center and block into the lathe between centers. Advance the tailstock center to secure the piece in the lathe.

Table 12-2. Gavel Materials.

Pieces	Description	Size	Material
1	Gavel Head	2⅛″ × 2⅛″ × 3½″	Walnut
1	Gavel Handle	1″ × 1″ × 11″	Birch

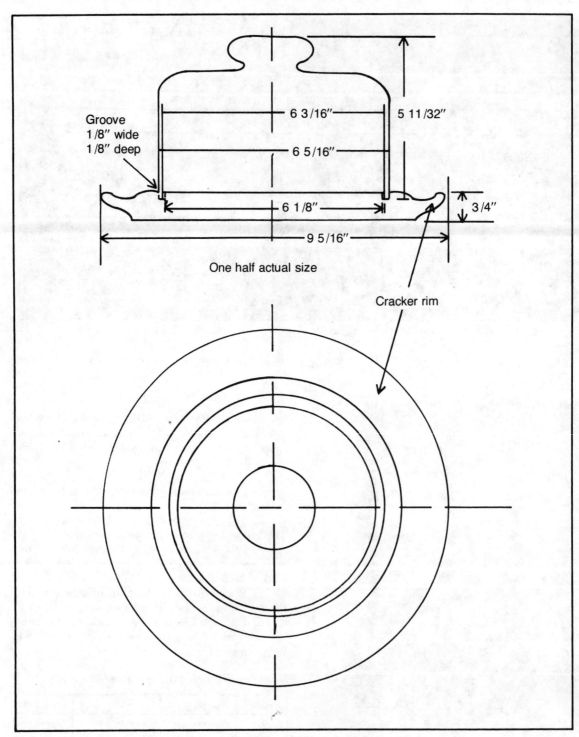

Groove
1/8" wide
1/8" deep

6 3/16"

5 11/32"

6 5/16"

6 1/8"

3/4"

9 5/16"

One half actual size

Cracker rim

Fig. 12-15. Cheese board and dome.

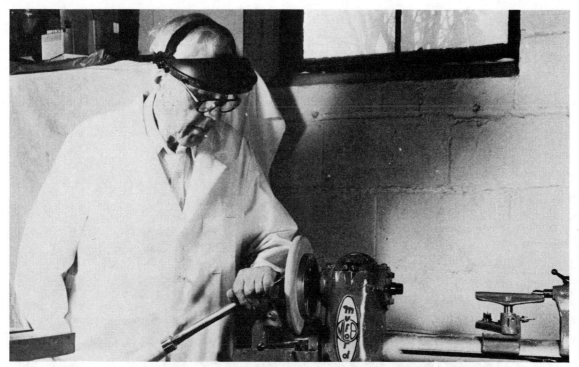

Fig. 12-16. Turning the cheese board with a "long and strong" gouge. Note the protective face shield.

Fig. 12-17. Sanding the cheese board while wearing a face mask.

Fig. 12-18. Completed cheese board and dome.

□ Adjust the tool rest, slightly below the center, about ¼ inch from the corners of the block as it is rotated.

□ Turn the block to the round with the round-nose (fingernail) gouge.

□ Make a gavel head template of heavy cardboard or thin plywood. See Fig. 12-20.

□ Turn the gavel to conform to the outline of the template.

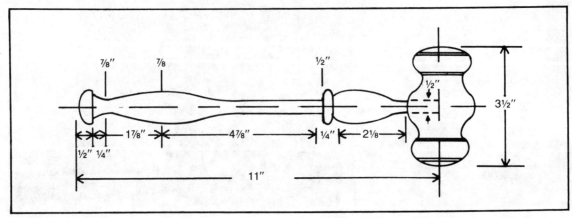

Fig. 12-19. Gavel.

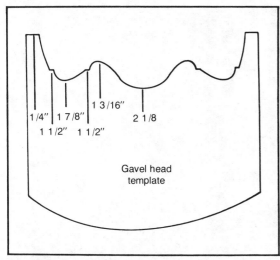

1 3/16"

1/4" 1 7/8"   2 1/8

1 1/2"   1 1/2"

Gavel head
template

Fig. 12-20. Gavel-head template.

☐ Sand the gavel head, first with medium sandpaper followed with fine sandpaper.

☐ Apply French polish to gavel head while the head is turning. Brush a small amount of white shellac (orange shellac if the color is not objectionable) on to the center of a long piece of folded cloth. Add one drop of linseed oil to the center of the shellac portion. Hold the cloth to the rotating gavel head with considerable pressure. Repeat the shellac/oil treatment until a substantial finish is built up. See Fig. 12-21.

☐ Cut off the head with the point of a skew while the lathe is turning. Catch the gavel head with your left hand so that it does not fall to the floor.

Gavel Handle

☐ Cut the rough stock for handle 1 × 1 × 12 inches.

☐ Draw diagonals across both ends of the birch stock.

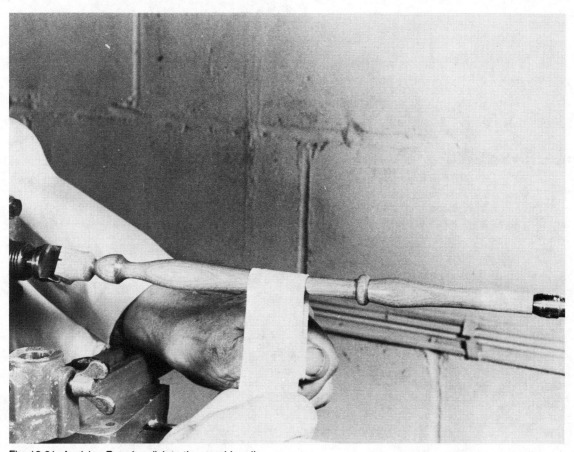

Fig. 12-21. Applying French polish to the gavel handle.

Fig. 12-22. V block used to bore a hole in the gavel head.

□ Make saw kerfs about ⅛ of an inch deep on one end. This end will be placed against the live center.

□ Drill ⅛-inch holes about ⅜ of an inch deep at the point where the diagonals intersect on both ends of the birch stock.

□ Remove the live center from the lathe and drive the spurs into the saw kerfs with a mallet.

□ Place the live center and the birch stock in the lathe between centers. Advance the tailstock center to secure the piece in the lathe.

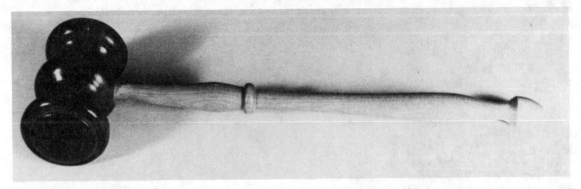

Fig. 12-23. The complete gavel.

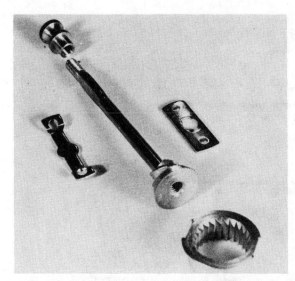

Fig. 12-24. Pepper mill mechanism.

□ Mark the "large" and "small" diameter positions of the handle on a thin stick about 12 inches long and transfer to the whirling stock with a long-pointed pencil. The stick should rest on the tool rest, about ¼ of an inch from the turning stock. *Caution:* Never use a steel rule or scale to transfer dimensions. This could lead to harm to the work, the scale, or possibly the turner.

□ At these major points, turn to the diameters as shown in Fig. 12-20.

□ Free-hand turn the rest of the handle. Refer frequently to Fig. 12-20.

□ Sand with medium and fine sandpaper.

□ French polish the gavel handle as described in the twelfth step.

□ Cut off the handle with the point of a skew. Catch with the left hand at the time of parting.

□ Sand the end of the handle and apply one or two coats of shellac.

□ Bore the handle hole in the head. Apply glue to end of handle and insert the handle into the hole in gavel head. See Fig. 12-22.

□ Apply furniture wax and polish. See Fig. 12-23.

PEPPER MILL

Woodcraft supplies three sizes of made-in-Germany pep-

□ Adjust tool rest slightly below the center with the clearance between the stock and the tool rest.

Turn the birch stock to the round with a round-nose gouge. Turn slowly to prevent vibrations.

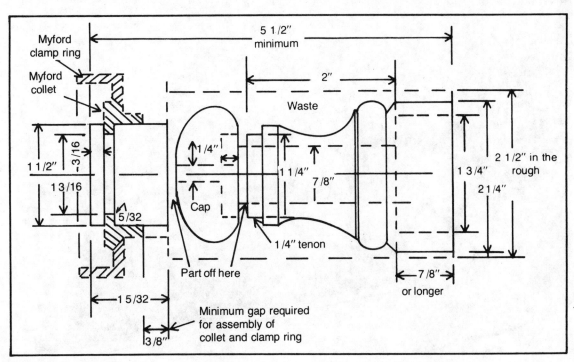

Fig. 12-25. Pepper mill layout.

Fig. 12-26. Preparing pepper mill stock to fit the Myford collet chuck.

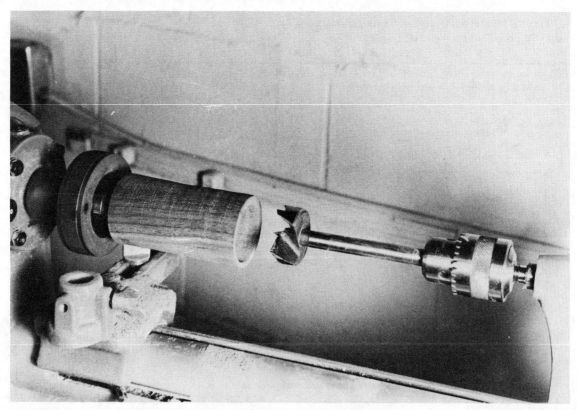

Fig. 12-27. Boring hole in the base of pepper mill with 1¾-inch multispur bit.

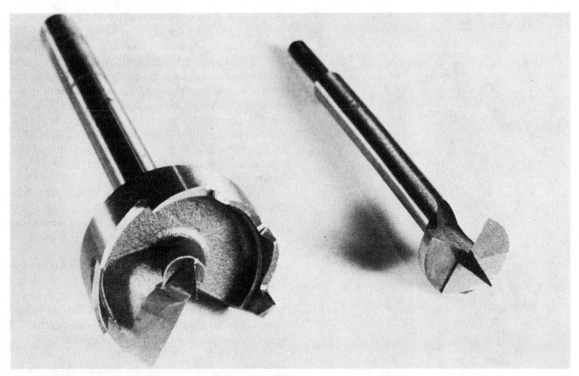

Fig. 12-28. 1¾-inch multispur bit and ⅞-inch power-bore bit.

Fig. 12-29. Turning the outside of the pepper mill with a conical plug in the base.

Fig. 12-30. The completed pepper mill.

per mill mechanisms with shafts 3½, 6⅞, and 10½ inches long (See Fig. 5-20). The 3½-inch shaft is designed for a pepper mill at least 3 9/16 inches high. The minimum height for a 6⅞-inch shaft is 6⅞ inches and 9⅞ inches for the 10½-inch-long shaft.

The toothed cup of the grinding mechanism fits over the matching toothed part on the end of the shaft. The "U" fixing clamp fits into the notches on the grinding cup's lip with two screws securing the grinding assembly to the pepper mill.

The driving washer is screwed to the center of the pepper mill's recessed portion in the underside of the cap so that the shaft slides easily through the ¼-inch hole in the cap. When the pepper mill is assembled, the washer will locate itself around the center of the shaft's driving wings. It is this assembly that rotates the grinder when the pepper mill cap is turned.

It will be necessary to expand the ¼-inch-diameter hole on the underside of the pepper mill cap to give the driving wings room when the entire mechanism is assembled. This tapering can be done with a countersink bit or craft knife. The clip is pushed horizontally into the

⅞-inch central bore and will hold the shaft in position during use. See Fig. 12-24.

Carefully study Fig. 12-25. The inside bore dimensions should be strictly adhered to. The outside design and dimensions can vary to suit the craftsman, but the outside wall thickness should be at least 3/16 of an inch.

The shaft hole in the cap should be ¼ inch in diameter. The length of the hole in the cap is 11/16 of an inch and the recess in cap ¼ inch so the total width (or height) of the cap is 15/16 of an inch. The diameter of the peppercorn chamber is ⅞ of an inch and the length is 2 inches.

The diameter of the hole for the grinding assembly is 1¾ inches and the minimum length is ⅞ of an inch. If the length of the hole is considerably longer than ⅞ of an inch, the craftsman might find it difficult to insert the screws holding the fixing clamp.

I used the Myford collet chuck to turn the pepper mill. There are a number of other chucks that could be used as well (see Chapter 3). The Myford collet chuck holds the work firm and secure, but it does have the disadvantage of using more stock than is needed for the project. A minimum of 1 5/32 inches of extra length must be allowed for the collet and clamp ring. The wood must be sufficiently long to allow for making the body, cap, as well as the waste held in the chuck and for parting off.

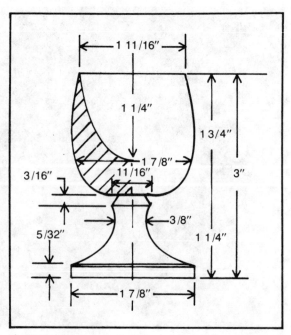

Fig. 12-31. Egg cup.

Any hardwood can be used for the pepper mill. I chose walnut because its color is close to that of pepper. See Table 12-3.

☐ Make full-size layout your design differs from mine. At the same time, a template for the outside shape should be made.

☐ Cut the stock for the mill. It must be at least 2½ inches square and at least 5½ inches long.

☐ Draw diagonals across the two ends. Saw kerfs 1⅛ of an inch deep on the end that eventually goes into the chuck. Drill a hole about ⅛ of an inch in diameter about ⅜ of an inch deep, where the diagonals intersect.

☐ Place the stock between live center and tailstock center and turn the portion of the stock that goes into the Myford collet chuck. The dimensions should be strictly adhered to. Turn the remaining stock to a 2¼-inch diameter. Remove stock from between centers. Turn the conical plug from 1-inch-thick hardwood stock. The large diameter is 1 13/16 inches and the small diameter is 1 11/16 inches. Remove plug from the lathe and place the Myford collet chuck on the headstock spindle. Place the

pepper mill stock in the Myford collet chuck. See Fig. 12-26.

☐ Place the 1¾-inch multispur bit in the tailstock. See Fig. 12-27.

☐ Advance the tailstock spindle at least ⅞ of an inch at approximately 500 to 700 rpm. The bottom of the stock should be flat.

☐ Bore the ⅞-inch diameter hole for the peppercorns. Use a multispur, spade bit or power-bore bit. The author used the power-bore bit. Bore completely through the length of the body and the ¼-inch tenon. See Fig. 12-28.

☐ Cut the ¼-inch tenon with a parting tool. The diameter of the tenon is 1¼ inches.

☐ Part off the body with a parting tool. The stock remaining in the chuck is the cap.

☐ Turn the recess in the cap to fit the ¼-inch tenon on the body.

☐ Bore a ¼-inch hole through the cap.

☐ Place the body of the pepper mill back into the cap and with the help of the conical plug inserted into the

Fig. 12-32. Turning outside of egg cup with a conical plug in place.

Table 12-3. Pepper Mill Materials.

Pieces	Description	Size	Material
1	Pepper Mill (Cap, body and waste) and waste)	2½″ × 2½″ × 5½″	Walnut
1	Conical Plug (not shown in drawing)	1″ × 1⅞″ diameter	Hardwood
1	Pepper Mill Mechanism		

1¾-inch hole in the bottom of the body. The tailstock center is inserted into the conical plug. The complete assembly is now secured between the chuck and the tailstock center.

☐ Complete the turning of both body and cap and sand with medium and fine sandpaper. See Fig. 12-29.

☐ Remove the body from the lathe. If the cap fits too tight to the tenon on the body, sand the recess in the cap until it turns rather freely on the body tenon.

☐ Part off the cap.

☐ Finish with polyurethane and install the mechanism. See Fig. 12-30.

EGG CUP

An egg cup is easy to turn and it has clean and trim lines. Other designs for egg cups are provided in Chapter 5.

I turned two egg cups: the first one in ash and the second one of birch stained with a mahogany stain. Ash is

Fig. 12-34. Birch egg cup.

the ideal wood for turning egg cups and goblets. It is strong and tough and the fibers tend to hold together in thin sections and small diameters. When I was a university student. I turned a small goblet of ash. The stem was less than ⅛ of an inch in diameter and the cup was egg-shell thin, allowing light to come through.

There are a number of chucks that can be used to turn the egg cup. I used the Myford screw chuck. See Fig. 12-31.

☐ Cut a piece of ash 2 × 2 × 4 inches.

☐ Draw diagonals across the two ends.

☐ In one end, bore a hole between ¾ and ⅞ of an inch deep where the diagonals intersect. The drill diameter should be equal to the core diameter of the screw in the screw chuck.

☐ Drill a ⅛-inch hole about ⅛ of an inch deep where the diagonals cross on the other end.

☐ Set the screw in the screw chuck to the extended distance of between ¾ and ⅞ of an inch. Secure the screw with the Allen set screw wrench.

Fig. 12-33. Ash egg cup.

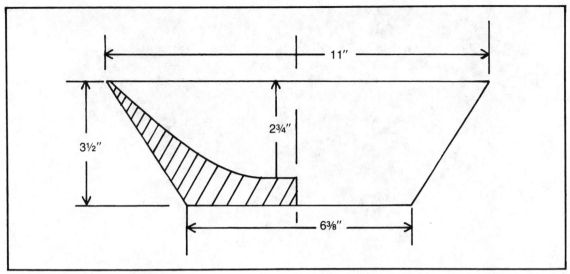

Fig. 12-35. Contemporary salad bowl.

☐ Attach the Myford screw chuck to the lathe and attach the ash stock to the screw chuck.

☐ Place a drill in the Jacobs chuck and place both in the tailstock. The size of the drill can be any size between ¾ and 1¼ inches. I use a ⅞-inch diameter power-bore bit. Bore the hole to the depth of 1 inch by advancing the tailstock spindle.

☐ Shape the inside of the egg cup, 1 11/16 inches wide by 1¼ inches deep, with a round-nose scraping tool.

☐ Remove the chuck and egg cup from the lathe and turn a conical plug between centers from 1-inch thick

hardwood. The large diameter should be 1¾ inches and the small diameter 1 9/16 inches. Remove the plug from the lathe.

☐ Place the chuck and stock back in the lathe.

☐ Place the conical plug inside the cup of the egg cup.

☐ Hold the plug in place with the tailstock center and turn the outside of the egg cup. Turn the smallest diameter last. See Fig. 12-32.

☐ Sand the egg cup while it is revolving in the lathe. Use medium grit followed by fine sandpaper.

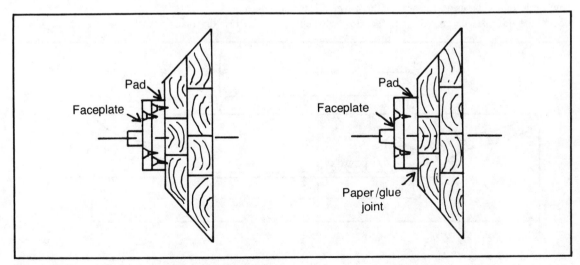

Fig. 12-36. Two methods of attaching work to faceplate.

Fig. 12-37. A contemporary salad bowl.

□ Finish with Deft, lacquer, or polyurethane. See Figs. 12-33 and 12-34.

CONTEMPORARY SALAD BOWL

A salad bowl is bound to challenge the skill of the wood-turner, particularly if he has not turned a faceplate of this size previously. For the beginning faceplate turner, it would probably be wise to turn a bowl of some inexpensive wood before starting on one of expensive hardwood.

This bowl was turned of mahogany, primarily because of its stability and ease of turning, however most any hardwood can be used. Because of the 4-inch thickness of the stock, it will probably be necessary to glue up

2-inch stock. For the fortunate craftsman with a jointer and thickness planer, this process will be rather easy. For the turner equipped only with a hand plane, planing stock to the accuracy required for gluing will be a long, tedious process; but it can be done with patience. It is good practice to alternate the grain of the wood. See Fig. 12-36.

The bowl should be turned on the outboard end of the lathe. Turning on the inboard side is apt to restrict the free movement of the gouge. See Fig. 12-35.

□ Glue up stock to the size of 4 inches thick by 12 inches square.

□ Draw diagonals across one face of the block.

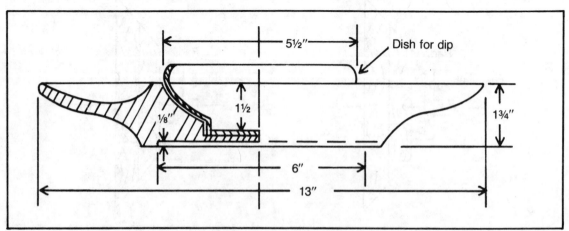

Fig. 12-38. Hors d'oeuvre tray.

From the intersection of the two diagonals, swing a 11½-inch-diameter circle with dividers or a pencil compass.

☐ Set the angle of the bandsaw table to 33 degrees and cut the circular disk. This angular cut will eliminate a considerable amount of the waste wood that will not have to be turned away.

☐ Cut a circular pad, 1 inch thick and 6 inches in diameter (the same size as the outboard faceplate). This can be stock from the scrap pile, either softwood or hardwood.

☐ Fasten the pad to the bowl stock with countersunk flathead screws. If this procedure is used, the screw holes in the bottom of the bowl should be filled after the bowl is completed with mahogany Plastic Wood and sanded flush when dry. The pad eliminates the possibility of doing damage to the faceplate.

An alternate method is the paper chuck technique that eliminates screw holes in the bowl. I used the paper/glue method. See Fig. 12-36.

A sharp, heavy knife is used to separate the bowl from the pad after turning, but first you must turn the bowl.

☐ Select a deep-fluted, square end, "long and strong" gouge. The ¾-inch size is preferred although the ½-inch gouge will do an adequate job. See Figs. 2-6 and 2-7.

☐ Adjust the lathe to turn at a slow speed.

☐ Check the gouge for sharpness. The end of the gouge should be straight across and the angle of the bevel should be approximately 40 degrees.

☐ Attach the faceplate, pad and bowl stock to the outboard end of the lathe.

☐ Turn the outside of the bowl first. Some turners turn the outside first then turn the bowl around and recenter and reattach the bowl to turn the inside. The pad makes this unnecessary because both the inside and outside can be turned at one sitting.

☐ The gouge should turn the front edge first. The gouge is held in an almost vertical position with the right hand over the top of the gouge near the cutting edge with hand holding the gouge securely to the top of the toolrest. The left hand holds the handle near the end. Some expert turners recommend that the handle should rest against the left leg for more stability and control.

☐ The handle is then raised and the gouge is rolled to the left. Keep in mind that the bevel of the gouge must rub the wood at all times. The gouge must never be used with a scraping action. The gouge is almost on its left side when the cut is completed.

☐ In turning from the large diameter toward the faceplate and pad on the outside of bowl, the process is reversed. Never turn from the smaller diameter toward the larger diameter. Cutting against the grain will cause all kinds of problems. The left hand holds the gouge against the toolrest near the cutting edge of the gouge. The right hand holds the handle securely near the end with the gouge in nearly an upright position.

The handle is gradually raised and the gouge is rolled to the right with the handle moving to the left. The gouge is nearly on its right edge when the cut is completed.

The tool rest should only be a pivot point for the gouge. The craftsman should avoid sliding the gouge along the tool rest while the tool is cutting. The pivot point on the tool rest can be changed on the tool rest, but never while the tool is cutting.

☐ After the rough shape is established, it is permissible to use the scraping chisel. The edge of the chisel should be straight or slightly rounded. The wire edge of the chisel should be turned with the burnisher after it is ground, in the same fashion as used on a cabinet scraper. The tip of the chisel should be slightly below the tool rest level with the handle raised to get a good scraping action. If small, silky shavings are not produced, it is an indication that the scraping chisel has not been properly sharpened or that the chisel is not being held in the correct position. Sanding should be held to a minimum using only fine sandpaper.

☐ Move the tool rest around to the front of the bowl to turn the inside. Some turners start from the outer edge of the bowl and work toward the center, while others start turning at the center. The author prefers the latter.

☐ With the square-end gouge, cut a conical hole in the center of the bowl. Twist the gouge to the left gradually lifting the end of the handle until the gouge is at a right angle to the face of the bowl.

☐ Carve a deep hole in the center and continue turning out surplus wood gradually working toward the outside edge of the bowl.

☐ Extreme caution must be taken when the gouge first enters the wood on each successive cuts because the gouge does not have a rubbing surface for the bevel at this stage and the gouge might go awry. Once the groove has been established, the bevel will be rubbing and the crisis is over if the corner of the gouge not cutting is not allowed to catch in the wood. This can also be a disaster.

☐ The cutting edge of the gouge is from the center of the gouge to the point on the left. The point on the right is the one to watch as it can kick up all kinds of mischief.

☐ The lower part of the palm of the right hand is behind the upper end of the gouge, resting on the tool rest close to the cutting edge of the gouge. The left hand holds the end of the handle. The left hand and handle should be held against the torso or leg, with the gouge in nearly a horizontal position.

☐ The gouge rests on its left side on the tool rest. Determine where you want the gouge to enter the wood on the next cut. Sometimes it is desirable to make concentric rings on the face by holding a pencil against the revolving bowl. The gouge is pushed into the wood, but only for a short distance. Once penetration has been accomplished the handle can be lowered. As the gouge point moves upward, it should be twisted toward the left to prevent the right corner of the gouge's cutting edge from catching.

☐ As the gouge continues to cut toward the center of the bowl, the handle is raised until it is nearly perpendicular to the bowl as the gouge nears the center.

☐ In making the last cut to establish the rim and the thickness of the bowl, it will be necessary to make a preliminary cut in the edge of the bowl. Because the outer edge of the bowl is traveling at a much faster rate of speed, it is apt to cause mistakes that might not otherwise happen and ruin the edge of the bowl. This preliminary cut is made with a parting chisel, the point of a skew, or the corner of a square scraping chisel. This establishes an entry point for the gouge and forms a surface on which the bevel of the gouge can rub.

☐ The inside of the bowl should be scraped in the same fashion as described in step 14, except the scraper should have a round nose. Keep in mind that the scraper should be rather blunt and the cutting edge should be pointed down to a slight angle by raising the handle of the scraper. If nothing but sawdust is produced instead of thin, silky shavings, the turner will know that the scraper has been sharpened incorrectly or he is holding the scraper in an incorrect position.

☐ Sand the inside of the bowl with fine sandpaper and remove the bowl from the waste pad by thrusting a thick knife blade or wide chisel into the paper/glue joint. Part of the paper will adhere to the pad, and the remainder will cling to the bottom of the bowl and must be sanded off.

☐ Fill the grain of the wood with dark mahogany paste filler. It might be necessary to make your own filler by mixing colors in oil with the natural-colored (cream) filler. Brush in the filler with a fairly stiff brush. Allow filler to remain on the surface for a few minutes and rub the filler into the grain with a piece of burlap. Wipe off the surface with a clean cloth. Allow filler to dry for at least 24 hours.

☐ Apply a thin coat of sealer (shellac, lacquer sealer, etc.,) and apply two or three coats of polyurethane by spraying or brushing. Polyurethane is nontoxic. When the last coat is dry, rub with #0000 steel wool. After salad is made in the bowl, wash the bowl with luke-warm water and soap and dry immediately. Never use hot water or allow the bowl to set in water. See Fig. 12-37.

HORS D'OEUVRE TRAY

A hors d'oeuvre tray is a very practical project and would be a wonderful gift to a relative or friend. The tray can be made of any hardwood; I used mahogany because of its beauty, stability, and ease of turning.

The dish in the center for the dip can be any round dish provided that the lower part is smaller in diameter than the top. I used one of the many that were stored in my china closet. See Fig. 12-38.

☐ Make full-size, cross-section drawing of the tray. The design can be altered to suit the taste of the turner.

☐ With a compass or dividers, swing the diameter (13¼ inches) of the tray on 1¾-inch or 2-inch stock, making sure that the center is easily observed. The diameter should be at least ¼ inch larger than the finished size to allow for waste in turning a perfect circle.

☐ Cut the circle with a bandsaw.

☐ Attach the outboard faceplate to the part of the disc that will eventually be the top of the tray. The screws should be placed in a portion of the tray that will eventually be waste.

☐ Turn the recessed part in the bottom of the tray ⅛-inch deep by 6 inches in diameter. Both Myford faceplates are 6 inches in diameter. See Fig. 12-39.

Turning the Underside of the Tray

☐ Turn the rest of the underside of the tray and sand with medium and fine grit sandpaper.

☐ Remove the faceplate and tray from the outboard end of the lathe and remove the faceplate from the tray.

☐ Place the faceplate in the recess turned in step 5, and attach to the tray with flathead screws. The screws must be placed so they will enter the thicker part of the tray.

☐ Place the faceplate and tray back on the lathe and turn the top of the tray. The deeper portion is turned with a square-end scraping tool while the rest is turned with the gouge, followed by a round-nose scraping tool to remove the rough grain. Sand with medium and fine

Fig. 12-39. Turning the underside of the hors d'oeuvre tray.

sandpaper while the tray is revolving in the lathe. See Fig. 12-40.

Turning The Top of the Tray

☐ Remove the faceplate and tray from the lathe and separate the two.

☐ Fill the screw holes in the bottom of tray with mahogany Plastic Wood. When dry sand flush.

☐ Finish tray with nontoxic polyurethane. See Fig. 12-41 and 12-42.

WIG STAND PLANTER

This is the second wig stand planter I have made. The first was made mahogany; this one is made of American black walnut. The first one was so richly admired by friends and relatives, because of its classical and traditional lines, that I decided to make a second one of different wood.

Originally, wig stand was topped by a large egg-shaped ball over which our ancestors placed their wigs for combing, powdering, and storing. Someone conceived the idea of converting the early American piece into a planter. As such it remains an attractive gem out of the past in the Colonial inspired home. It goes well in almost any style home except the ultracontemporary. This piece, in different styles and designs, was cherished by Colonial gentry in the middle 1700s in the Williamsburg area.

One reason for the selection of this piece of furniture is that with a minimum of expensive hardwood the craftsman can build a valuable heirloom that will endure indefinitely. Another reason for the selection is the large number of operations represented (although the major operations are spindle turning and faceplate turning).

The wig stand planter can be built of any of the common cabinet hardwoods (mahogany, cherry, walnut, teak, etc.). I chose walnut for this stand. See Table 12-4.

Laminated Ring

☐ Cut a backing piece of 13/16-inch white pine or some similar material at least 11⅝ inches in diameter. See Fig. 12-43.

☐ Draw two circles with a compass, one 11⅝ inches in diameter and one 8½ inches in diameter, on the backing piece using the same center mark.

☐ Glue a piece of heavy paper on each side of the center, but do not cover the center mark.

Fig. 12-40. Turning the topside of the hors d'oeuvre tray.

Fig. 12-41. The completed hors d'oeuvre tray.

Table 12-4. Wig Stand Planter Materials.

Pieces	Description	Size (Rough Sizes Only)	Material
16	Laminated Ring	1/4″ × 3 1/2″ × 8 1/4″	Walnut
3	"S" Scroll Ring Support	7/8″ × 2 1/2″ × 5 1/8″	Walnut
3	Short Turnings for Ring Support	1 1/4″ × 1 1/4″ × 5 1/2″	Walnut
1	Top Shelf	1 3/8″ × 8″ × 9 1/2″	Walnut
6	120° Overlays	3/16″ × 4 1/2″ × 6″	Walnut
3	Long Turnings	1 1/8″ × 1 1/8″ × 15″	Walnut
1	Bottom Shelf	1 5/8″ × 8″ × 9 1/2″	Walnut
3	Legs	1 1/8″ × 3″ × 9 1/2″	Walnut
12	Rosettes	3/16″ × 3/4″ × 3/4″	Walnut

☐ Glue up the 16 90-degree quadrant laminations into a ring. Glue up one layer at a time. Be sure enough clamps are on hand. After the glue is dry, glue the ring to the heavy paper on the backing piece.

☐ Drill a 1/32-inch hole through the center of the backing piece. This hole will assist in lining up the faceplate later.

☐ Attach outboard faceplate to the backing piece and laminated ring with flathead screws.

☐ File a registration mark on the faceplate and

Fig. 12-42. A hors d'euvre tray with hors d'oeuvres.

mark another registration, adjacent to the mark on the faceplate with a pencil or ball-point pen. This precautionary measure assures that the faceplate and the workpiece will be properly aligned if it is necessary to detach the faceplate.

☐ Make a pattern or template of the cross section of the ring on cardboard to check the turning of the ring. See the lower drawing in Fig. 12-43.

☐ Place the faceplate and workpiece on the outboard end of the lathe. If the lathe will swing a 12-inch diameter on the inboard side, it can be used. It is easier, however, to turn faceplate work on the outboard end of the lathe.

☐ Set the speed of the lathe at its lowest rate of rotation. Be sure that the tools are sharp. Turn the ring slowly and check with the template frequently. See Fig. 12-44.

☐ Sand the laminated ring while it is rotating. The speed of the lathe can be increased while sanding. Use successive grades of sandpaper. For best results use folded sandpaper.

☐ Remove the ring from the paper and backing piece with a sharp chisel. Work slowly and carefully around the perimeter of the ring. Sand off the paper that adhered to the ring.

S Scroll Ring Supports

☐ Make a pattern for the S scroll from heavy paper. The laminated ring sets on top of the S scroll ring supports. See Fig. 12-45.

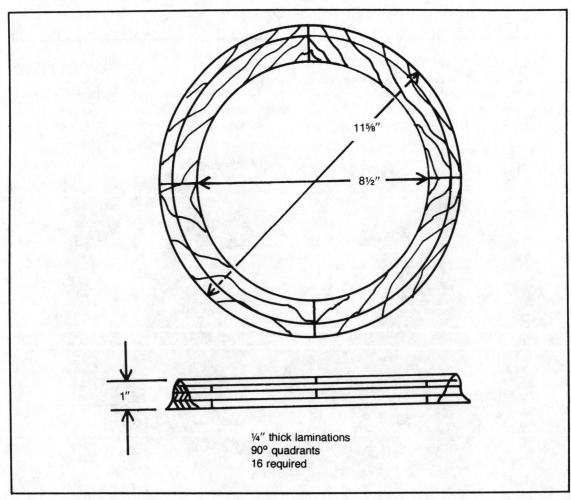

11⅝"

8½"

1"

¼" thick laminations
90° quadrants
16 required

Fig. 12-43. Laminated ring.

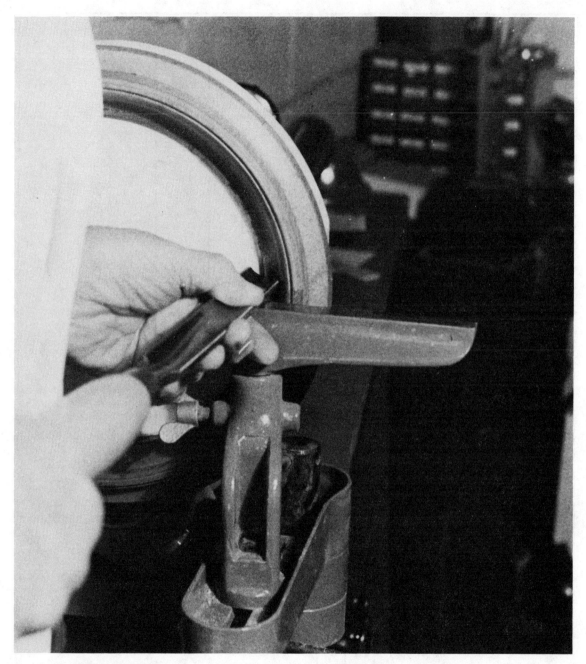

Fig. 12-44. Turning a laminated ring.

☐ Transfer the outline of the pattern to self-adhesive paper. Apply the self-adhesive patterns to the walnut stock.

☐ Saw out the S scrolls with a bandsaw. In order to cut the short radius curves at the two ends, it is necessary to make a series of saw kerfs to the edge of the curves unless a very narrow bandsaw blade is used. See Fig. 12-46.

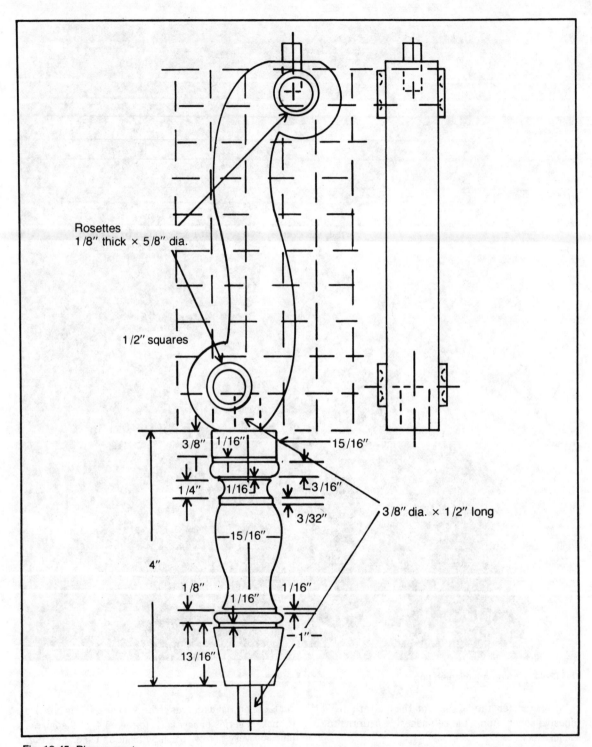

Rosettes
1/8″ thick × 5/8″ dia.

1/2″ squares

3/8″   1/16″   15/16″

1/4″   1/16″   3/16″

3/32″

3/8″ dia. × 1/2″ long

15/16″

4″

1/8″   1/16″   1/16″

1″

13/16″

Fig. 12-45. Ring support.

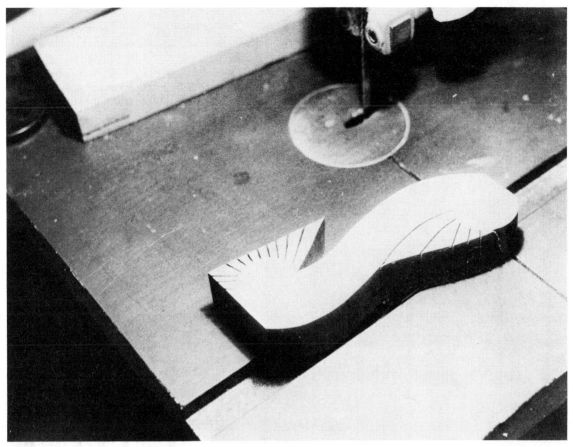

Fig. 12-46. Saw kerfs to assist in cutting short radii curves.

□ Sand the S scroll with successive grades of sandpaper. Bore the ¼-inch hole for the dowel at the top of scroll and a ⅜-inch hole at the bottom of the scroll.

Short Turning For Ring Support

□ Cut the stock for the three short turnings.

□ Mark the diagonal across the ends of the cut stock with a centering jig or with a scale. The centering jig can be used on both round and square stock.

□ Saw a saw kerf about ⅛-inch deep on the diagonals on one end of the short turnings. Drill a 1/16-inch diameter hole where the two kerfs intersect to accommodate the center of the spur drive center. If the hole is not drilled, the spur center is apt to split the wood when the spur center is driven into the saw kerfs.

□ Drill a small hole (about 1/32 of an inch in diameter) where the pencil lines intersect on the other end of the stock. This hole is to accommodate the tailstock center. See Fig. 12-47.

□ Remove the spur center and tailstock centers from the lathe and drive them into the stock held in a vise until the centers are firmly seated. Use a mallet for driving in the centers. Never use a hammer. The stock should never be driven into the center while the center is in the lathe because it might do damage to the lathe bearings. Insert the centers and stock into the lathe and turn the stock with a gouge until it is round. See Fig. 12-48.

□ Make a template of thin wood to indicate the major incisions and crucial diameters. A small V cut should be made at the edge of the template at every marked point to allow a sharply pointed pencil to slide into the rotating stock without wandering. Never use a scale or rule against rotating stock. Mark the incisions and diameters on the rotating stock. See Fig. 12-49.

□ Select the lathe tools for making the incisions. The parting tool is the one most generally used.

□ Set the calipers to the correct dimensions. The

caliper adjusting nut should be held away from the operator and between the middle finger and the finger adjacent to the little finger. This prevents the adjusting nut from vibrating and losing the correct setting. The calipers should be held in the right hand and the handle of the lathe tool should be held along the forearm of the left arm. For left-handed persons the tools are reverse. See Fig. 12-50.

☐ Check the diameter with the calipers after each cut with the lathe tool. Continue using the lathe tool and calipers alternately until the calipers barely slip over the turning. Never use calipers on stock that is not perfectly round. It could lead to a serious injury. Make all the necessary incision cuts. Finish turning the piece with appropriate lathe tools. Sand rotating stock with successive grades of folded sandpaper.

Top Shelf Of Wig Stand Planter

☐ Study Fig. 12-51. Note carefully how the grain

runs in the six 120-degree overlays (three on top and three on the bottom). The top and bottom shelves are essentially the same as far as the outside contour is concerned.

☐ Make the pattern of the shelf on heavy paper. Lay the pattern on 1⅜-inch thick stock and mark the contour. Saw the curves with a bandsaw. Sand the curves with an upside-down belt sander held in a vise. See Fig. 12-52.

☐ Make six 120-degree overlay segments. Be sure the angles are exactly 120 degrees.

☐ Tape three overlays for the top. Tape the other three for the bottom. See Fig. 12-53.

☐ Make the pattern of overlay segments about 3/16 of an inch larger, all the way around, than the 1⅜-inch thick base shelf pattern. Trace the pattern on the overlay segments and cut the outline on the bandsaw. Roll all the edges with rasp, file, and different grades of sandpaper.

☐ Glue the overlay segments to the base shelf with white glue. Be sure there are enough clamps available to

Fig. 12-47. Spur drive center and tailstock center.

Fig. 12-48. Turning to the round.

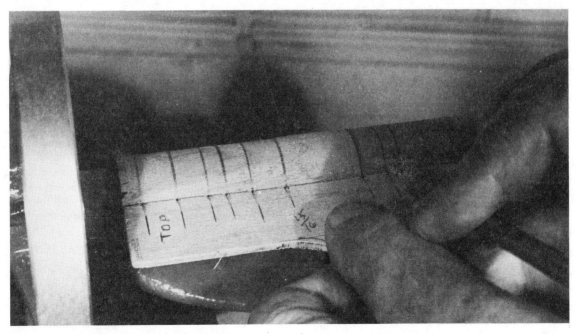

Fig. 12-49. Marking incisions of short turning.

Fig. 12-50. Establishing crucial dimensions on short turning.

do the job. Place wooden pads under the jaws of the clamps. Glue the bottom segments in the same fashion.

☐ When glue is dry, sand the top and bottom by hand, orbital sander, or finishing sander. A portable belt sander is hard to control on a piece this small.

Long Turnings For The Wig Stand Planter

☐ Make a template for the long turning. See Fig. 12-54.

☐ Cut stock to a rough size of 1⅛ × 1⅛ × 15 inches. Mark diagonals on the ends and saw kerfs for the spurs on the drive center.

☐ Place stock in the lathe and turn the stock to the round. Mark the incision points with the template while the lathe is running. Establish crucial dimensions with calipers and lathe tool.

☐ Finish turning the piece with appropriate lathe tools. Sand the rotating stock with successive grades of folded sandpaper.

Bottom Shelf

☐ Cut stock for the bottom shelf (Fig. 12-55). Mark with the same pattern as used to mark the top shelf.

☐ Cut the contour with the bandsaw. Sand the edges with the upside-down belt sander.

☐ Lay out the dovetail mortises for the legs on the underside of the bottom shelf. The dovetail is ⅝ of an inch long, ¾ of an inch across the wider part, and ½ inch across the narrow part.

☐ Cut dovetail mortises with a dovetail saw and mortise chisel. Leave a little stock to be removed when the individual legs are fitted.

☐ Fasten the side of shelf with the dovetail mortises to the faceplate. Turn the recessed portion to the dimensions indicated in Fig. 12-55. Then sand the two flat faces by hand, after removing the piece from the faceplate.

Legs

☐ Make the pattern for the legs as shown in Fig. 12-56.

☐ Trace the pattern on 1⅛-inch stock. Cut the rough blanks for legs on the bandsaw. See Fig. 12-57.

☐ Cut the dovetail tenons with the dovetail saw. See Fig. 12-58.

□ Shape the legs to conform to the dimensions shown on the drawing with spokeshave, Surform, rasps, and sandpaper. A drum sander or the end of an upside-down portable belt sander can be used to advantage here. See Fig. 12-59.

□ Fit the leg dovetails into the dovetail mortises in the bottom shelf and glue the legs in place.

Rosettes

□ Cut enough 3/16-inch stock for 12 rosettes.

□ Draw 12 circles ¾ of an inch in diameter on the stock.

□ Cut the circles with a jigsaw or coping saw.

□ Cut a circle of ½-inch stock on the bandsaw or jigsaw at least 2 inches in diameter and mount on the faceplate. I used the Dremel Motor-Lathe and the Dremel miniature lathe tools.

□ True up the wood faceplate and inscribe a ⅝-inch diameter on the face while it is turning in the lathe.

□ Drive three small brads into the faceplate inside the inscribed circle.

□ Cut off the heads of the brads, leaving 1/16 of an inch of the brad protruding. File the brads to a sharp point.

□ Drive the rosette stock onto the sharp brads with a wooden mallet and turn to conform to the dimensions shown in Fig. 12-3. Glue the rosettes to the S scroll supports as shown in Fig. 12-3.

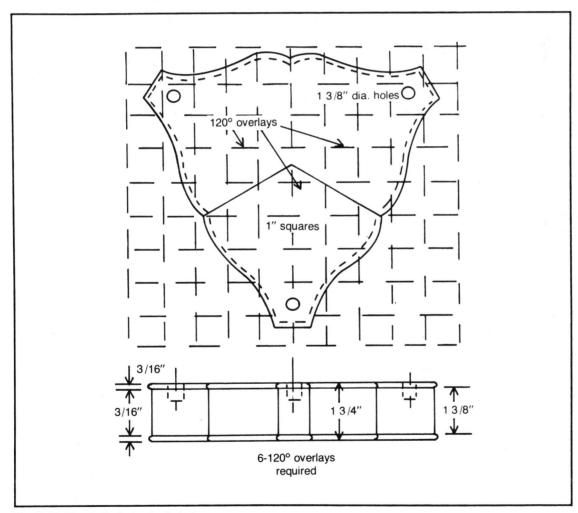

Fig. 12-51. Top shelf of wig stand planter.

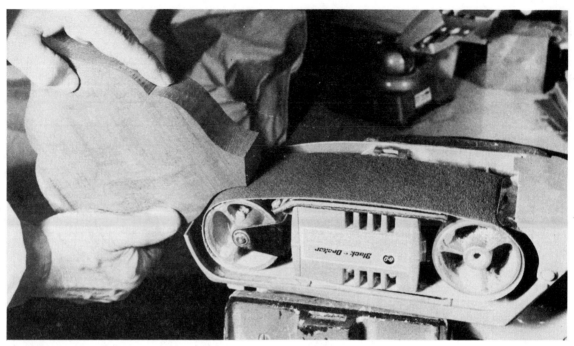

Fig. 12-52. Sanding curves of shelf on upside-down belt sander.

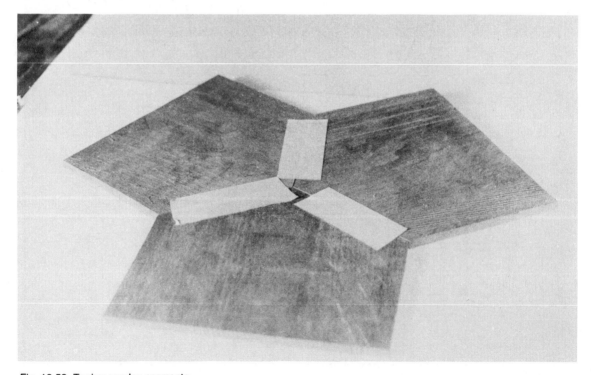

Fig. 12-53. Taping overlay segments.

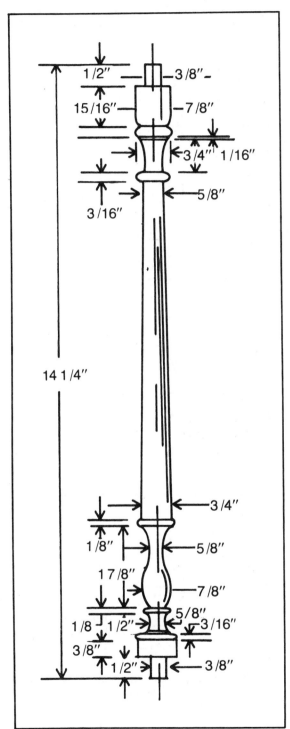

Fig. 12-54. Long turning for wig stand planter.

Assembly

☐ Bore ¼-inch diameter holes in the tops of the S scrolls ½ inch deep.

☐ Cut three ¼-inch dowels ¾ of an inch long.

☐ Drive the three ¼-inch dowels into the holes at the top of the S scrolls after glue has been applied. One-quarter inch of dowel should protrude from the top of the scroll.

☐ Bore ⅜-inch-diameter holes, ½ inch deep, in the bottom of the S scrolls to receive the dowel-turned ends of the short turnings.

☐ Bore three holes ¼ inch in diameter, ¼ inch deep, in the laminated ring 120 degrees apart.

☐ Glue short turnings to the S scrolls.

☐ Glue the short turning S scroll subassembly into the laminated ring. The top of the S scroll should point away from the center of the wig stand planter.

☐ Before the glue has had a chance to set, place the subassembly on top of the top shelf. It might be necessary to force the short turning S scroll subassembly into position before the glue is set. When it is properly positioned over the three "horns" of the shelf, draw circles around the turned ends of the short turnings. Mark the centers with an awl and bore ⅜-inch-diameter holes ½ inch deep in the top of the top shelf.

☐ Bore three ⅜-inch diameter holes ½ inch deep on the underside of the top shelf and on the top of the bottom shelf.

☐ Position the long turnings in place.

☐ Test assemble the entire wig stand planter.

☐ Disassemble the parts not yet glued.

☐ Glue, reassemble, and clamp.

Finish

☐ Sand the project with 4/0-150 sandpaper after the glue has set.

☐ Make a glue size of hot water mixed with Le-Page's or Franklin liquid animal glue. Use at least 13 parts of water to 1 part of glue.

☐ Apply the glue size to the entire project with a natural or synthetic sponge. Apply only enough size to moisten the wood—no puddles. This step is particularly important if a stain is to be applied. After 8 to 10 hours, sand the project with 6/0-220 sandpaper.

☐ Apply a sealer washcoat of thin shellac or lacquer sealer. At least twice as much thinner should be used as there is sealer material. This washcoat prevents the stain from sinking in more rapidly in some places than others, and it provides a casing around the filler which prevents

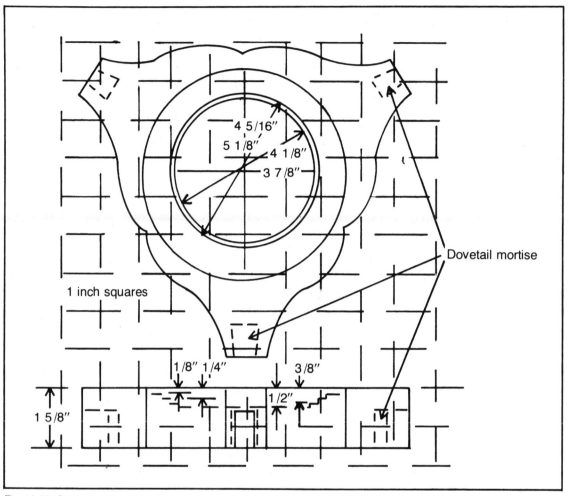

Fig. 12-55. Bottom shelf of wig stand planter.

the oil from the filler from sinking into the wood too rapidly.

☐ Apply stain. If the project contains no sapwood, it might be advisable not to stain. I did not use stain on the walnut wig stand planter.

☐ Apply paste filler. For walnut or mahogany, the filler should be darker than the stained wood. When the filler starts to dull, rub it with the lower part of the palm of your hand. Follow with rags or pieces of burlap rubbing across the grain. Remove the filler from incisions and corner with a rag over a sharpened stick.

☐ Apply two thin coats of lacquer sealer or shellac. When dry, sand with 8/0-280 or 9/0-320 abrasive paper. Use #0000 steel wool on the turnings.

☐ Apply a glaze you prefer. It does a lot to enhance

the finish of traditional furniture.

☐ Apply one coat of shellac or lacquer sealer or clear spray Deft over the glaze coat. This coat must be applied as a spray. If the finish is brushed on the glaze will smear.

☐ Apply three coats of clear lacquer, varnish, or polyurethane. If a flat or dull finish is preferred, do not apply the flat coat until the last coat because it does not have the body of the gloss finishes.

☐ Rub the finish with rottenstone and oil if a high gloss, "piano" finish is preferred.

☐ Apply furniture polish or wax. Avoid waxes with a paraffin base. Buff the wax until an even polish is attained. See Figs. 12-60 and 12-61.

208

EARLY AMERICAN CANDLESTICK

This Early American candlestick is made in two parts. The upper part is turned between centers. The base is turned on a faceplate or chuck. Because of the number of operations performed, it makes a fine instructional project in schools or other training situations.

Pine is not the best wood for turning and for that reason tools must be kept extra sharp. It is advisable to distress this project sparingly and to use a glaze to emphasize aging.

Procedure:

Top

☐ Cut a piece of white pine stock 5½ inches long (1-inch allowance for waste) by 1¾ inches square.

☐ Draw diagonals across the two ends to establish centers.

☐ Indent centers with a center punch or awl.

☐ Saw a saw kerf, about ⅛ of an inch deep, on one end on one of the diagonals. The live or drive center will enter the saw cut for positive drive.

☐ On the end opposite the saw kerf, bore a ⅞-inch diameter hole about ½ of an inch deep to hold the candle. Small brass rings are available to insert into the hole.

☐ Take the drive center from the lathe and drive the spurs into the saw kerf. Use only a wooden mallet.

☐ Advance the tailstock center until it enters the center depression left by the ⅞-inch bit.

☐ Turn the stock to 1⅝-inch diameter.

☐ Make a template or marking stick to mark out the natural divisions out of a piece of wood about 1-inch wide

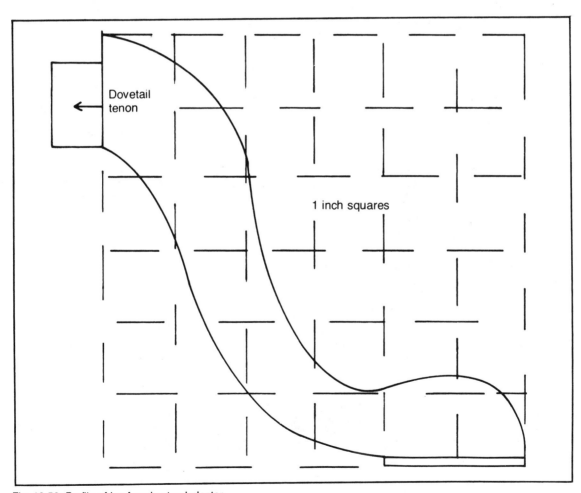

Fig. 12-56. Profile of leg for wig stand planter.

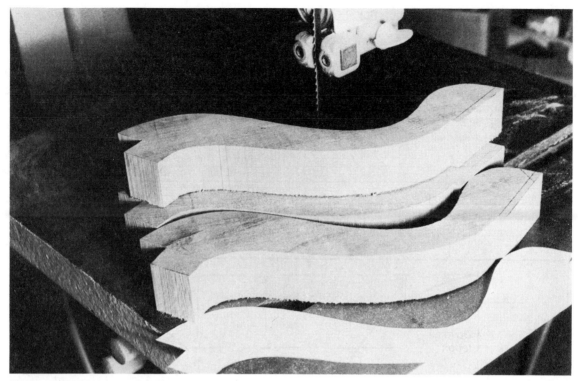

Fig. 12-57. Rough bandsawed legs with pattern.

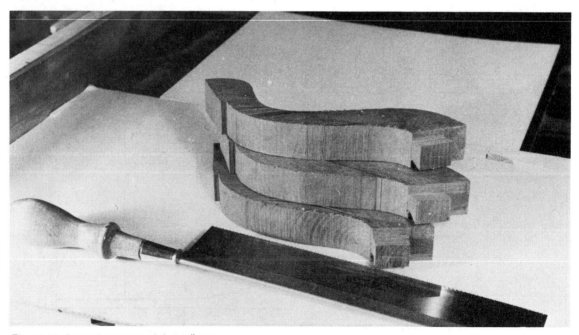

Fig. 12-58. Dovetail tenons and dovetail saw.

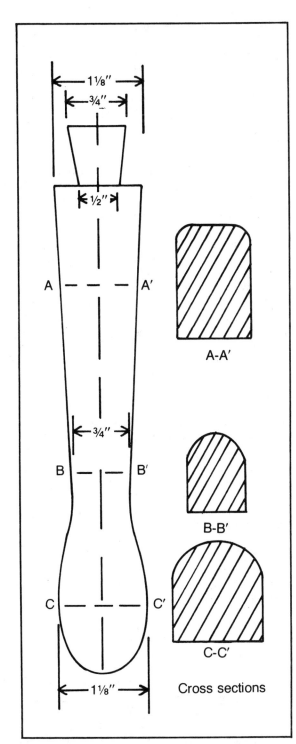

Fig. 12-60. Wig stand planter assembled.

and ⅛-inch thick. Make a small V cut at each mark so a long pencil point will enter the V when marking.

☐ Adjust the tool rest to about ¼-inch from the stock and slightly below center.

☐ Hold the marking stick about ⅛ of an inch from the revolving stock after it is turned round and with a sharp pencil mark the beads and grooves on the rotating stock. Note: Never use a scale, rule, or other measuring tools close to or against rotating stock. The measuring tool can be easily damaged or broken.

☐ Turn the stock to the dimensions shown in Fig. 12-62 with a variety of lathe tools (parting tool, skew, round nose and diamond point). Be sure to turn the ¾-inch- × -½-inch-long dowel that goes into the base very accurately.

☐ Use folded sandpaper for sanding the beads. Be careful not to flatten the tops of the beads. Use coarse sandpaper to smooth all end grain before using finer sandpaper.

Base of Candlestick

☐ Cut a circle of waste stock from the scrap box at

Fig. 12-59. Top view of leg for wig stand planter.

Fig. 12-61. Wig stand planter with accessories and plant.

bandsaw, and glue to the paper on the waste stock.

☐ When the glue is dry, turn the white pine to a 4-inch in diameter.

☐ Turn to the size and shape as depicted in Fig. 12-62.

☐ Turn the dowel hole ¾ of an inch in diameter and ½ inch deep in the center of the base. Stop the lathe, from time to time, to test whether the dowel on the spindle turning will fit. It should fit the base fairly snug, but with allowance for glue.

☐ Apply glue to the spindle dowel and insert the spindle into the base. Advance the tailstock center until it enters the candle hole. This will guarantee that the spindle is on straight and will hold the spindle in place until the glue has had time to set.

☐ Remove any excess glue after the glue has set. Back off the tailstock and remove the faceplate from the waste stock and candlestick.

☐ With a sharp knife or chisel, carefully pry the candlestick from the waste stock. Part of the paper will adhere to the candle stick base and part to the waste stock. Sand the base of candlestick until the paper is removed.

CUTTING BOARD

Cutting boards have many uses, vegetables, meats and cheeses and many other items may be cut into small pieces on the board. The cutting board can also be used as a server of hors d'oeuvres and as a platform for hot dishes.

Usually cooking oils are used to finish cutting boards; I used polyurethane. The cutting board, finished with polyurethane, should be left to cure for a number of days before using, otherwise the polyurethane is apt to leave an undesirable taste or odor.

It is highly desirable that the wood for cutting boards be laminated. Solid, one-piece cutting boards are apt to warp after being wiped off with a damp cloth a number of times. Under no circumstance should cutting boards be immersed in water.

Board

☐ Cut enough ¾-inch-thick, 1¾-inch-wide maple stock to make an 8-inch square.

☐ Glue up the stock with a good-quality glue.

☐ Clamp with three or four short bar clamps.

☐ After the glue is dry, plane the stock down to 1⅝ inches thick.

☐ Sand one face that goes next to the faceplate.

least ½-inch thick and 5 inches in diameter, on the bandsaw.

☐ Fasten the circle to the faceplate with flathead screws and center as close as possible.

☐ Smooth up the face with a square-nose chisel.

☐ While the lathe is running, scribe a 4½-inch-diameter circle on the waste stock.

☐ Cut a circle of paper 4⅜ inches in diameter and glue to the circle of waste stock inside the 4½-inch circle.

☐ With a pencil compass, swing a 4¼-inch circle on ¾-inch-thick pine, cut to the compass line with the

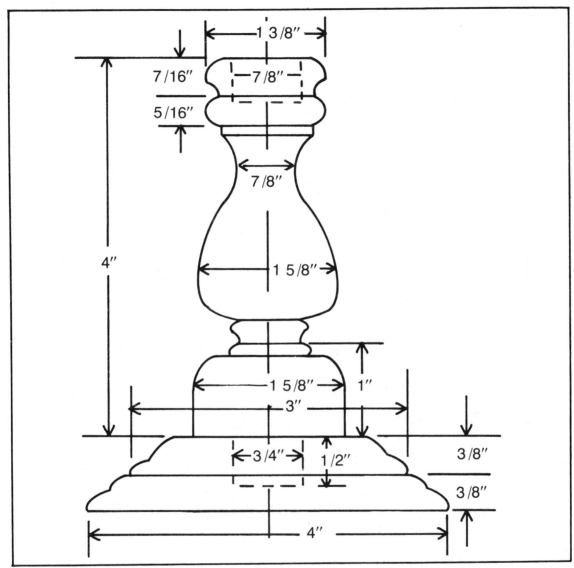

Fig. 12-62. Early American candlestick details.

□ On the same face, draw diagonals to establish a center.

□ From this center, swing a 7-inch-diameter circle with a pencil compass or dividers.

□ Bandsaw a circle of stock about ¼ inch outside the 7-inch-diameter penciled circle.

□ Mark and cut a circle from ¾-inch scrap stock about 8 inches in diameter.

□ Fasten this piece of scrap stock to the faceplate with flathead screws aligning the center mark with the hole in the faceplate.

□ Glue a piece of paper to the cutting board stock and glue both the wooden faceplate made in the step before last.

□ This method, which is known as glue/paper chucking, will eliminate screw holes in the cutting board.

□ Attach the faceplate, the wooden waste faceplate and the cutting-board stock to the lathe. It can be attached

213

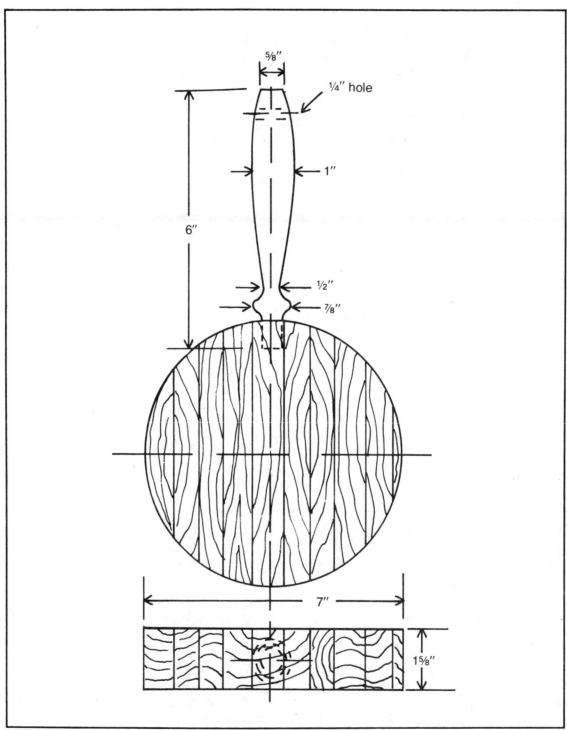

Fig. 12-63. Cutting board details.

Fig. 12-64. The completed cutting board.

to either the outboard or inboard spindle.

☐ Turn the cutting board to 7 inches in diameter. Sand both the edges and the face, first with fairly coarse sandpaper 2/0-100, followed by 5/0-180 paper, rounding over the corners.

☐ With a wide, sharp chisel, tap gently at the glue line all around the edges of the turning. Insert a sharp knife at the glue/paper line and the turning will break loose from the wooden faceplate. About half of the paper will cling to the board and the other half to the faceplate. Sand the paper from the cutting board.

☐ Bore a ½-inch hole about ¾ of an inch deep in the center of the edge for the handle. See Fig. 12-63. Be sure the hole is bored directly toward the center of the board.

Handle

☐ Cut a piece of maple stock 1¼ × 1¼ × 8 inches; this allows 1 inch of waste at each end.

☐ Draw diagonals across each end to establish centers.

☐ Make a saw kerf, about ⅛ of an inch deep, on one of the diagonals. This end will be used at the drive center.

☐ Drill a 1/16-inch hole, on both ends, at the centers that have been indented with an awl.

☐ Remove the drive center from the lathe and drive the spurs into the kerf. Use only a wooden mallet. A metal hammer is apt to ruin the center.

☐ Place the drive center and stock into the lathe and advance the tailstock center to enter the center at the right end.

☐ Turn the handle to the right size and shape. Be sure the dowel end that goes into the board is held to an exact ½-inch diameter.

☐ Cut off the two ends in the waste stock with the parting tool after the handle has been sanded with fine sandpaper.

☐ Bore a ¼-inch hole, ⅝ of an inch from the end opposite the dowel end. Make a V block out of scrap wood to place on the drill press table to prevent the handle from turning.

☐ Glue the handle into the board. See Figs. 12-63 and 12-64.

☐ Finish the handle and board with polyurethane or cooking oil if you prefer.

☐ Cut an 8-inch or 9-inch length from a rawhide shoe or boot lace and thread the piece through the hole in the handle. The cutting board can then be hung on the wall as a decorative piece.

Appendix A

Suppliers and Manufacturers

A & M Wood Specialty
358 Eagle St., North
Cambridge (Preston)
N3H 4S6 Ontario, Canada

*Domestic,
imported,
and exotic
hardwood lumber*

Albrecht, Robert M.
18701 Parthenice St.
Northridge, CA 91324

*Domestic,
imported,
and exotic
hardwood lumber
and PEG
(polyethylene
gloycol 1000)*

American Hardwood Co.
1900 East 15th St.
Los Angeles, CA 90021

*Domestic,
imported,
and exotic
hardwood lumber*

American Machine and
Tool Co.
4th and Spring St.
Royersford, PA 19468

*Power
woodworking
tools*

American Woodcrafters
Box 919
Piqua, OH 45356

*Veneers,
hardwoods,
carvings,
and turning blocks*

American Wood Working Co.
Montello, WI 53949

*Domestic
Hardwoods
and Manu-
facturer of wood parts*

Atlas Press Co.,
2019 N. Pitcher
Kalamazoo, MI 49007

*Power and
hand tools*

Austin Hardwoods, Inc.
2125 Goodrich
Austin, TX 78704

*Domestic
and imported
hardwood
lumber*

Baer American, Inc.,
Dept. W-B103
RT 2, Box 152
Edgerton, WI 53534

*Manufacturer
of "Heavy-
weight" Wood-
turning lathe*

Bedford Lumber Co., Inc.
Box 65
Shelbyville, TN 37160

*Domestic
hardwood lumber*

Beauty-Wood Industries
339 Lakeshore Rd. E
Mississauga, Ontario, Canada

*Hardwoods
and Soft-
woods*

The Board Store
Box 205
Bangor, EI 54614

*Kiln-dried
hardwoods*

Collins Hardwood Co.
500 W. Wesley
Denver, CO 80223

*Domestic
hardwood lumber*

Chester B. Stern, Inc.
2708 Grant Line Road
New Albany, IN 47150

*Foreign
and domestic
hardwood
and veneer*

Classic Grain
Hardwood Co.
902 E. Hughes Access Road
Tucson, AZ 85706

*Hardwoods,
wholesale only*

Constantine & Son, Inc.
2065 B. Eastchester Road
Bronx, NY 10461

*Furniture
woods,
tools, hardware
finishing material and
many other items*

Cotton Hanlon, Inc.
Cayta, NY 14824

*Domestic,
imported, and
exotic hardwood lumber*

Craftsman Wood
Service Co.
1735 West Cortland St.
Addison, IL 60101

*Tools, hardwoods,
Veneers, finishing
materials,
toy parts and many other
items for the woodworker*

Craftwoods
(Div. of O'Shea
Lumber Co.)
York Road and Beaver
Run Lane
Cockeysville, MD 21030

*Foreign hardwoods,
domestic hard-
woods, veneers and
cabinet
plywoods*

The Crane Creek Co.
Box 5553
Madison, WI 53705

D.A. Buckley
R 1, W. Valley, NY 14171

*Native American
hardwoods*

Deft
17451 Von Karman Ave.
Irvine, CA 92714
or
411 East Keystone Ave.
Alliance, OH 44601

Finishing materials

Diehl Machines
P.O. Box 465
Wabash, IN 46992

*Automatic wood-
turning machines*

Dremel
Div. of Emerson
Electric Co.,
Racine, WI 53406

*Small electrical power
woodworking tools,
including lathe
and woodturning
tools*

Du-er Tools
5448 Edina Ind. Blvd.
Minneapolis, MN 55435

*Power woodworking
tools*

Educational Lumber Co.
21 Meadow Ct. Box 5373
Asheville, NC 28803

*Appa-
lachian hard-
woods and
veneers*

Emco-Lux Corp.
2050 Fairwood Ave
Columbus, OH 43107

*Universal
combination
power wood-
working tools*

Exotic Woodshed
65 N. York Road
Warminster, PA 18974

*Domestic,
imported, and
exotic
hardwood lumber*

Fair Price Tool Co.
La Canada, CA 91011

*Hand clamps, work-
benches, vises, chisels,
hand tools, books, and
sharpening stones*

*PEG (polyeth-
ylene glycol 1000)
stabilizer and chemical
seasoning agent. retail
and bulk*

The Fine Tool Shop
1200 E. Post Road
Westport, CT 06880

*Power tools,
measuring and
lay-out tools, hardware,
clamps, books, drills*

Forest City Tool Co.
Ex-Cell-O Corp.
P.O. Box 788
Hickory, NC 28601

*Woodworking
machines, saws,
cutter knives, and
mill supplies*

Fox Super Shop, Inc.
6701 W. 110th St.
Bloomington, MN 55438

*7-in-1
super shop
multi-purpose
power tool*

Frog Tool Co., Lyd.
548 North Wells St.
Chicago, IL 60610

*Representatives for My-
ford lathes and
quality hand wood-
working tools*

General Woodcraft
100 Blinman St.
New London, CT 06320

*Domestic
and
imported
hardwood, plywood
and veneer*

Gilliom Mfg. Co.
St. Charles, MO 63301

*Power tool kits
to build
your own power tools*

Glenn Wing
1437 S. Woodward Ave.
Birmingham, MI 48011

*Representatives for
Rockwell,
Bosch, and
Stanley Power Tools*

GMAMS
Box 19651
Rimpan Station
Los Angeles, CA 90019

*Manufacturers of the
GIZCO Wood-turning
duplicator*

Goodspeed Machine Co.
15 Elm St.
Winchendon, MA 01475

*Industrial
woodworking ma-
chinery*

Green Mountain
Cabins, Inc.
(Weird Wood) Box 190
Chester, VT 05143

*Hardwood, soft-
wood, boards, slabs,
and free-
form cut ovals*

Hattersley &
Davidson, Ltd.
803/817 Chesterfield Road
Sheffield S8 OSR, England

*6-in-1 universal
lathe chuck*

Hayes Patterns
6 Willow St. Dept. W21
Wodburn, MA 01801

*Woodworking
patterns*

Henegan's Wood Shed
7760 Southern Blvd.
West Palm Beach, FL 33411

*All kinds
of lumber*

Hobbywoods
1305 Eastern Ave.
Baltimore, MD 21231

*Domestic, imported
and exotic hard-
wood lumber*

Hoge Lumber Co.
New Knoxville, OH 45871

*Domestic
hardwood
lumber*

Holz Machine Co.
45 Halladay St.
Jersy City, NJ 07304

*Power wood-
working tools*

House of Hardwoods
610 Freeman St.
Orange, NJ

*Hardwood,
plywood, veneers,
carving blocks
and burls*

Industrial Arts
Supply Co.
5724 W. 36th St.
Minneapolis, MN 55416

*PEG (polyeth-
ylene glycol 1000)*

International Woodworking
Equipment Corporation
11665 Coley River Creek
Fountain Valley, CA 92708

*Man-
ufacturer
of HAPLO
Model AHDK Standard
Woodturning Lathe and
KA-TS3 Copier.*

Interstate Hardwood
Co. Inc.
850 Flora St.
Elizabith, NJ 07201

*Hardwoods.
No mail orders*

John Harra Wood
and Supply Co.
39 W. 19th St.
New York, NY 10011

*Domestic,
imported, and
exotic hardwood
lumber*

Johnson's Workbench Box 278 Charlotte, MI 48813	*Domestic, imported, and exotic hardwood lumber*	New England Hobby Supply, Inc. Manchester, CT	*Bell Yankee Chucker to use with dremel lathe*
Jones Sheet Metal, Inc. 1524 First Ave. Mankato, MN 56002	*Manufac- turer of the LeGwns wood- turning duplicator*	Nor Cal Walnut Products 1365 Walnut Ave. Redding, CA 96001	*Walnut lathe blocks*
Lake Superior Lumber Co. Box 600 Iron Mountain, MI 49801	*Domestic hardwood lumber*	Northfield Foundry and Machine Co. Northfield, MN 55057	*Power tools*
Leichtung, Inc. 701 Beta Drive Cleveland, OH 44143	*Professional (German) wood bits and depth adjusting collars, workbenches, hand tools, portable power tools, chisels, gouges, etc.*	Oliver Machine Co. 445 6th St. Grand Rapids, MI 49504	*Power wood- working tools*
		Paul Killinger Hardwoods 4309 Butler Circle Boulder, CO 80303	*Imported and exotic hardwood lumber*
Lemco Tools, Inc. Box 1664 Dept. E Sedalia, MO 65301	*"Diaccurate" woodturning tools*	Penofin Co. 819 J Street Sacramento, CA 95814	*Penetrating oil finishes*
Lemont Specialties Box 271 Lemont, PA 16851	*PEG (polyethylene glycol 1000)*	Poitras, Danckaert Woodworking Machine Co. 891 Howell Mill Road., N.W. Atlanta, GA 30318	*Power wood- working tools*
Mattison Machine Works Rockford, IL 61101	*Mattison automatic industrial mass-producing lathes*	Polamco 755 Greenleaf Ave. Elk Groove Village, IL 60007	*Power woodworking tools*
Maurice L. Condon Co., Inc. 248 Ferris Ave. White Plains, NY 10603	*Domestic and foreign hardwoods and softwoods*	Powermatic Division Houdaille Ind. Inc. Morrison Rd. Box 70 McMinnville, TN 37110	*Power Wood- working tools*
Midland Walnut Co. Box 262 Savannah, GA 64485	*Domestic hard- wood lumber*	Precision Concepts 4200 Westgrove, Box 918 Addison, TX 75001	*Power wood- working tools*
Myford Limited Beston, Nottingham England	*Myford lathe and acces- sories*	Raab-Kirk Co. P.O. Box 208 Corvallis, OR	*Vertical wood- turning tools*
Native American Hardwoods West Valley, NY 14171	*Domestic hard- wood lumber*	Ring Master, Inc. P.O. Box 8527A Orlando, FL 32856	*Perfect con- centric ring cutter*

Robert M. Albrecht
8635 Yolanda Ave.
Northbridge, CA 91324

PEG (polyethylene glycol 1000)

Rockwell International
400 N. Lexington Ave.
Pittsburgh, PA 15208

Power woodworking tools

Russ Zimmerman
RFD3, Box 57A
Putney, VT 05346

Myford lathe distributor

The Sawmill
P.O. Box 329
Nazareth, PA 18064

Exotic and precious woods, wholesale only

Sears Roebuck and Co.
Dept 141
925 S. Homan Ave.
Chicago, IL 60607

Woodworking tools and supplies

Shopsmith, Inc.
750 Outer Drive
Vandalia, OH 45377

Five major power tools packaged into one

Spielmans Wood Works
188 Gibraltar Road
Fish Creek, WI 54212

PEG (polyethylene glycol 1000)

Sprunger Corp.
Box 1621
Elkhart, IN 46515

Power woodworking tools

Tannewitz Division
3940 Clay Ave., S.W.
Grand Rapids, MI 49508

Power woodworking tools

Toolmark Co.
6840 Shingle Creek Parkway
Minneapolis, MN 55400

Lathe duplicator Attachment

TOTAL Shop
P.O. Box 16297
Greenville, SC 29606

Manufacturers of a combination 5-in-1 power woodworking machine

Turnmaster Corp.
11665 Coley River Circle
Fountain Valley, CA
92708

Manufacturers of the glaser screw chuck

Turn-O-Carve Tool Co.
P.O. Box 8315
Tampa, Florida 33674

Lathe turning duplicator

Wadkin Ltd.
Green Lane Wks.
Leicester, England
LE5 4PF

Power woodworking tools

Watco-Dennis Corp.
Michigan Ave. at 22nd St.
Santa Monica, CA 90404

Danish oil wood finish

Weird Wood
Box 190
Chester, VT 05143

Hardwoods and softwoods in boards, slabs and freeform cut ovals

W. I. G. (Wood Is Good) Co.
Box 477
Lakewood, CA 90174

Wood-carving tools and blocks

Wilkens-Anderson Co.
4525 West Division St.
Chicago, IL 60651

PEG (polyethylene glycol 1000)

Willard Brothers
Woodcutters
300 Basin Road
Trenton, NJ 08619

Wood flitches, slabs, mantle clocks, carving blocks, dimension and unusual woods

Woodcraft Supply Co.
313 Montvale Ave.
Woburn, MA 01801

Tools hardware, finishing materials, craft supplies, books, etc.

Wood Shed
1807 Elmwood Ave.
Buffalo, NY 14207

Hardwoods and veneer

Woodshop Specialties
Box 1013
East Middlebury, VT 05740

Stationary woodworking machines and related accessories

Woodstream Hardwoods
Box 11471
Knoxville, TN 37919

Retail and wholesale exotic and domestic hardwoods

The Woodworker's Store
21801 Industrial Blvd.
Rogers, MN 55374

*3000 wood-
working
items and
domestic hardwood lumber*

Woodworker's Tool Works
222-224 S. Jefferson St.
Chicago, IL 60606

Tools

Woodworker's Supply, Inc.
P.O. Box 14117
Albuquerque, NM 87112

*Wood-
working tools*

Wood World
9006 Waukegan Road
Morton Grove, IL 60053

*Foreign and do-
mestic hard-
woods*

Woodworks
Box 79238
Saginaw, TX 76179

*Hardwoods and
dowels*

Yates/American
Machine Co.
Roscoe, IL 61073

*Power
woodworking
and industrial
woodworking machines*

Appendix B

Design Idea Sources

Books

Educational Affairs Department *Creative Design for the Industrial Arts Teacher*. Dearborn, Michigan: Ford Motor Co.

Gloag, John *Industrial Art Explained*. New York: The Macmillan Co.

Gump, Richard *Good Taste Costs No More*. New York: Doubleday & Co.

Hatjie, Gerd and John Peter, editors *New Furniture*. New York: George Wittenborn, Inc.

Kaufman, Edgar Jr. *Fifty Years of Danish Silver*. New York: Museum of Modern Art.

Kaufman, Edgar Jr. *Prize Designs for Modern Furniture*. New York: Museum of Modern Art.

Kaufman, Edgar J. *What's Modern Design?* New York: Museum of Modern Art.

Noyes, Eliot F. *Organic Design*. New York: Museum of Modern Art.

Nelson, George *Chairs*. New York: Whitney Publications.

Nelson, George *Living Spaces*. New York: Whitney Publications.

Olivetti *Design In Industry*. New York: Museum of Modern Art.

Read, Herbert *Art and Industry*. New York: Horizon Press, Inc.

Ritchie, Andrew C. *Good Design in Your Business*. Buffalo, New York: The Holling Press, Inc.

Scott, Robert *Design Fundamentals*. New York: McGraw-Hill Book Co.

Schultz, Inc., Wittenborn *Idea Book*. International Design Annaual. New York.

Sekely, Dezso *Contemporary Industrial Arts Projects*. Bloomington, Illinois: McKnight & McKnight Publications.

Van Doren, Harold *Industrial Design*. New York: McGraw-Hill Book Co.

Wallace, D. *Shaping America's Products*. New York: Reinhold Publishing Corp.

Catalogs and Brochures

A.B.C. of Modern Furniture
The Herman Miller Furniture Co.
Zeelan, MI

Furniture Catalog
Jens Risom, Inc.
49 East 53rd St.
New York, NY

Knoll Associates, Inc.
575 Madison Ave.
New York, NY

Furniture Catalog
Van Keppel-Green
Beverly Hills, CA

Magazines
Arts and Architecture
3305 Wilshire Blvd.
Los Angeles, CA

Design Quarterly
Walker Art Center
1710 Lyndale Ave.
South Minneapolis, MN

Fine Woodworking
The Taunton Press
52 Church Hill Road
Box 355
Newtown, CT 06470

Workbench Magazine
Modern Handcraft, Inc.
4251 Pennsylvania
Kansas City, MO 64111

Industrial Design
Whitney Publications
18 East 50th St.
New York, NY

Glossary

abrasive—Another term for sandpaper.

auger—A boring bit used with a hand brace.

bead—A raised, semicircular protrusion on turned stock.

bed—The base of a lathe on which the headstock, tool rest saddle, and tailstock rests.

Bodger's lathe—A primitive lathe operated by wrapping string around the workpiece.

bow lathe—A bow string wrapped around the stock operates the lathe.

burl—A growth on a tree that might be described as a tree wart. It has no grain direction.

burnisher—Used to turn the wire edge of a scraping tool or scraper. Also called a ticketer.

butterfly nut—A hand-operated nut with two wings.

calipers—Used to measure outside diameters of round, spindle stock.

Carnauba—A wax from a Brazilian palm tree.

center, four-spur—A four-prong drive center, used primarily with softwood.

center, two-spur—A two prong drive center, used primarily with hardwood. Sometimes called a fork chuck or a prong chuck.

centering jig—A device for marking centers on square and round stock.

centers—Cylindrical-shaped devices, usually ground to a Morse taper, that support spindle turnings on the lathe.

center-tailstock—Sometimes called dead centers as opposed to live or drive centers.

chisel—A cutting tool with a rectangular or square cross section.

chuck—A lathe attachment for holding workpieces. It is generally used on the headstock spindle without the aid of the tailstock.

club foot—An enlarged end of a leg.

collet—A two or more part, expanding, contracting device for holding tools or workpieces.

"color dynamics"—A multicolor system for painting machines and shop areas.

cone pulley—A series of adjacent, different-size pulleys for varying lathe speeds.

contour gauge—A device with overlapping thin leaves that duplicates irregular-shaped objects.

countersink—An angle or bevel shape bored into a hole. Often used for flathead screws. Also the name of the tool used for this purpose.

"cyclone"—A part of a dust collecting system.

depth gauge—A tool for measuring the depth of holes and depressions.

diamond or spear—Terms used to describe spear-shaped scraping tools used on the lathe.

dividers—A tool used for scribing circles or marking out equal divisions.

dowel—A uniform turned part of different diameters, usually to fit a hole of the same size.

duplicator—A lathe attachment for making multiple turnings exactly alike.

faceplate turning—Turning that involves only the headstock. Spindle turnings involve both the headstock and the tailstock.

ferrule—A short, metal tube to prevent the splitting of a tool handle.

FHB—An abbreviation for "flat head bright." A term generally used to describe flathead screws.

Fingernail gouge—Another name for a spindle-turning gouge. So named because of the shape of the cutting edge.

fork chuck—Another term for a two-spur center.

forstner—A special bit used primarily for counterboring.

freewheel lathe—A ratcher bicycle sprocket is the major component of this lathe.

French polishing—A method of finishing while the lathe and workpiece are revolving. The components are shellac and oil.

gap-bed lathe—A lathe with a gap in the base which allows larger faceplate work to be turned than would ordinarily be possible.

gouge—A cutting tool with a "U" shaped, curved cross section.

hand brace—A tool used with auger bits for boring holes in wood.

headstock—The heavy casting at the left end of a lathe that provides the power for turning.

headstock spindle—A part of the headstock that transfers the power and holds the live center or faceplate. It is sometimes called the headstock mandrel.

hp—An abbreviation for horse power.

inboard turning—Turning on the headstock spindle end that points toward the tailstock.

independent chuck—Another name for a four-jaw chuck.

Jacobs chuck—Used to hold bits and drills. When fitted with a Morse taper, it can be used in the headstock or tailstock of a lathe.

jig—Any homemade device to hold work or a tool for repetitive operations.

kerf—A cut made by a saw.

kiln—A large ovenlike structure for drying lumber.

laminate—Stock made by building up glued layers of wood.

"long and strong"—A term used to describe heavy purpose, long-handled gouges and chisels.

mandrel—A dowel-like projection from a wooden faceplate on which stock with a hole in it, the same size as the dowel, is placed for turning.

Morse taper—Most lathe headstock spindles, tailstock spindles, and centers are ground to #1 or #2 Morse taper.

mortise—A square or rectangular hole into which a tenon is inserted.

multi-spur bit—A large bit with numerous teeth around the cutting edge.

offset turning—A type of turning on centers other than the true centers.

outboard turning—Turning on the headstock spindle (or mandrel) that points away from the tailstock.

PEG—An abbreviation for Polyethylene Glycol 1000 used to treat and stabilize green lumber.

pilot hole—A hole bored to guide a screw or larger drill.

pummel—The square portions left on spindle turnings.

respirator—A face mask to prevent dust from entering the lungs.

revolving center—A special tailstock center used to prevent burning the end of spindle turnings.

RPM—An abbreviation for "revolutions per minute."

serviette—Another name for a table napkin.

skew—A chisel, sharpened on both edges. The edge is slanted or angled to the rest of the chisel. It is sometimes called a long-cornered chisel.

slip—A abbreviated term for slip stone. A stone used to whet cutting tools.

spindle turning—Turning that is done between the live center (drive center) and the dead (tailstock center). Often called turning between centers.

splated wood—Splated wood is caused by a partial decaying process in some white lumber that lends beauty to turnings.

split turning—The term given to two pieces temporarily joined together before turning. The halves are generally used for decoration on pieces of furniture.

steady—An abbreviated term for steady rest used to keep slender turnings from vibrating.

stick lacquer—A material used to fill small holes and depressions. Must be melted with a heated iron or knife and "burned" into the hole.

stick shellac—A material used to fill small holes and depressions in wood that is to be finished with a shellac/varnish finish. Must be melted with a heated iron or knife and burned into the hole.

tailstock—The heavy casting at the lathe right end.

tenon—A square or rectangular projection with a shoulder that fits into a mortise.

ticketer—Another name for a burnisher.

tool rest—Provides support for lathe cutting tools.

tool rest saddle—Rests on the lathe base (bed) and supports the tool rest.

treadle lathe—A lathe using a flywheel and treadle and allows the work to turn in only one direction.

universal chuck—A 3-jaw chuck generally used for metal turning.

wheel dresser—A device used to remove debris from a grinding wheel.

wire edge—A rough edge produced by grinding.

Bibliography

"Beyond the Bowl." *Fine Woodworking.* January/February 1982: 108.

Bjorkman, Donald C. "Shop-Made Bowl Lathe." *Fine Woodworking.* November/December 1981: 78.

Blandford, Percy W. *The Woodturner's Bible.* Blue Ridge Summit, PA: TAB Books Inc., 1979.

Capotosto, R. J. "Decorator Balance Scale." *Workbench.* June 1981: 33.

Child, Peter. *The Craftsman Woodturner.* New York, NY: Charles Scribner's Sons, 1982.

Child, Peter. "Woodworking Chisels." *Fine Woodworking.* September/October 1979: 70.

Child, Peter. "Spindle Turning." *Fine Woodworking.* September 1978: 60.

Christoforo, R.J. *Modern Power Tool Woodworking.*

Crabb, Tom. "Turning without a Lathe." *Workbench.* February 1982: 68.

Cramlet, Ross C. *Wood Turning Visualized.* New York, NY: Glencoe Publishing Co., Inc., 1973.

Creitz, E. Carroll. "Turning without Screw Holes." *Fine Woodworking.* November/December 1980: 82.

Darlow, Mike. "Turning Thin Spindles." *Fine Woodworking.* July/August 1980: 70.

Duffy, Thomas J. "Bolection Turning." *Fine Woodworking.* January/February 1979: 69.

Engler, Nick, ed. "Hands On! The Homeshop Magazine." Dayton, OH: A Shopsmith Publication.

Engles, Nick. "Geometric Turnings." *Fine Woodworking.* July/August 1981: 54.

Ensinger, Earl W. *Problems in Artistic Wood Turning.* Woburn, MA: Woodcraft Supply Corp., 1978.

Feirer, John L. *Cabinet Making & Millwork.* Peoria, IL: Bennett Publishing Co., 1982.

Fine Woodworking Magazine, eds. *Fine Woodworking Design: Book Two.* Newton, CT: The Taunton Press, 1979.

Fine Woodworking Magazine, eds. *Fine Woodworking Techniques.* Newton, CT: The Taunton Press.

Fine Woodworking Magazine, eds. *Fine Woodworking Biennial Design Book.* Newton, CT: The Taunton Press, 1977.

Forrester, Kent. "The Flageolet." *Fine Woodworking.* Fall 1977: 80.

Getting the Most Out of Your Lathe. New York, NY: A.S. Barnes and Co.

Gilson, Bob. "Tool Rests and Turning Tactics." *Fine*

Woodworking. July/August 1980: 61.

Gustavson, Ragner, Olsen, Olle. *Creating in Wood with the Lathe.*

Hall, Fran William. "Inlaid Turnings." *Fine Woodworking.* July/August 1981: 56.

Hedin, R.S. "Lighthouse Project." *Popular Mechanics.* July 1976.

Henderson, H.L. *The Air Seasoning and Kiln Drying of Wood.* Albany, NY: Henderson Publishers.

Hjorth, Herman. *Machine Woodworking.* New York, NY: Glencoe Publishing Co., Inc.

Hodges, Lewis H. *The Master Craftsman's Illustrated Woodworking Manual with Projects.* Blue Ridge Summit, PA: TAB Books Inc., 1981.

Hodges, Lewis H. *66 Weekend Wood Furniture Projects.* Blue Ridge Summit, PA: TAB Books Inc., 1977.

Hogbin, Stephen. *Wood Turning: The Purpose of the Object.* New York, NY: Van Nostrand Reinhold, 1980.

Holtrop, W.F. *Operation of Modern Woodworking Machines.* New York, NY: Glencoe Publishing Co., Inc., 1966.

Holtzapffel, John J. *Hand or Simple Turning: Principles and Practices.* New York, NY: Dover Publications, Inc., 1976.

Holtzapffel, John J. *The Principles and Practice of Ornamental or Complex Turning.* New York, NY: Dover Publications, Inc., 1973.

Kelsey, John. "The Turned Bowl." *Fine Woodworking.* January/February 1982: 54.

Klenke, William W. *Art of Wood Turning.* Peoria, IL: Bennett Publishing Co., 1954.

Krenou, Stephen. *Wood Turning.* New York, NY: Van Nostrand Reinhold Co.

Kribs, David. *Commercial Foreign Woods on the American Market.* New York, NY: Dover Publishing Co.

Kuepper, A.R. "Lathe Rotating Stand." *Workbench.* March/April 1981: 129.

"Lathe-turned Tea Set is Miniature Heirloom." *Workbench.* June 1979: 58.

LeCoff, Albert. *Gallery of Turned Objects.* Provo, UT: Brigham Young University Press, 1981.

"Legacy of Harry Nohr." *Fine Woodworking.* July/August 1980: 59.

Lory, David. "Turning Thin and Finishing with Epoxy." *Fine Woodworking.* July/August 1980: 60.

"Luna Lathe From Sweden." *Workbench.* June 1979: 80.

Mastelli, Rick. "Tips from the Turning Conference." *Fine Woodworking.* November/December 1979: 72.

Meader, Robert F. *Illustrated Guide to Shaker Furniture.* New York, NY: Dover Publications, Inc.

Miller. "Turn Wood Scraps into Mushroom Sculptures." *School Shop Magazine.* January 1979: 39.

Nish, Dale L. *Artistic Woodturning.* Provo, UT: Brigham Young University Press, 1980.

Nish, Dale L. *Creative Woodturning.* Provo, UT: Brigham Young University Press, 1975.

Oldin, Maj-Britt. "An Assortment of Lathe Turning." *Workbench.* June 1979: 4.

Pack, Ted. "Five Basic Spindle Laminations." *Fine Woodworking.* July/August 1981: 52.

Pain, F. *The Practical Wood Turner.* New York, NY: Sterling Publishing Co., 1979.

Plumier, Charles. *L'Arte De Tourner.*

Rebhorn, Eldon. *Woodturning.* Bloomington, IL: McKnight & McKnight Publishing Co., 1970.

Rodd, John. "Old-Fashioned Turner's Gauges." *Fine Woodworking.* November/December 1979: 74.

Sainsbury, John. *Sainsbury's Woodturning Projects for Dining.* New York, NY: Sterling Publishing Co., 1981.

Seale, Roland. *Practical Designs for Wood Turning.* New York, NY: Sterling Publishing Co., 1979.

"Shopmade Wood Lathe." *Workbench.* December 1979: 100.

Smith, Robert E. *Machine Woodworking.* Bloomington, IL: McKnight & McKnight Publishing Co.,

Smith, Wendell. "Turning for Figure." *Fine Woodworking.* November/December 1981: 75.

"Sprunger 10" Gap-Bed Lathe." *Workbench.* June 1980: 116.

Starr, Richard. "Last was Best." *Fine Woodworking.* January/February 1982: 61.

Starr, Richard. "Freewheel Lathe Drive." *Fine Woodworking.* March/April 1979: 65.

Stokes, Gordon. *Modern Wood Turning.* New York, NY: Sterling Publishing Co., 1979.

Stokes, Gordon. *Woodturning for Pleasure.* Englewood Cliffs, NJ: Prentice-Hall, Inc., 1980.

Stubbs, Del. "Turning up Your Lathe." *Fine Woodworking.* November/December 1980: 80.

Thorlin, Anders. *Ideas for Woodturning.* Englewood Cliffs, NJ: Prentice-Hall, Inc., 1980.

"Trestle Table is Lathe-turner's Delight." *Workbench.* June 1979: 28.

Wagner, Willis H. *Modern Woodworking.* South Holland, IL: Goodheart-Wilcox, Co., Inc., 1980s.

Waltner, Willard and Elma. "Eight-Piece Salad Set." *Workbench.* October 1979: 80.

Waltner, Willard and Elma. "International Egg Cups." *Workbench.* February 1982: 52.

Ward, David. "Sanding and Finishing on the Lathe." *Fine Woodworking*. July/August 1981: 58.

Widdicombe, C.I. "Recipe-card Holder is Woodturning Projects." *Workbench*. August 1979: 28.

"Wood-lathe Fundamentals—From Faceplate to Tailstock." *Workbench*. June 1979: 33.

Index